Dad
Happy Father's
Day. 2007.
   Lots of love,
      Danna + Ken

LAUNCHING
HISTORY

LAUNCHING
HISTORY
— The Saga of —
Burrard Dry Dock

FRANCIS MANSBRIDGE

HARBOUR PUBLISHING

Published by

HARBOUR PUBLISHING CO. LTD.

P.O. Box 219
Madeira Park, BC Canada
V0N 2H0
www.harbourpublishing.com

Edited by Audrey McClellan
Cover and page design by Warren Clark

Front cover photo
The 10,000-ton ship *Westend Park*, one of 41 Victory ships built by Burrard Dry Dock for use in World War II, is launched down the slipway. 27-2309

Back cover photos
Top Left: In 1916, the construction of the first Wallace-built schooner, the *Mabel Brown*, marked the start of a new type of schooner with five masts but no topmasts. 27-2649
Top Middle: In 1988, the *Henry Larsen* became the last icebreaker built by Burrard. It was named for the skipper of the St. Roch, the yard's most famous ship. 27-4188
Top Right: Burrard Dry Dock employees Phyllis Plume (left) and Maria Bouvier were among thousands of women temporarily hired by Burrard during World War II. 9613
Bottom: The cruise ship *Britannia*, in the new dry dock in 1987, demonstrates the dramatic changes in ship construction experienced by Burrard. 27-4196

Unless otherwise noted, all photographs are courtesy North Vancouver Museum and Archives.

Printed in Canada

Harbour Publishing acknowledges the financial support of the Government of Canada through the Book Publishing Industry Development Program (BPIDP) and the Canada Council for the Arts, and the Province of British Columbia through the British Columbia Arts Council, for its publishing activities.

THE CANADA COUNCIL FOR THE ARTS SINCE 1957 | LE CONSEIL DES ARTS DU CANADA DEPUIS 1957

National Library of Canada Cataloguing in Publication Data

Mansbridge, Francis, 1943-
    Launching history

    Includes bibliographical references and index.
    ISBN 1-55017-280-8

    1. Burrard Dry Dock Co.—History. 2. Shipbuilding—British Columbia—North Vancouver—History. I. Title.
VM301.B87M36 2002   338.7'62383'0971133   C2002-910761-X

A stillness absolute as death
Along the slacking wheels shall lie

...

And over that tremendous town
The silence of eternal night
Shall gather close and settle down

From Archibald Lampman's
"The City of the End of Things"

CONTENTS

Acknowledgements

As a newcomer to the world about which I am writing, I am much indebted to many people who helped dispel some of my ignorance. Rollie Webb not only read and commented on the manuscript, but also added much from his extensive historical knowledge. The hull list in Appendix 2 is perhaps the most important of his many contributions. Thanks also to Robert Faulkner for his assistance with the hull list. Len McCann, curator emeritus of the Vancouver Maritime Museum, generously contributed many constructive comments from the depth of his knowledge in maritime history. Will Morrison's background both in shipbuilding and as a writer provided a valuable reference point.

Thanks to the many people I interviewed—Bob Logan, Jack Cash, George Tomlinson, Robert Downing, George MacPherson and John Fitzpatrick provided a valuable workers/union perspective; Tom Knox and George Matthews spoke as foremen; and David Wallace, John Wallace, Bill Hudson, Tom Duncan, David Alsop, Dale Jenkins and Peter Saunders expressed the views of those who shaped the direction of the company—although it is interesting how similar their positions have become with a few years' perspective. Tapes and transcripts of their interviews are on deposit at the North Vancouver Museum and Archives.

Thanks also to my institution, the North Vancouver Museum and Archives, through whose foresight the photographs and other records of the shipyard were preserved, for giving me the freedom to use this material. And thank you to the photographers and others in the company who gathered a rich record of the company's activities. Building is a lot easier with a solid foundation.

Introduction

The history of North Vancouver's waterfront has been primarily industrial, with shipbuilding front and centre. While many yards came and went, Burrard Dry Dock, originally Wallace Shipyards, remained. Over 400 ships—from small tugs to naval construction and vessels for BC's ferry fleet—were hammered, riveted and welded by thousands of workers. Three generations of the Wallace family guided the yard through most of its history, displaying unusual skill in sensing the early signs of economic and social change, staying one step ahead of most of their competition. Through most of the 1900s, Burrard provided much of the transportation and industrial support that has shaped Canada's West Coast.

But now the buildings just east of Lonsdale Quay are rapidly disappearing as developers go to work on what was once the largest shipyard in Canada. While a few buildings are being retained, and the former machine shop will house a new museum, in a few years expensive condos and trendy shops will show little evidence of almost a century of shipbuilding.

The history of the company is from one perspective an industrial romance in which an ambitious young immigrant named Alfred Wallace made a Horatio Alger-like rise to success through hard work and nerve, with his son Clarence solidifying that success and ultimately becoming lieutenant-governor of British Columbia. It's also a comedy in the classic sense, a tale of success and accomplishment, but with darkening overtones as the business became a casualty of the global economy and an indifferent federal government.

The company's strong sense of its corporate history has greatly facilitated the current work. J.S. Marshall's commissioned unpublished history was an invaluable resource, as were both the clipping files the company maintained with assiduous care from its earliest days and the company newsletters published at various times from the 1940s on. Many of the corporate records have been salvaged and preserved by the North Vancouver Museum and Archives, although disappointingly few survive from the years before 1950.

Perhaps most important for this book is the rich visual record of some 5,000 photographs acquired by the North Vancouver Archives that date from the earliest years of the company. Jack Wardlaw, Jack Cash, John McGinnis and John Helcermanas are among the photographers who documented the workers in these yards and their achievements with unusual skill and sensitivity. The mostly black-and-white images are an apt medium for communicating the gritty vitality of shipyard work.

As with any account, this one is necessarily selective. Related shipyards, especially Yarrows and North Van Ship Repairs, are historically significant, as is the union movement, but their stories are mainly outside the scope of this narrative. My emphasis is on the vicissitudes of the company, the building and history of significant ships, and the men and women who made them possible. Passion, imagination and some remarkable personalities make this a story of enduring interest.

CHAPTER 1

Laying the Foundations: 1894–1913

The land may vary more;
But wherever the truth may be—
The water comes ashore,
And the people look at the sea.

From Robert Frost's
"Neither Out Far Nor In Deep"

As the 1890s dawned in British Columbia, the pace of development quickened. Sewell Moody and Captain Edward Stamp—the two lumber barons whose vigour and imagination began in the 1860s to set the early direction for Burrard Inlet—were both dead, although their mills carried on. The gold rush had come and gone, trailing economic and political development in its wake. British Columbia had become a province and joined the Canadian confederation in 1871. A new society was taking shape, one that combined the brash aggressiveness of the frontier with the eccentricity that finds the West Coast congenial soil.

The City of Vancouver had been incorporated in 1886 with a population of 1,000, followed quickly by its almost total destruction by fire—but this setback was temporary. With the arrival of the Canadian Pacific Railway (CPR) the next year and its choice of Vancouver as western terminus, the city's future as BC's industrial and commercial hub was assured. At the same time, the need for marine transportation as an extension to the railway became apparent. In 1889 the legendary Union Steamship Company began its coastal service, carrying people and goods to and from lumber and fishing camps along the province's rugged West Coast. Canadian Pacific Navigation Company and other lines also did a thriving business transporting passengers and goods among the communities of the northwest. The magnificent *Empress of India*, *Empress of China* and *Empress of Japan*—products of British shipyards—began service from Vancouver to the Far East in 1891.

The first Granville Street bridge opened in 1888, and streetcar service to New Westminster began in 1891. Industries such as BC Sugar Refinery (1891) set up shop. Before the turn of the century, Vancouver had replaced Victoria as the centre of population and commercial activity on Canada's West Coast, becoming BC's focal point for entrepreneurial initiative, with a population of 13,709 in the 1891 census. Alfred Wallace was among the most energetic and innovative of the many young men who challenged this land with their energy and talents.

Alfred Wallace: His Early Years

Wallace's background shaped him for a life as a shipbuilder. Born in 1865 in Devonport, a town on the English Channel adjacent to Plymouth, Alfred (Andy) Wallace was one of ten children, the third and youngest son of Samuel Tozer Wallace and Jane Pope Wallace. Samuel Wallace, a master craftsman and shipbuilder, worked in the picturesque seacoast village of Brixham, Devon. From at least the sixteenth century, craft from Brixham had fished the North Sea, and by 1818 Brixham vessels were fishing as far afield as Dublin Bay. By the end of the nineteenth century the Brixham trawler had developed into the largest and most powerful of British fishing craft; a boat-building industry for this fleet naturally developed.

Wallace senior worked with Devon elm and oak to build finely crafted boats for four shipyards. Besides 80- to 90-foot fishing vessels, he built larger ships such as three- and four-masted schooners, employing as many as 40 men.

When he was 11, Alfred was apprenticed to his father at Brixham; he became a journeyman shipwright in 1883, moving in 1884 to work at the shipyards in Grimsby, in northeastern England. Experience as a ship's carpenter on voyages that took him to Stockholm and then

Bombay gave him a first-hand awareness of the importance of sound ship construction, although he had formal education in neither engineering nor business. On his return to England he continued working in Grimsby. In nearby Cleethorpes, a small town on the Humber estuary, he met Eliza Eugene Underhill; they were married December 27, 1887.

In 1889 the young couple immigrated to Canada, where Alfred found work with Polson Iron Works in Toronto, a bustling city with an active harbour and shipbuilding industry for the Great Lakes trade. When later that year the company secured a contract from Canadian Pacific for the construction of the *Manitoba*, a steel passenger steamship for service on

Lakes Huron and Superior, Alfred Wallace was one of the workmen sent to Owen Sound on Georgian Bay to lay out and build the new shipyard and ship. After its launching, Wallace stayed to work at a shipyard in Collingwood. When the work ended, Vancouver and salt water beckoned, with the promise of assembling three steel ships prefabricated in Scotland (the *Comox*, the *Capilano* and the *Coquitlam*) for the new Union Steamship Company. This took place on Coal Harbour, near where the Westin Bayshore Resort now stands.

Alfred Wallace, an energetic young man of 25, arrived in Vancouver with John McColl and a number of his other workmates on February 22, 1891. Wife Eliza arrived later. Her husband's first jobs included helping build the yacht *Miramichi* for Captain William Watts and working for the respected shipbuilder Andy Linton and Associates on the sealing schooner *C.D. Rand* and other vessels before taking a number of short-term jobs in shipyards and sawmills. Work for shipwright Henry Darling's Union Steamship Company later paid off in a number of contracts with this line, although Darling turned down an offer from Wallace to go into partnership.

Alfred and Eliza's first residence was in what is now Vancouver's West End at 1117 Richards Street. After Wallace built a house next door at 1113, he and his friend and former Ontario workmate John McColl spent their weekends and evenings (after a regular day's work) building lifeboats in the backyard for the CPR steamships. Days were never long enough; wife

Above: Alfred and Eliza Wallace as a young couple in their finery. 8083

Eliza came out to hold a lantern for them so they could continue work as the evenings darkened. She was also "holder-up" when Wallace drove copper rivets in the hulls of small boats—his first female employee.

In 1894, with the profits from this work and with a loan of $800 from McColl, Wallace and T. Thompson opened a small shipbuilding yard just east of the north end of the Granville Street bridge on land leased from the CPR.

The Beginning: The False Creek Yards

The burgeoning fishing and logging industries drove early BC shipbuilding. Wallace drew on the experience gained with his father for the first jobs in his new yard. He built flat-bottomed lapstreak fish boats for the Fraser River fishing fleet, then larger boats of the Columbia River type. With six men and two helpers he was able to increase production from two to seven boats a day by using a solid boat frame upside down, around which the boats were built, with an overhead

trolley to convey material. Thompson objected to "working himself to death for those damned fishermen," so Eliza Wallace bought him out and became her husband's partner. He never had another. No doubt few could match his burning energy and drive.

When Wallace started building boats, he had little competition in Vancouver. The 1894 city directory lists only four boatbuilders in the area, compared to 12 in Victoria. Captain William Watts had a large yard on Burrard Inlet, and Andy Linton a smaller one on False Creek. Many of the early shipbuilders appeared to become involved with shipbuilding because the economic opportunity presented itself, switching to other types of construction when the economic winds shifted. Wallace stayed with shipbuilding and ship repair, where both his skill and passion were focussed. He was keenly competitive in business dealings. When a local yard operated by Japanese Canadians bid on a contract to build 300 fishing boats for two northern canneries at $125 a boat, Wallace responded with a bid of $78.

His first registered vessel, the 30-foot scow

TWO GENERATIONS of McColls were intimately connected with 70 years of the Wallaces and the life of the shipyard. John McColl declined Alfred's proposal of a partnership, but lent him $800 to get started in 1894. He was Alfred's first employee in the False Creek operations, with his two sons continuing to work for Wallace Shipyards. Earl, noted for his genial manner and hearty laugh, joined the company in 1913 at the age of 16. He worked at a variety of jobs—making shells during World War I, storesman, purchasing—but David Wallace recalls that Earl's drinking on the job (his wife would not let him drink at home) was a persistent problem. However, as he was such a long-time intimate of the family, Clarence Wallace refused to have him fired. Earl retired in May 1960, and died in December of the same year. Earl's brother Jim started with the company in July 1917 as an office boy. He worked in the plating, shipwright and patternmaking shops before joining the mould loft in 1930, and was foreman loftsman from the late 1930s to his retirement in 1963.

Jim McColl (left) and Red Ross, a riveter known for his sense of humour, enjoy a lighter moment in 1957. 27-769

Lighthouse No. 2, built for the Federation Brand Company, was completed in the False Creek yard in 1896. He soon branched out into building motor launches and constructing tugs for use as cannery tenders. Between 1896 and the end of 1913, Wallace's obsessive drive resulted in the completion of 105 vessels registered at the Port of Vancouver.* Scows and tugs constituted the bulk of these, but down the ways also slid ferries, yachts, schooners and barges. His customers were a diverse lot, with Packers Steamship Company (eight tugs), the department of public works (eight tugs and scows), Vancouver Tug and Barge (seven scows) and Sir John Jackson (four scows) among the best. His efficient workmanship brought him steady business.

In 1898 Wallace expanded, building another shop on False Creek just west of the Granville Street bridge. A new engine that was part of the project had sufficient power to operate a marine ways. George Doidge, who would continue as shipwright's foreman and dockmaster with Wallace for nearly 50 years, started working for him in 1896. One day, as Andy Wallace was off to San Francisco, he left Doidge with an order

to build a marine ways. Doidge recalls: "I didn't know much about building marine ways, but in those days when Andy said 'build something' you went ahead and built it with your head and hands." He used his ingenuity to build a marine railway 40 feet wide and 100 feet long, with a capacity of 150 tons, which enabled the company to work on larger ships. When a diver was needed for the construction, Doidge simply stripped off his clothes and dove in.

Doidge lived a rich and colourful life, which included being nearly killed during the Riel rebellion. His first shipbuilding job was a sternwheeler for the Red River. When Burrard built a new dry dock in 1925, he took charge of pontoon construction and became dockmaster, docking over 3,000 ships without a single accident. He epitomized the dedicated competence that made the Wallace yard so successful; in 1942 at the age of 76 he was still capable of putting in

---

* Rollie Webb states that a hull list was not completed until the start of World War I, when a list was compiled from the registrar's office in Vancouver. Vessels registered at other BC ports were ignored, as were unregistered vessels. Webb states that he has found a total of 115 for this period, though this may not be all-inclusive as other unregistered vessels may have existed.

Top: Building Columbia River fishing boats at Alfred Wallace's first yard on False Creek, circa 1897. The old Granville Street bridge is on the right. 27–2712

more than 24 hours at a stretch. In March 1944 the company magazine, *Wallace Shipbuilder*, described him as "Andy's right hand man and staunchest friend." He died November 13, 1946.

The discovery of gold in the Yukon in 1896 galvanized the economy of the West Coast, drawing it out of a depression (that did not appear to greatly affect Wallace's business), and helped propel Wallace into the world of major shipbuilding. On May 30, 1898, the company launched the 486-ton *James Domville*, a sternwheeler, for service in the Yukon. The owners were the Klondike, Yukon, and Stewart River Pioneers Company, with Lieutenant-Colonel James Domville, a New Brunswick Member of Parliament, managing director. Polson Iron Works of Toronto, Wallace's former employer, supplied the sternwheeler's engines as Wallace cultivated the networks that helped sustain his success. The *Vancouver Daily World* of May 30 gives an upbeat account of the happy occasion of the launch:

Mrs. Captain McLean christened the new steamer, breaking a bottle of wine over her bows. Mesdames Mcgowan and McConnell, who were also present had many words of praise for the boat and Col. Domville's speech was one of the most happy he ever uttered. The health of Capt. McLean was proposed and everything passed off very joyously indeed. The *James S. Domville* will leave for the north on the 8th prox. in tow of the *Manuense* and through passages to Dawson are now being booked by the two steamers. The *World* predicts great success for the new steamer.

The ship transported would-be gold seekers and their equipment from St. Michaels at the mouth of the Yukon River to the goldfields of the Klondike; it was the first ship bearing the British flag to do so. Bill

Above: Looking south past Wallace's boat-building sheds to the Granville Street –Third Avenue bridge, circa 1899.
27-3895

Jealouse, a pioneer member of the Royal North West Mounted Police, and during World War II a guard at Burrard, recalled the ship as "sturdy and strong with a real personality," although its career was brief. It ran aground in the Whitehorse rapids in the spring of 1902, becoming one of the many relics of the gold rush.

Other projects soon followed, with Wallace's Union Steamship connections paying off. The new marine ways gave him the capacity to convert the *J.R. McDonald*, a schooner launched at Ballard, Washington, in 1890, to a coastal passenger ship for Union Steamship. It was renamed the *Cassiar*, a corruption of the name of the Caska First Nations, meaning "creek." Bow McLachlan engines and boilers were brought in from Scotland for the ship. Vancouver still did not have the capacity to build compound and triple expansion engines, although for some years companies such as Victoria's Albion Works had built engines for sternwheelers and other vessels on the Canadian West Coast. The *Cassiar's* reconstruction provided cabins, complete with

electric light, for 42 berths, with total accommodation for 144 passengers. With a modest speed of nine knots, and 17.5 miles on a ton of coal, the ship had a useful radius of nearly 400 miles.

Relaunched on September 28, 1901, and captained by Charles Moody, the *Cassiar* transported freight, passengers and mail to and from BC coastal logging camps, often bearing a load of canned salmon on the return. Known as the "Loggers' Palace," it was the most famous ship on the West Coast. Its saloon hosted many memorable occasions, especially on trips with loads of loggers heading down to Vancouver after hard work in the bush. Sometimes the party got a little out of hand, but crew such as Arthur Jarvis, known as the "Black Mate," were generally equal to the task of subduing overly enthusiastic loggers.

In its 1,730 voyages and 750,000 miles of steaming, it hit its share of rocks, but was stranded only once, near Simoom Sound in 1917. After this accident it was again refurbished and rebuilt by Wallace Shipyards. In 1923 it was retired and sold to a US

Top: The Cassiar *at the Union Steamship Company's dock at the foot of Carrall Street.* Vancouver Maritime Museum 13451

fishing company in Puget Sound, resuming its original name, *J.R. McDonald*. Six years later it became a floating dance hall on Lake Washington.

The elegant *Kestrel* was the company's first government contract and first ship intended for deep-sea navigation. It stretched the yard's capabilities, as the mould loft was not large enough, so the men had to lay the ship down in sections. Laying out its ram bow sectionally was especially difficult. The *Kestrel* was launched with great fanfare on February 14, 1903, after a lengthy construction process that started in June 1901 and cost over $80,000. Built for the federal department of marine and fisheries, the *Kestrel*'s purpose was to stop American poachers from raiding British Columbia fishing grounds. It had Maxim machine guns mounted on the foredeck and a five-pounder to provide muscle. The reporter for the *Daily World* of February 14 again offered eloquent testimony to the sumptuous workmanship. Ships were not mere transportation; they expressed a culture that valued a fusion of practical workmanship with aesthetics.

The fittings and trimmings in all parts of the boat are in quartered oak, richly polished, the numerous pilasters surmounted with Corinthian capitals finished in gold. Steam heated, electric lighted, carpeted with the best Brussels, finished with everything that experience could suggest or ingenuity devise, the officers' quarters are all that the most fastidious could demand. Two bathrooms, supplied with both hot and cold water, form part of the equipment. Forward, the accommodation provided for the men is just as complete if not quite so elaborate. The very ports, which are of Mr. Wallace's invention, are worth special mention. Set in a solid, square metal frame, they are fitted with inch and a quarter plate glass, while provision has been made for a mishap in an extra rubber cushion with galvanized plugs and patent adjustments.

Above: Wallace's yard and Robertson and Hackett's sawmill at the foot of Granville Street, circa 1902. The Kestrel *is under construction on the left. Completed fishing boats are tied together on the right.* 27-2713

One of the *Kestrel*'s summer cabin boys in the early years was Alfred's eldest son, Clarence, who in a November 15, 1982, *Vancouver Province* interview recalled drills on the main deck under the eyes of Captain Newcome. The ship's exploits included firing four rounds into the Seattle fishing cruiser *Charles Levi Woodbury*, which had been poaching in Canadian waters. Later it was sold to private interests, finishing its career as a trading ship in the South Seas before being lost during a voyage from Fanning Island to Honolulu in 1919.

Wallace's business prospered and his family grew.

Clarence had been born June 22, 1894, and Hubert followed March 3, 1899. The combination of the family's need for space and Alfred's business success led to their move in 1902 from Richards Street to a much larger house at 1165 Davie Street. The 1913 Fire Insurance maps show this magnificent residence on a double lot, with a floor plan approximately 40 feet square, or about twice the size of any other house on the street. Its two and one-half storeys plus basement comprised about 4,000 square feet, including two parking spaces.

Wallace recognized the importance of networking

THE TERM "ton" originated from "tun," meaning a cask of wine. Originally it had nothing to do with weight, but rather referred to the number of casks a ship could carry. Several different ways of estimating tonnage have developed over the years to provide various measurements. It came to be accepted that one ton equalled 100 cubic feet, so the registered tonnage of the ship is its contents in cubic feet divided by 100. Gross registered tonnage is all space below the upper deck as well as permanently closed-in space on that deck. Net registered tonnage is the gross tonnage less certain allowed deductions for space that is not available for carrying cargo. Deadweight tonnage (dwt) is the carrying capacity of the ship in actual tons of 2,240 pounds. In a modern freighter the gross tonnage is half again as much as the net tonnage, and the deadweight tonnage two and one-half times the net. Gross tonnage is generally the designation used in this text.

Top: The Kestrel, *built for the department of marine and fisheries, nearing completion. The keel was laid June 22, 1901, although the launch did not take place until February 14, 1903.* 27-2709

to ensure business success, a view of life that his children, especially Clarence, would refine to an even greater art. R.E. Gosnell's 1906 *History of British Columbia* indicates that the Wallaces were members of the Methodist Church, while Alfred Wallace "belongs to the Western Star Lodge, IOOF, and is a prominent Mason, holding membership in Mount Herman Lodge, AF & AM, of which he is now senior deacon in the Royal Arch chapter; and in the Lodge of Perfection, having attained the fourteenth degree of the Scottish rite."

North Vancouver Ferry No. 2

North Vancouver had started to boom in 1900, and ferry service across the inlet became a priority, particularly for those whose business success hinged on the increased value of land resulting from easier access. The first of the many ferries built by Wallace Shipyards was the *St. George*, named after Colonel Alfred St. George Hamersley, president of the North Vancouver Ferry and Power Company. Launched in 1904 at the False Creek yard for service across Burrard Inlet, it suffered a change of name to the more prosaic *North Vancouver Ferry No. 2* in 1911.

The steel frame was constructed at Polson Iron Works in Toronto and then Wallace's men built the rest of the ferry. John McColl completed the upper works using BC cedar. It was the first double-ended ferry for the Lower Mainland, enabling wagons and cars to board at one end and roll off the other. Two runways for vehicles on the main deck were flanked on the outer side by commodious cabins. The upper deck was roofed but not enclosed. At 131 feet it was the largest vessel for inland water use constructed by Wallace Shipyards while it was at False Creek. Captain Mooney was

in charge during the early years of its service, with Chief Engineer Hurd and Assistant Engineer McWilliams presiding over the engine room. R.R. Spicer was later captain for 27 years.

The ship's life became interwoven with the community's. Moonlight cruises up the North Arm were occasions for dancing on the open deck, often to the music of Harpur's orchestra. At other times North Shore organizations hired it for their outings. Until 1936 it faithfully plied the waters of Burrard Inlet, transporting an estimated 30 million passengers and 2 million vehicles. But the huge cost of necessary renovations in a time of depression led to its retirement from active service. It was sold in 1937 to the North Shore Junk Company for $3,000. In August 1938 Gibsons Brothers Lumber Company turned it into a camp for loggers. Fire ended its existence in February 1939; the ship now rests on the bottom of Nootka Sound.

Right: The Wallaces moved into this imposing residence at 1165 Davie Street in 1902. 8086

Moving to the North Shore

Across Burrard Inlet the magnificent mountains and verdant forests of the North Shore beckoned the dreamers who journeyed to the West Coast looking for the "promised land." North Vancouver became the focus of many grandiose projects and the graveyard of most. A few dreamers combined their imagination with a core of hard practicality. No one fused these characteristics better than "Andy" Wallace. (Alfred was commonly known as Andrew. Many of his fishermen friends were Scots and related more easily to a Scottish name. The English Alfred would not do, hence Andy was picked.)

Wallace's business required more space and perhaps deeper water than was available at his False Creek site. In his *Echoes of the Ferries*, Rodger Burnes notes that there had been some doubt as to whether the *St. George* would be able to pass through the draw span on the old Granville Street bridge to get out to Burrard Inlet. There was, he states, only six inches to spare on each side. Although several of the barges built for Vancouver Tug and Barge in the False Creek yards had beams up to 32 feet, or three feet wider than the ferry, their lack of a superstructure may have allowed them to pass beneath the bridge. Taller vessels were likely to hit the roadway, which extended beyond the supporting pylons of the bridge.

In 1904 Wallace, thanks in part to his wife's frugal financial management, bought Lots 5 to 8 in Block 176, DL 274, just east of the foot of Lonsdale, at what would be the centre of waterfront activity in North

Above: The St. George, *later* North Vancouver Ferry No. 2, *under construction in the False Creek yards. The Granville Street bridge is to the left behind the boat.* 27-2705

Vancouver. At that time, Charles H. Cates had recently established the first business on the North Vancouver waterfront; in 1904 he built the first wharf in North Vancouver (apart from the ferry dock) and in 1907 added boat repairing facilities and a sawmill. McDougall-Jenkins Engineering works was established on the east side of Lonsdale in 1909.

On April 6, 1905, Wallace submitted a proposal to the North Vancouver council to establish a shipyard on the North Shore. Also in that year he incorporated the business as Wallace Shipyards Limited, with his wife as president; W.J. Bowser, a solicitor (and later premier of BC), as vice-president; and Wallace himself as secretary-treasurer. In September 1906, almost immediately after electric power reached the North Shore, Wallace started setting up facilities in this location. Perhaps he was also encouraged by talk of a bridge from the North Shore to Vancouver, with the possibility of rail service, although the actual completion of the Second Narrows bridge was nearly 20 years away.

The move certainly did his business no harm. In each of 1905 and 1906 he had launched seven hulls with total gross tonnage of 1,054 and 360 respectively. In 1907 he launched 17 hulls with a gross tonnage of 2,194, although only two of these (the first of seven barges for Vancouver Tug and Barge) were built at the new yard. The first registered vessel built on the North Shore was the wooden scow *V.T.B. 1*.

The last registered vessel from the Granville Street yard was the *Helen M. Scanlon*, a wooden stern-wheeler built for the Brooks Scanlon Lumber Company in 1909 and later renamed the *William H. Ladner*. A fire in the early morning of May 14, 1910, destroyed the original yard, although it had been idle for more than a year, all activity having shifted by this point to the North Shore. The *Province* that came out later the same day estimated the loss at not more than $3,000. Ritchie Contracting soon set up business in the space.

On the North Shore, Wallace saw he would need more facilities to build larger ships and traded on some of his acquired credibility as a respected shipbuilder and provider of employment for more municipal support. During early 1908 the North Shore newspaper, the *Express*, contained frequent references to Wallace and his presentations to the city council. In March the council agreed to guarantee the company's bonds to the extent of $20,000, the money to be used to build a 1,600-ton marine railway. While some people raised concerns that current debenture loans of $519,600 might have overextended the city's finances, the project went ahead and was completed in late January 1909 at a cost of about $30,000. This enabled Wallace to transfer all operations to the North Shore. The first ship on the cradle was the *Camosun*. The marine railway provided a steady source of revenue for the company from the repair of smaller vessels. It also provided employment for many of the local citizens. North Vancouver's growth to a sizeable community featured the shipyards front and centre.

Wallace never lived on the North Shore, retaining a physical and emotional distance that allowed him to be an astute player in the incestuous world of North Vancouver business and politics, effectively protecting and promoting his own interests. The *Express* of December 9, 1910, described his proposition: "[I]f the city council of North Vancouver was willing to grant them certain concessions which include exemption from taxation for a number of years it is the proposal of the company to fit the boat up [the *Zafiro*] as a salvor for operation on the coast." The requested relief from taxes would also allow his company to expand further, perhaps establishing a foundry, with implications of more jobs for the local citizens. The relief was apparently not granted. On February 10, 1911, the *Express* reported his complaints about his assessment of $275 a foot on the water frontage. When informed that the assessment was upheld, Wallace gave notice that he would appeal to a judge, though he appears not to have pursued that alternative.

North Vancouver Ferry No. 3

In 1910 Wallace won the contract to add another ferry to join the two already shuttling back and forth between Vancouver and its northern cousin. His bid of $118,000 for the *North Vancouver Ferry No. 3* was $7,000 lower than that of his closest competitor.

The 1,176-ton ferry, the first built on the West Coast with a steel hull (which was constructed by the North Vancouver firm McDougall-Jenkins), had two boilers, two sets of fore-and-aft compound engines, two six-foot, nine-inch cast steel propellers, and could generate 12 knots. It was launched February 27, 1911, to the sweet sounds of civic support. The *Express* of February 28 quoted Vancouver politician J.M. Bowell as saying that "the city could not do better than help Mr. Wallace." After its maiden voyage on March 18, the reporter for the *Express* was enthusiastic. "The saloon and cabins are richly finished in red beam and red brick which show up to perfection on the white painted background of native cedar…Decorations in beautiful scenes from the Rockies effectively embellish otherwise vacant scenes of the interior." The privileged guests on this first trip enjoyed themselves

thoroughly. Although "a slight haze was discernible, it did not affect the view of those whose epicurean delight is solely in devouring the scenery and drinking in the fresh, pure atmosphere."

But apparently many of the honoured passengers were drinking in a lot more than the pure atmosphere, and the haze may have been induced by the refreshments provided. The initial euphoria generated considerable reaction. The April 25 *Express* described a meeting of city council at which the ratepayers' association questioned the cost of the new ferry from a number of aspects. The association especially took a jaundiced view of the use of taxpayers' money for refreshments on the maiden voyage, which included $84 spent on champagne. H.C. Wright, who perhaps not coincidentally had just missed being elected to council in the previous election, tried to rain on the parade by calling the *No. 3 Ferry* "a disgrace to North Vancouver."

Wallace was not amused. Eight years later he could still work up a good head of steam over the temerity of council discussing his business in an open meeting.

Top: North Vancouver Ferry No. 3 *crossing Burrard Inlet.* 2384

I would remind you of the way in which this firm was treated at the conclusion of the contract for building *Ferry #3*, when the questions of extras and demurrage were freely aired in open Council meetings and this firm criticized at some length in the reports which appeared in the local press…Our annual accounts for repairs to the ferries have been discussed in open Council meetings and imputations which are circulated throughout the Province by means of the Press continue to give the public the opinion that the veracity and trustworthiness of this firm as a business institution cannot be relied on.

As he no doubt realized, in spite of the rhetoric, Wallace did not have a lot to worry about. The tide was definitely flowing in his direction, aided by spectacular growth in North Vancouver and the Lower Mainland generally. According to the *Express* of June 6, 1911, "Since the completion of the famous *North Vancouver Ferry No. 3*, upon which it is estimated some 450 people have expressed opinions, condemnation and praise being about equally divided, the shipyards have had some 110 vessels of various kinds upon its ways in process of repair and under construction in the plant."

The *No. 3 Ferry* stayed in regular use until 1948 with only one fatality, and that a suicide. As Captain James Barr writes in his *Ferry Across the Harbour*, the ship was "a cow to handle but in her time she made a lot of money for the City of North Vancouver." It was sold in 1952 to Gulf of Georgia Towing for use as a floating store and shipwright's workshop, but the company disposed of it two years later to Nelson Brothers. The registry on the ship was closed in November 1966, at which time it was in use at Bella Bella as a net storage loft.

Above: The Point Grey *was the first steel tug built by Wallace (1911). This photo was probably taken after the company lengthened it in 1917. This increased its bunker capacity for long wartime hauls of airplane spruce, ordered by the aeronautical division of the Imperial Munitions Board.* 27-2700

Adapting to Local Needs

Early in the twentieth century, West Coast shipyards were not at the forefront of innovations in shipbuilding and ship repair technology. Major advances in machinery and construction continued to come from Britain, as did many of the prototypes for ships. But local yards, including Wallace's, adapted British models to the needs of the northwest. In particular, they developed a type of tug suited to the West Coast's maritime needs.

Elsewhere tugs were either of the large deep-sea variety or small harbour tugs. The type developed for the West Coast, especially for towing log booms and working with the canneries, was mid-sized, 70 to 100 feet long with a 20- to 25-foot beam. Major differences included more open deck space because they did more work in open water, and larger propellers

because of the slow speeds needed, particularly when towing log booms.

Wallace's tugs were built of wood rather than steel, which was becoming the industry standard. On the West Coast, wood was plentiful, cheap and of excellent quality. Between 1898 and 1913 the company launched 49 tugs, all but one of which, the *Point Grey*, were constructed of wood. In 1912 a new 600-ton-capacity marine railway on the east side of the machine shop assisted in the repair and conversion of tugs and small scows, complementing the larger 1,600-ton marine railway.

Wallace's first large tug was the 79-foot *Albion*, launched in 1899, while the 77-foot *Progressive* (1906) and the 100-foot *Ivanhoe* (1907) were two of his best known, designed specifically for towing logs on the West Coast. Other tugs of 70 feet or more in length included the *Unican* (1902), *Squid* (1903), *Belfast* (1904), *Clayburn* (1906), *Daring* (1907), *Spray* (1907), *Celtic* (1907), *B.C.P.* (1907), *Noname* (1908), *Olallie* (1912) and *Freno* (1912). These tugs helped shape marine and logging development on BC's West Coast.

The Terminal Steamship Company operated the *Unican*, an 89.2-foot tug launched in 1902 and soon renamed the *Belcarra*, on the North Arm and Howe Sound. It was the largest tug built by the Wallace yards to this time. In January 1910 it was sold to Sechelt Steamship Company and put on northern routes, but soon ran into trouble. On September 16, 1910, it left Vancouver under the command of Captain J.E. Fulton and encountered thick fog after leaving Pender Harbour. Thinking he was at Dempsey's Camp, Fulton headed at top speed to what he believed was the light at the end of the landing. Unfortunately the light was inland, and the *Belcarra* ground to a rocky halt well short of it. While all on board escaped safely, the tug slid into deep water and sank. Captain Fulton was absolved of responsibility for mistaking the light but was found guilty of reckless navigation for proceeding at top speed through thick fog.

The *Progressive*, captained by Alfred Lewis, made history by towing the first Davis raft across Hecate

Above: The Progressive, *a steam tug, on the marine railway at the False Creek yards before 1923. Later this was the location of the blacksmith shop. The building level with the top of the cradle is the boilerhouse, with the electrical department on the second floor.* 27-2704

Strait in 1917 from Masset Inlet to Georgetown, near Prince Rupert. In 1937 it was converted to diesel, with 350-horsepower engines; in 1952 it was brought in for new bulwarks and guardrails, becoming the *D.A. Evans* in 1955. Most of its life was spent towing freight barges between Vancouver and Powell River before it was finally retired from service in 1964.

Arthur H. Moscrop, who had apprenticed with Andrew Wallace, supervised construction of the *Ivanhoe*, built for George Wilson. Moscrop's daughter recalls that he would pin up blueprints of the boats he was building on the walls of his office in their house at Pine Street and 4th Avenue. She would follow her father deep into the forest as he searched for special timber for ships' knees and for the prow bend in the keel. The *Ivanhoe*'s decks were built of four-inch, clear, edge-grained fir that had been air dried, a five-year process that gave the wood more suppleness than kiln drying. Moscrop shared with his employer a belief in the value of fine construction and thoroughness. Later he went on to start his own yard.

The *Ivanhoe* helped launch the Kingcome Navigation Company's fleet in 1912–1913. It was converted in 1938 to a Union 600Z-type diesel that made it the most powerful tug on the West Coast, capable of towing log booms over 500 yards long and 100 yards wide. Former captain Bill Dolmage considered it the finest tug ever built in BC. It remained in active service towing logs along the West Coast until 1971, after which it became the floating home of Les Withey and his wife at Silva Bay, Gabriola Island. Don Napier, an advertising executive with a passion for boats, purchased it in 1972 and established the Ivanhoe Heritage Foundation in 1983 to refit and restore the old tug to its 1938 external configuration. Malcolm McLaren and his company disassembled the engine and tried to rebuild it, but ran into many difficulties. Eventually McLaren's company was owed so much money it informally took possession of the ship. The *Ivanhoe* is still afloat, the oldest surviving wooden hull on the Canadian West Coast, now docked at the Cowichan Bay Maritime Centre.

Such ships won Wallace increased respect from local customers as well as others farther afield. Britain, after all, was a long and expensive voyage away, especially in the days before the Panama Canal, and it made sense to do as much as possible locally. However, the British yards were still much more proficient with building steel hulls, which may explain why in late 1910 Wallace secured the contract for completing only the superstructure, cabins and general fittings for the Union Steamship's *Cheslakee*, named after a Native community on the Nimpkish River. Designed by A.J. Robertson of North Vancouver, this steel single-screw vessel's hull and main deck were completed at Dublin Dockyard, and engines installed in Belfast by MacColl and Company. It left Belfast June 29, 1910, under the command of Captain J.W. Starkey, arriving in Vancouver September 16. The superstructure was built of wood, which was cheap on the West Coast, and the track record of those who worked with it was good. (This unusual two-stage manner of construction was also used for the *Princess Victoria*, which had been completed on the West Coast after its voyage out from Britain. The division of labour in this case had been occasioned by the threat of a strike in the English yards. This experiment does not appear to have been repeated.)

The *Cheslakee* joined the *Cassiar* and the *Comox* as a Union Steamship vessel serving the communities on the West Coast. Unfortunately the weight of the Wallace-built superstructure gave it a permanent list, making it roll and sway "like a harpooned whale." On the early morning of January 7, 1913, on a trip from Vancouver up the coast under Captain John Cockle, heavy seas forced an emergency docking at Van Anda. While most escaped, six passengers and one crew member were drowned and the *Cheslakee* sank to the bottom. Some reports suggest that 11 loggers, not listed as official passengers, also drowned. This was the only accident in Union Steamship's history involving loss of life.

The BC Salvage Company's *Salvor* raised the ship,

which was taken to BC Marine Dry Dock in Victoria, where it was cut in half and a 20-foot midsection inserted. Reborn as the *Cheakamus*, its stability was much improved. In 1942 BC Marine converted it into a tugboat, and the US navy bought it after the war. A short time later it was transferred to the Foss Launching and Towboat operation in Seattle, and in 1950 it was transferred again to the Puget Sound Maritime Historical Society. The society did not have the money to maintain it, so it was scrapped in Seattle in the 1950s.

Surviving Fire and Leaner Times

In the early morning of July 11, 1911, the most destructive blaze in the brief recorded history of the North Shore struck Wallace's business, destroying the greater part of his shipyard and throwing 200 men out of work. Fortunately the absence of any wind prevented the fire from spreading to nearby North Vancouver businesses. Total loss of property was estimated at $150,000 to $200,000, only part of which was covered by insurance. Luckily the office building

and marine ways were saved.

At the time of the blaze, Wallace and his family were in England, where as loyal British subjects they attended the coronation of King George V. When they returned a few days after the fire, Wallace again took the opportunity to complain about local service and was quoted in the July 18 *Express* saying: "As I consider the rate of taxation to which I am subject disproportionate and ridiculous with the fire protection offered an industry in North Vancouver, it is extremely unlikely that the Wallace Shipyards will be built on their old site." Taxes paid for 1914 were $3,269.66.

Wallace hinted that he was considering alternative sites on the North Arm, but after a compromise on the subject of taxation he agreed to stay, and within six weeks of his return from England the yard was operating again.

In spite of the general economic downturn in 1913, the yard remained busy. On January 28 four vessels—the *Defiance*, *Storm King*, *Orontes* and *Mastodon*—were being serviced or repaired. The Union Steamship Company gave the repair work of

Top: The Cheslakee *in service.* Vancouver Maritime Museum 12530

all its fleet to the Wallace yard; the complete rebuilding of the wrecked *Vadso* was a major project in 1914. New construction included nine scows, a dredge hull and HMCS *Naden*, built for the hydrographic department of the government of Canada and designed by the noted marine architect R.L. Newman. This graceful two-masted schooner was used for its original purpose for one season only, working in the Skeena area under Mr. Davies as a tender to the surveying ship *Lillooet*. In 1918 it was lent to the navy and commissioned as a tender to the Naval College for training in sail. In 1925 Lieutenant J.W. Hobbs purchased the

Top: The aftermath of the July 1911 fire, with the marine ways still intact. 27-308

Above: The Naden, *built in 1913 for the hydrographic department of the government of Canada.* 27-2699

ship, renamed it the *Mabel Dell* and again used it as a training vessel for naval reserve seamen. Eventually it became a Hollywood movie star's yacht.

The history of Burrard Dry Dock would have been very different if Alfred Wallace had reached an agreement with Sir Alfred Yarrow, owner of Yarrows, the famous British shipyard on the Clyde. Yarrow wanted a plant outside Britain that would be unaffected by the ominous clouds that were about to burst into World War I and that could take advantage of the possibility of construction work for the nascent Canadian navy. Yarrow and Wallace discussed the sale of Wallace's company, but Yarrow considered it too small and lacking in railway trackage to bring in steel and other materials. The Second Narrows bridge, which would provide that needed link to the mainland, remained a paper project. Yarrow purchased the Bullen plant (BC Marine Railway) in Victoria in 1913 for $300,000; the adjoining government dry dock could accommodate vessels up to 480 feet. Three-quarters of the shares of the new company were issued in Sir Alfred's name and the remainder in the name of his son Norman, who eventually operated the plant, although for the first years it was run by R.D. Keay.

Yarrows and Wallace (later Burrard Dry Dock) were the major companies in their respective cities for most of the next half century, with Burrard buying out Yarrows 32 years later. But much was to happen before then. The outbreak of World War I delayed the building of a fixed crossing to the North Shore and other major industrial initiatives, but in the long run the war, and the opening of the Panama Canal in 1914, initiated major and permanent changes in maritime endeavours and the whole Canadian economic, social and cultural fabric. Certainly Wallace's business would be transformed. In the meantime, Alfred Wallace, affluently corpulent, looked like a man who could handle just about anything.

Above: A successful family—Alfred and Eliza Wallace with sons Clarence (left) and Hubert in 1912 or 1913. 8087

Ocean Ventures: 1914–1920

I remember the black wharves and the slips,
And the sea-tides tossing free;
And Spanish sailors with bearded lips
And the beauty and mystery of the ships,
And the magic of the sea.

From Henry Wadsworth Longfellow's
"My Lost Youth"

Early War Years: The Wallace Yards Expand

Before World War I, no facilities existed in BC for building ocean-going ships. In 1916 the provincial government, with Wallace's former associate W.J. Bowser now the premier, decided to change that, as the war had greatly stimulated the need for new ships. BC's lumber trade especially was suffering from a lack of vessels to carry its lumber to market. The BC Shipping Act (1916) encouraged the building of ocean-going ships through a generous subsidy of five dollars per ton deadweight as well as other financial enticements. In addition, the Imperial Munitions Board and the French government ordered numerous ships. The October 1939 issue of *Harbour and Shipping* states that during and immediately after the war, BC shipyards launched 21 auxiliary wooden schooners, 69 wooden steamers and 45 steel steamers. Loans guaranteed by the provincial government helped establish 17 new shipyards on the West Coast.

These years saw the birth of shipbuilding as a major industry in British Columbia.

War was the engine that drove the shipyards, as Britain in its beleaguered state looked to its colonies for help. In 1915 Alfred Wallace received his first major contract through Britain's Imperial Munitions Board—it was to manufacture shell casings. H.B. Taylor, a British engineer, set up the shell production line to produce 18-pound high explosives ordinance. Each was machined down to the last half-thousandth of an inch. These had to pass rigorous examination by a corps of trained inspectors. Good shells could be fired consistently into a three-foot square at 5,000 yards; even a slightly defective shell might fly 50 yards wide of the mark.

One of the junior employees was Wallace's older son, Clarence. He started with the shipyards in 1912 at the age of 18, after he graduated from St. Andrews College, and became head of the purchasing department in 1914 at the age of 21. Three days after the outbreak of war he joined the BC Horse Regiment with two friends, Laird Gordon and Harry Letson, and ended up with the Fifth Battalion Canadian Infantry in France. After being gassed and wounded in the second Battle of Ypres, losing a little finger, he was sent to McGill Hospital in Buckinghamshire. The result of his gassing was a bad cough that persisted to the end of his life, more than 60 years later.

When he was demobilized because of his injuries, Clarence had the choice of receiving a monthly pension for life or a smaller lump sum. His son David

BIG JIM ANDREWS, all six feet, two inches of him, worked as rigging boss for Burrard for 30 years. He drove piles for the first North Shore cradle in 1908 and launched 83 ships, beginning with the *Mabel Brown*. During World War II he helped superintend the layout of the South Yard, directing the building of all derricks at both the North and South Yards. As described in the *Wallace Shipbuilder* of August 1943, "He's the man who stands high on the bow of the ships as they slide down the ways...the cargo ship figure-head that all Burrard is proud of." While no one questioned his dedication, as boss of the bull gang he wielded a great deal of power that he used arbitrarily to select those who would be honoured with work. Those who tried to establish procedures and fight grievances were always the first to be laid off, at least until the union was able to establish more control over hiring and firing procedures. His son Jim worked for Burrard from 1925 to 1958, for much of the time as foreman rigger-labourer.

Jim Andrews, one of Burrard's longest-serving employees, in 1957. 27-376

Above: Making high explosive shells in the machine shop. 27-94

states that his father and a couple of buddies opted to take the lump sum—"and they had a party that took over the whole damn hospital." Clarence returned to work in the shipyard. He married Charlotte Shaw and they had four sons: Blake, Philip, Richard and David.

Meanwhile, Clarence's younger brother Hubert entered the Royal Military College in Kingston, Ontario, in 1916. From there he joined the Royal Flying Corps (later the Royal Air Force) to receive training as a pilot. He started work for the shipyards in 1919, remaining intimately connected with the company for the rest of his life.

No. 2 Yard:
The *Mabel Brown* and its Sisters

Sailing ships were definitely on their way out in the early years of the twentieth century, but during World War I their fortunes temporarily revived. By 1916, foreign tramp steamers and subsidized trading vessels had withdrawn from the lumber trade to more profitable work nearer the war zone. The resulting shortage of tonnage inflated freight rates and trebled the value of ships. Suddenly building wooden sailing ships became an attractive proposition, especially in parts of the world like the West Coast where wood was cheap and plentiful. During the pre-war years, wooden schooners were being built in great numbers in Puget Sound—Hall brothers at Port Blakely, Washington, had built 108—and it was relatively economical to equip yards for this purpose.

In June 1916 Wallace purchased 21 acres on the foreshore of DL 265, Block 22, west of the main shipyards, for $165,000 from H.H. Lonsdale and James P. Fell. This property, known as the Lonsdale Fell Fill, was bounded on the north by the south boundary of the Pacific Great Eastern Railway right-of-way, on the east by Bewicke Avenue and on the west by Fell Avenue. In a letter to city council dated June 2, 1916, Wallace, never a wallflower, makes his pitch for good service.

Above: Mrs. H.W. Brown, wife of the ship's purchaser, in the frame of the Mabel Brown. 27-2641

We would therefore be glad if the City of North Vancouver would erect a suitable bridge and construct the necessary roadway on the east side of the property in order that we may land many materials at the Plant which may be shipped by North Vancouver Merchants or from Vancouver Merchants by the City Ferries. We also make application for suitable water system for fire protection and for use generally in connection with the work.

The June 2, 1916, *North Shore Press*, ever eager to boost local projects, celebrated this occasion as "a sunbeam in the darkness." The citizens must now "rise to the occasion of such prosperity as stands on the city's threshold."

Hyperbole aside, this was indeed ideal land for shipbuilding, extending "level as a board" from the foreshore to deep water. Here, with men such as Frank Davie, Louis Larsen, Bob Blackstock and Jim Andrews, Wallace constructed No. 2 yard and contracted to build three modern auxiliary schooners for H.W. Brown's Canada West Coast Navigation Company for $121,200 each. He engaged J.H. Price from the US to design and supervise the ships' construction. The first building on the site was a two-storey structure, 50 by 150 feet, with a corrugated roof. The upper storey was to be used as a laying-out loft, and the ground floor as a woodworking shop.

Wallace soon contracted to build a further three schooners for Canada West Coast Navigation Company for $131,200 each. Cameron-Genoa Mills Shipbuilders Ltd. in Victoria, a company that had no previous shipbuilding experience, also built six. All were designed primarily to carry lumber, each having a capacity of between 1.5 million and 1.6 million board feet. They were constructed of local Douglas fir, a non-strategic material, supplied by the Vancouver firm Walsh Day Lumber Company. Engines were European-designed 91-horsepower (nominal horsepower or nhp) Bolinders.

The keel for the first of the Wallace-built

Top: Three of the schooners under construction at No. 2 yard in 1917. 27-2635

schooners, the *Mabel Brown*, was laid June 15, 1916, at the No. 2 yard. The structure of those that followed was virtually identical, although the last two—the *Mabel Stewart* and *Marie Barnard*—were three feet longer. Vessels built to this pattern came to be known as the "Mabel Brown" type. These were "bald-headed" schooners because they had no topmasts; the main sails were hoisted from the deck with steam winches, which reduced the need for experienced seamen. The five masts of the *Mabel Brown* were set into the deck itself, with the main mast four feet through at the base and 14 storeys high.

When it came time for the *Mabel Brown*'s launch, all did not go well. Before the throngs of expectant viewers, the schooner stubbornly refused to budge from its comfortable home, as the filled land on which it had been built had settled. A Scottish expert finally coaxed it into the water, but when it started on its launch it left before the bottle of wine could christen it. Alfred Wallace sprinted after the retreating ship, smashing against the hull a flask of whiskey that he just happened to be carrying with him.

The *Mabel Brown*'s reluctance to enter the water was well founded. As Dick Hammond wrote many years later:

∼

The *Mabel Brown* and her five sisters were obsolete when they were designed. Over-masted and under-engined, they were indeed not one thing or the other. A five-masted full-rigged ship needs a large crew to operate it, far more than would be economically practical. And unless the sails can be furled quickly, any sudden squall of wind could be dangerous. The two Bolinder semi-diesels were too small to drive such a heavy ship; they were undependable and old fashioned before they were installed. The war had brought a surge of mechanical advances in its wake and although this was hardly obvious at the time, the day of the sailing cargo ship was over.

On its maiden voyage to Australia with a load of lumber, commanded by Captain W. Boyd, the *Mabel Brown* soon ran into trouble when shrinking planks caused serious leaking (it had been constructed from green lumber). The engines quit, as did the pumps they drove. The ship went over on its side, in which awkward position it drifted for five or six months. When discovered, the crew was starving and there were rumours of cannibalism. It was refitted, ending its days under the Norwegian flag as the *Redemptor*, storm-damaged in the Novin Sea in December 1921 and scrapped in 1922.

The *Janet Carruthers* had a more successful launch on April 28, 1917, but troubles ensued. Its engines suffered cracked cylinders and a broken shaft on its first trip out of Vancouver, and it travelled from

Right: The Mabel Brown, *afloat at last, with all sails set.* 27-2649

Honolulu to Australia under sail. When it reached Apia it was badly disabled, and although temporary repairs got it going, its deck was a shambles, with the rigging twisted and torn. It eventually reached Adelaide under tow. After a voyage back across the Pacific it left Puget Sound again on January 20, 1919, but on January 22 it ran aground four miles north of the Grays Harbor bar, the captain mistaking Grays Harbor Light for North Head. Six men who tried to leave the wreck drowned when their boat was flipped over. Declared a constructive loss on January 30, 1919, the wreck was sold for $11,000 to James H. Price, former president of Cameron-Genoa Mills Shipbuilders of Victoria, and the ship's original designer. The new owner pumped oil from *Janet Carruthers*' tanks in an attempt to refloat it, but the Washington State commissioner responded by charging the salvagers with polluting the clam beds. The ship broke up.

Top: Lights enable work to continue on the Geraldine Wolvin *all night.* 4968

Other auxiliary schooners built by Wallace in No. 2 yard—the *Jessie Norcross, Mabel Stewart, Marie Barnard* and *Geraldine Wolvin*—were all named after the wives of Great Lakes shipowners. Captained by Peter Mathieson, the *Wolvin* made five crossings of the Pacific, including the first crossing for the Canada West Coast Navigation Company. It also had an eventful life, being severely damaged by a typhoon on one trip and surviving an engine-room fire on another.

The *Jessie Norcross* was also devastated by an engine-room fire and in fact sank, although it was successfully raised. Its crew, composed of miners and loggers who had taken to the sea, were equally buoyant. They made several successful trips transporting lumber to Australia and the East. Along with the *Mabel Brown, Mabel Stewart* and *Geraldine Wolvin*, the *Norcross* was taken over at Marseilles by a Paris company in April 1919. The *Wolvin* and *Norcross* were sold to Egyptians for $8,800 each in 1922. The *Mabel Stewart* was sold to Greek interests, renamed the *Calimeris* and totally destroyed by a fire off Gibraltar. The *Marie Barnard* also found a home with Greek shipowners, who renamed it the *Agapi*.

The schooners were not a profitable venture for Wallace—he lost $30,000 on each ship—and he was glad to lease No. 2 yard to William Lyall Shipbuilding Company in June 1917 for about $70,000, while retaining the right to complete boats already on the ways. Lyall Shipbuilding operated there only until the end of its three-year lease in 1920, although in those few years it launched numerous vessels.

It is true that the "Mabel Brown" ships were the end of an era: wooden ships that relied partly on sail when steel steamers were already the norm in most parts of the world. Still, they were beautiful ships and some gave good service. More importantly they catapulted the Wallace yards into the world of ocean-going vessel construction. Art Jones, writing in 1954, remembers those days nostalgically, the intervening years no doubt sweetening the memory:

⌇

The "Mabel Brown" vessels were good sea-boats, and had fairly good lines. They weren't clippers or old-time packet boats when it came to speed, just a general average of six miles per hour. The best week I can remember we logged 1100 miles. That was north of New Zealand and the engines running all the while. After being in the Australian square-rigger grain ships, these five-masted schooners seemed like a sailor's dream of heaven. A wheelhouse, electric light, steam to hoist the anchor, compressed air winches to hoist sail. No brass and no varnish work to look after. No chipping hammer. One yard instead of ten or fifteen, and only two persons on the ship who knew what it was for. One was the skipper, the other myself. There were no gaff topsails so the boys didn't need to go any higher aloft after dark than the top bunks.

Above: The Wallace Shipyards sign is on top of the old machine shop, which was located between two marine railways. The nearest one supports the Ballena. *The bunk scow in the foreground belongs to PWD Dredge* Mastodon, *berthed in the background alongside the Russian freighter* Azov, *the* Melmore *and two unidentified vessels, circa 1910s.* 02-16D

The War Ships

In April 1917 British and Allied shipping losses totalled 555,056 gross tons, while new production was only 69,711. The British authorities, alarmed at the destruction being inflicted by the German U-boats, sent a team of experts to Canada to investigate the facilities for steel shipbuilding. They were not encouraged by what they saw. Canadian expertise in steel shipbuilding was minimal, but the British had little choice. The Imperial Munitions Board placed orders with 10 Canadian firms to build 41 steel ships from 1,800 to 8,800 tons. There were further orders for 47 with wooden hulls at a dwt of 3,300.

It may have been because of the financial drain of the "Mabel Brown" types, or perhaps Wallace sensed that steel shipbuilding was the way of the future, but the yard built no wooden vessels for the war. It completed three steel ships: *War Dog, War Power* and *War Storm.* No doubt encouraged by Wallace's solid track

Above: The men from the office are dwarfed by the huge propellers of the War Dog *on May 17, 1917. The workers stand discreetly in the background.* 27-2672

record, Dingwall Cotts and Company of London ordered the *War Dog* through its Vancouver office for the Kishimoto Steamship Company of Osaka, Japan; as the war caused the withdrawal of British shipping from the Pacific, the Japanese expanded. According to historian G.W. Taylor, "The increases in costs, difficulties in getting steel, and the inability of the British and Scandinavian yards to make firm commitments for delivery, had made B.C. more competitive." No further business, however, came from the Orient.

The Imperial Munitions Board took over the *War Dog* when it was completed. It was a small freighter of 3,046 tons, costing $484,500—the first steel cargo vessel built in BC. Designed by naval architect J.D. Baker, with construction supervised by R.E. Ellis, it was launched in May 1917 with a crowd of 2,000 to 3,000 in attendance. *War Power* and *War Storm* followed

Top: The War Storm *ready for service.* 27-2617
Above: The deck of the War Dog, *March 5, 1917.* 27-2666

shortly, costing $736,000 and $943,000 respectively, as prices escalated.

The 1,300-horsepower triple expansion reciprocating engines for all three vessels were built in the engine works of the Wallace Shipyards under the direction of H. Bakewell Taylor, chief engineer and assistant superintendent of the yard. These were the first engines of any considerable size to be constructed in BC—the propeller was 15 feet in diameter. Wallace also engined the *War Cayuse* and the *War Atlin* built by Lyall, and the *War Tanoo* built by Western Canada Shipyards on False Creek. He imported boilers from England for the *War Dog*, but those for the latter two

War vessels built by Wallace were fashioned at Granville Island's Vulcan Iron Works by local boiler-makers. The North Shore Iron Works built winches and deck machinery for the *War Dog*. With the exception of the boilers and the deck and engine-room auxiliaries, practically everything in a Wallace ship could now be built in the company yards.

While these ships were useful for the war effort, the British did not generally keep them around after the Armistice. In 1920 the *War Dog* went under the Italian flag, renamed *Roverbella*; it was scrapped in Genoa, Italy, in 1933. *War Power* was sold to the French, becoming successively the *Antoinette*, the

Top: Boilers similar to those built for War Power *and* War Storm *by Vulcan Iron Works.* 27-3759

Top: Workers at the Greene Electric Furnace in the Wallace Foundry on Granville Island. 27-3754

Above: Workers lay out the design for the Canadian Volunteer *in the new mould loft, 1918.* 27-143

Monette and the *Tristan Vieljeux*. In 1939 it was the Greek steamer *Keti Chandris*.

Lucrative wartime contracts led Wallace to expand the original yard and ancillary businesses. Frustrated by slow deliveries from the US and eastern Canada, Wallace established the Wallace Foundry on Granville Island on September 27, 1917, with a capital of $75,000, not only to supply engines for the *War* series of ships, but also to undertake contracts for the Imperial Munitions Board. In April 1919 the foundry turned out a propeller that, at nine tons, was the largest ever cast in Canada to this time. All propellers for the 27 Imperial Munitions Board steamers built on the West Coast were cast in BC shops. On March 7, 1930, Wallace Foundry's plant and equipment (but not the company) was sold to Vulcan Iron Works for $50,000. When the latter company was liquidated in 1934, the Wallaces reacquired the assets and operated it once more until 1939.

In early 1918 Wallace purchased the lot in North Vancouver immediately adjoining the old ferry landing, where the company developed a new plate shop

Top: The yards around 1918, with materials ready for a new project. 27-21

and spacious mould loft, as well as other facilities. Wallace established a new sawmill and joiner shop (No. 2 stores building) in 1920 and purchased the Brackman-Ker milling building at Lot 14, Block 176, for use as a sheet metal and copper shop.

He also continued his running battle with the North Vancouver politicians, using thinly veiled threats to lever concessions from the fledgling municipal government. "[W]e write to protest against the exorbitant rates which are now charged on loads of freight, consisting of supplies and raw material, which are now daily delivered to us by team and motor truck." Later in the same letter he suggests that it is "an extremely shortsighted policy for the City of North Vancouver to adopt measures which tend to drive

industries away from North Vancouver rather than induce them to locate here." Though he may not have won every battle, Wallace, a valued contributor of taxes and jobs, was generally well treated by his municipal host.

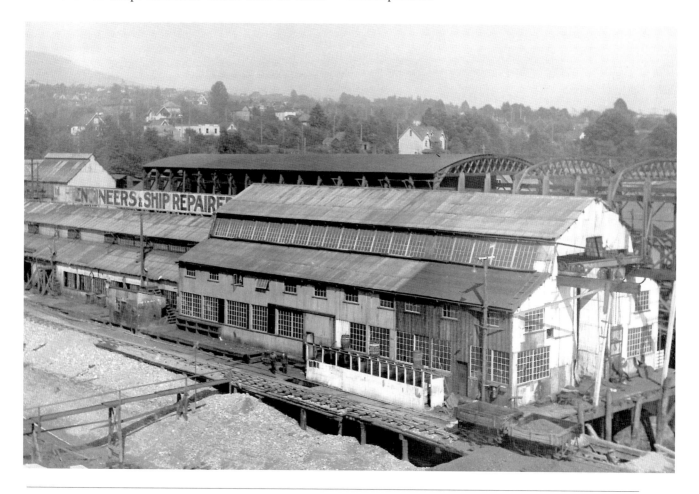

Top: One of Burrard's first trucks, circa 1920, with, left to right: Fred Kasel (driver), Fred Clendenning (patternmaker) and Joe Irvine (patternmaker). The propeller blade is for the Canadian Transporter. 27-265

Above: The original machine shop, circa 1920. It was built in 1911 and was later used as No. 1 stores building. It is still standing, now preserved as a heritage building. 02-16A

Merchant Marine Contracts

World War I built up Canada's sense of nationhood and pride of accomplishment, and as the war drew to a close, the Canadian government realized that it might be possible to parlay domestic shipyards' experiences building ocean-going steel vessels for Britain into a peacetime industry. The shipyards could build ships for a merchant marine that would be an extension of Canada's railways, transporting goods in either peace or war. C.C. Ballantyne, minister of marine and fisheries, initiated a Canadian Government Merchant Marine (CGMM) shipbuilding program that gave contracts to all the major yards in Canada, providing much-needed work for returning servicemen.

These were good years for shipbuilding in Canada, as the shortage of ships caused by the war had tripled the construction cost per ton in Britain and made the Canadian industry competitive—for a few years at least. Demand was high. The Australian lumber market was profitable, while in 1919 the British timber controller placed an order with the Association of Timber Exporters of British Columbia for 70 million feet of timber and ties for the British railways. Ships were needed to transport the lumber.

In March 1918 Wallace was the first to receive contracts for six ships for the CGMM at a cost of nearly $7 million, beginning with the *Canadian Volunteer* and the *Canadian Aviator*. The former was the first BC-built steamer to be handed over to the new Canadian mercantile marine. Wallace also built

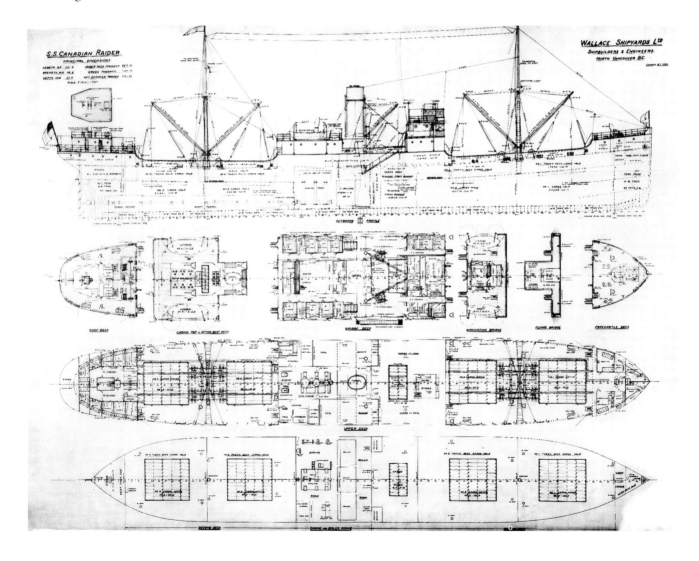

Above: Plans for the Canadian Raider, *which were also used for the other* Canadian *ships built by Wallace Shipyards.* 27-2724

its 1,800-horsepower (indicated horsepower or ihp) engines. The main coal-fired boilers, built by Vulcan Iron Works, were 15 feet, 6 inches in diameter and 11 feet, 6 inches long; the heaviest to be built in BC at 50 tons each, they provided a modest service speed of 11 knots. All castings were made by the Wallace Foundry. Wallace also built the *Canadian Raider*, *Canadian Trooper*, *Canadian Highlander* and *Canadian Skirmisher* for this series. The latter two were considerably larger, at 5,370 and 5,373 tons, with three boilers rather than two.

In late March 1918, A. Johnson, deputy minister of marine, wrote to Canadian shipyards to suggest they hire women to assist with these contracts. The response was at best tepid. While the Vancouver yard John Coughlan and Sons stated that it was already using women in the drafting department who were "chiefly relatives of soldiers serving at the front," Wallace's company was not interested.

⁓

[We] have come to the conclusion that at the present time it is not practicable to employ women in any of the branches of the trade mentioned in your letter. Take for example carpentering and Rivetting. We doubt very much if women have the necessary constitution to stand this extremely heavy work. In the former trade, it is a matter of lifting and erecting heavy shores. In the latter we find that it is necessary for even a man to have a first class physique in order to stand the jar of the pneumatic rivetting hammers.

Top: The Canadian Volunteer, *first BC-built Canadian government steamer to be handed over to the new Canadian Government Merchant Marine.* 27-2607

Prince Rupert for the job in April 1919, but before the end of 1920 the Prince Rupert builders went into liquidation.* Alfred Wallace transferred H.J. Turney, secretary of Wallace Shipyards, to the northern city as manager of the project and also sent along his second son, Hubert, to oversee and gain some experience. The two hulls, one of which was well advanced, and the other half finished when Wallace took over, were successfully completed before the end of 1921 and registered as the *Canadian Britisher* and the *Canadian Scottish*. The former later went under the Chinese flag as the *Ping An*, then was bought by the Japanese and renamed *Heian Maru* of Yokohama. The *Canadian Scottish* became the Greek steamer *Mount Parnassus*. In 1939 it was sold to Germany and renamed the *Johann Schulte*, going down off Norway in 1940.

Between 1918 and 1920 the Canadian government commissioned 63 new steamships, built in 17 Canadian shipyards and financed on a cost per ton basis rather than cost-plus. The cost per deadweight ton of ships built for the CGMM was $192, comparing favourably with Japan ($187 a ton), Britain ($185 a ton) and the US ($200 to $220 a ton). BC shipbuilders were paid $10 a ton more than those in the east because of higher labour rates ($7 a ton more) and higher freight rates.

It would take another war for women's constitutions to be accepted as adequate.

The men performed their duties well. They laid the keel of the *Canadian Aviator* within three hours after the *Canadian Volunteer* left the ways on April 5, a record for the Pacific coast. The May 1919 issue of *Harbour and Shipping* noted that the *Canadian Aviator* would employ "an entirely white crew." These were difficult times for those who were not white men and wanted or needed to earn a living in building or working on ships.

In January 1921 Wallace Shipyards received one more government contract—to complete two CGMM ships that were originally to be built by Prince Rupert Drydock and Shipyard. That company leased the Grand Trunk Pacific Railway's dry dock in

But the Canadian Government Merchant Marine ships did not live up to Minister Ballantyne's hopes. While they opened up new trade routes, especially to the West Indies, and established service to the Orient, Australia, New Zealand, Europe and eastern Canada, they were mostly a money pit—generally more expensive, less fuel efficient and less efficient at handling cargo than others built immediately after the war. Although a continued strong demand for shipping services made them profitable in 1919–1920, and they made a profit of over $70,000 in the first nine

---

* The Prince Rupert dry dock's less than glorious career ended in 1955 when it was towed down to Seattle.

Top: The keel was laid and centre girder erected for the Canadian Aviator *three hours after the* Canadian Volunteer *was launched.* 27-2587

months of 1926, losses were more the rule. Declining freight rates led to a loss of nearly $2 million in 1921, and a crippling total of $82 million before the merchant marine was disbanded in 1936.

The ships were sold off to other owners between 1923 and 1936. The *Canadian Volunteer* became the *Cornwallis* and then by 1939 the *Magister of Jamaica*, turning up in Vancouver in May 1946 with 1,800 cases of Jamaica rum. The *Canadian Aviator* was sold in Montreal and renamed *Cavalier*. The *Canadian Highlander* became the *Saint Lindsay* of Newport, South Wales. The *Canadian Raider* became the Norwegian *Tenax*, then the Spanish *Mari Dolores*, and in 1939 the *Antonio-De-Sattoustegui*, also of Spain. From 1965 it sailed from Fowey in Cornwall, England, with cargoes of china clay for Italy, surviving to 1977.

Top: Miss Begg lets fly with the champagne for the 1957 launch of the self-unloading barge Crown Zellerbach No. 5. *Above: Mrs. Stevens, wife of MP H.H. Stevens, preparing to launch the* Canadian Aviator, *displays the more sedate demeanor expected of a society matron of 1919.* 27-2593, 27-1947

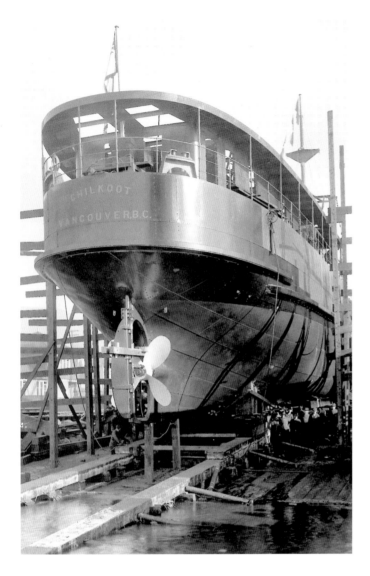

In 1939 the *Canadian Skirmisher* was the *Colborne* of Montreal. The *Canadian Trooper* was sold in 1930 to G. Paul Knudsen of Bergen, Norway, to become the *Lundhaug*. Several of the last ships (the exact number is uncertain) were purchased by a young Aristotle Onassis in one of his first steps to becoming a shipping magnate.

The *Chilkoot*

As the lucrative wartime contracts wound down, the shipyards sought other business. Alfred Wallace had worked for the Union Steamship Company on his arrival in Vancouver, and now the connections paid

off. The *Chilkoot*, built for Union Steamship immediately after the war, was launched by Miss Constance Darling, elder daughter of Henry Darling, the designer. The *North Shore Press* of February 27, 1919, described the event:

> Miss Darling swung the bottle of wine against the steel prow as it moved away. The container of the precious beverage, however, proved to be a stubborn quantity for it bounded away from the side of the ship without exploding. However, a workman quickly caught the string and swung the bottle aloft, bringing it back sharply against the steel plates. A burst of foam before the vessel left the ways signified that the christening had been truly carried out despite the few seconds delay.

Built for service along the West Coast, this $225,000 ship was capable of 12 knots, making it the fastest local cargo carrier in the business. Its 725-horsepower (ihp) war-surplus engines came from Builders Iron Foundry in Providence, Rhode Island, USA, and its Scotch marine boilers from Vulcan Iron Works in Vancouver. With spaces for 20,000 cases of canned salmon, convenient working hatches and a 20-ton lift capacity, it was the class of coastal shipping. First commanded by Captain James Findlay, it had room for a crew of 21, including officers, and its fuel capacity gave it a range of 2,500 miles.

The *Chilkoot* served the coastal area past Prince Rupert up to Wales Island until it was sold in 1934 to the Border Line for a bargain basement price of $40,000 and renamed the *Border Prince*. Gerald Rushton, who wrote the history of the Union Steamship Company, regretted the *Chilkoot*'s loss, arguing that when World War II broke out, its value was five times what had been received. In 1958 it was completely reconstructed for the northern coastal service of Northland Navigation Company and renamed *Alaska Prince*.

Top: The Chilkoot *ready for launching.* 27-2565

Changing Times

Shipbuilding had changed during the war in ways that Andy Wallace grasped better than most. At the end of the war some people still claimed that wood would remain the material of choice for ships, arguing that in the post-war world, wood was plentiful but steel was not and that replacement of steel infrastructure destroyed by the war would have priority over ships. They were wrong. Wallace, positioning his company for the construction and especially the repair of steel ships, was right. An added advantage for his yard, which had limited possibilities for physical expansion, was that steel shipbuilding takes up less space than wooden shipbuilding. The Canadian government also made it clear that steel rather than wood shipbuilding was its priority.

By 1920, shipbuilding in BC had been transformed. Instead of producing mostly wooden ships for local use, some companies were now building international ocean-going steel ships. It did not take local politicians and businessmen long to realize that the industry was dropping a lot of golden tax eggs in their basket. As the *Vancouver Sun* noted on May 26, 1918, "Shipbuilding has taken the lead of all industries in this province. The result is apparent on every hand, with an estimated number of 5,000 employees in Vancouver alone, and a total of close to 10,000 employees in all plants." By 1919 shipbuilding was worth $30 million a year in BC, with Wallace and John Coughlan and Sons accounting for half that amount.

In May 1918, Wallace Shipyards employed between 900 and 1,000 men. The only local shipyard employing more was Coughlan, which employed

Above: The Wallace Pipe Band on a trip to Seattle–Tacoma during World War II. 27-1166

A series of agreements between Wallace and the City of North Vancouver council beginning January 2, 1916, strengthened his community support at the cost of social equality. These and subsequent agreements re-inforced Wallace's commitment to hire white male North Vancouverites in return for concessions in water rates and taxes. An agreement dated December 24, 1920, committed the company to employ "not less than forty white workmen, in addition to the respective numbers the Company has already…agreed to employ, all of whom shall be permanent residents of said City of North Vancouver." In return he was guaranteed up to 2,500 gallons of free water a day and a fixed tax assessment of $50 a foot. These and other agreements were written up as bylaws by the city council (which struck similar agreements with other North Vancouver companies) and ratified by the provincial government.

While this overt racism cannot be justified, those lucky enough to work for the yard were treated like members of an extended family. In July 1918 C.M. Stewart founded an athletics club to promote interest in outdoor sports. Company baseball and football teams attracted many employees to both play and watch. Union Steamship vessels transported workers and their families to yearly picnics on Bowen Island.

between 2,600 and 2,800 before a fire in May 1918 caused it to cut the payroll to about 1,500. At this time Coughlan was the largest employer in Vancouver, although in 1923 it closed down its shipbuilding operations and turned back to fabricating steel for office buildings.

These were huge social occasions, cementing the bonds that led to company loyalty and long-time service. Later, during World War II, the Wallace Pipe Band became a well-known ambassador for the yards. From one perspective these recreational, social and team activities were replications of the workplace,

Top: Tug of war, 1957. 27-1039

reinforcing work ethic values and the subordination of the individual to a group/team effort in an atmosphere of camaraderie.

THE SHIPYARD workers who lived in North Van socialized with one another pretty well. You see, in those days we knew everybody in the shipyard. Then, of course, they used to have the picnics to Bowen Island at that time. Union Steamship, or Burrard, I don't know which, had their annual picnic every year. We'd all pile on the Union Steamship boat and go to Bowen Island and have a day there and then back in. And it used to cost us a dollar for a ticket. We'd take the whole family and take a lunch.

Dick Broadhurst in *A History of Shipbuilding in British Columbia*, p. 44.

Beyond the heady achievements of the war and immediate post-war years lay rocky waters. The boom, encouraged by extremely high freight rates because of the shortage of tonnage, lasted only until 1921. By this time the tonnage deficit had been made up, causing freight rates to fall rapidly. With steel plate at $102 a ton compared to $55 a ton in Britain, and shipwrights earning $36.30 for a 44-hour week as compared to $16.50 in Britain for a 50-hour week, local yards found it difficult to compete. The Canadian government was reluctant to either fund a Canadian navy or establish laws that would protect the local shipbuilding and repair industry, so with a few exceptions, the British yards got the major contracts.

By the early 1920s, most of the BC shipbuilding companies that had sprung up during the war were closed. In 1921 S. and R. Wallace (no relation to Alfred) set up a wooden boat-building business that

Top: 1910s elegance shows its muscle, but with all hats properly in place. 8882

lasted until about 1928, building at least 12 registered vessels. The Burdick brothers set up Pacific Salvage on the waterfront just west of Lonsdale Avenue in 1925. But for most of the inter-war period, Wallace Shipyards (which became Burrard Dry Dock in 1921) remained the only significant shipyard in the Lower Mainland.

AT LEAST until the later years, Burrard Dry Dock was not only a place to work, but also a way of life. The loyalty and sense of belonging the Wallaces fostered was to a large extent responsible for the company's success. Social and sports activities included bowling, golf, billiards and annual fishing derbies. During World War II the company had what was reported to be the largest bowling league in the world. Annual picnics included tugs-of-war, children's races, relay races and a variety of other activities. Wallace also sponsored baseball and football teams, and the football club became BC champion in 1918–1919. In 1942 four members of this team—Alec McInnis, John Melville, Billy "Dirty" Drumond and Duggie Brown—were still working for Burrard.

Top: The Wallace Shipyards baseball team, circa 1920. 27-709

CHAPTER 3

A Few Good Ships:
1921–1939

I knew Sam Curry. He was a first class plater from Harland and Wolff in Belfast. He was awful cranky—being a good plater, he expected his helper to anticipate the next move on the job, and if he didn't, Sam would get mad. But there was another side to Sam. He and his wife helped many people in Lynn Valley. In fact, they often shared whatever Sam earned with those who were having it worse than they. This was a real sacrifice, for Sam only got a day or two now and then. It was real kindness on their part.

Robert John Speers in *A History of Shipbuilding in British Columbia*

Princess Louise: It *Is* Possible

After World War I, the CPR needed a replacement for the ill-fated *Princess Sophia*, which had been lost on Vanderbilt Reef on October 25, 1918, along with more than 350 passengers and crew. The CPR's Captain James Troup tried negotiating with the Denny yard on the Clyde in Scotland, but it was unable to guarantee delivery of another coast liner until the following year. Other established British shipbuilders were backlogged with orders to replace tonnage lost during the war. So the CPR turned to BC for tenders on its next passenger liner for West Coast service.

Wallace's connections did no harm. E.W. Beatty, president of the CPR, was the son of Henry Beatty, head of the shipping company that ordered the construction of the *Manitoba*, on which Wallace had worked as a foreman 30 years earlier. Previously Victoria's Bullen yard had built the *Princess Beatrice* (1903), the *Princess Royal* (1906) and the *Princess Maquinna* (1913) for the CPR. Now Wallace submitted the lowest bid for a 4,032-ton ship at a cost of $1.5 million, and with the recommendation of F.W. Peters, general superintendent of the CPR, won the contract to construct the *Princess Louise*, named after the first vessel brought to the Pacific for the CPR coastal service in 1878. The original had been built by John English and Sons in New York in 1869.

While neither the size nor the cost of this ship was significantly greater than projects the yard had built previously, a *Princess* needed style and elegance. Like the wartime ships that were built to a standard plan devised in another country, the CP liner's drawings, machinery, furnishings and steel plate came from Scotland, but it also brought unique challenges to be solved by Canadian expertise. Masts, derricks, boilers and engines were all made in Vancouver or New Westminster. Frank Gildersleeve, the architect who oversaw inside decoration of the Hotel Vancouver, was in charge of interior decorating for the *Princess Louise*. All woodwork was done in BC, and all the material, with the exception of hardwoods, came from BC forests. An observation room was framed in Honduras mahogany.

In his unpublished history of Burrard Dry Dock, J.S. Marshall described the library, which contained bookcases with leaded panels and a floral motif of Canadian dogwood, as well as the smoking room, framed in black walnut with large plate glass windows. This room was decorated at each end with representations of Siwash Rock and the Lions. There were also two multi-panelled skylights, one with motifs representing each Canadian province and the other representing BC industries. (These two windows are now in the Maritime Museum of British Columbia in Victoria.) The first-class dining saloon, framed in natural oak, seated 140. Reflecting the expected clientele, accommodations were available for 300 first-class and 44 second-class passengers on three decks, while 90 officers and crew took care of their needs. In the bow, beyond the cargo hold, was room for 10 Chinese cooks and 10 third-class Asian passengers.

Robert Allan, formerly chief draftsman for the Fairfield Shipyards in Glasgow, outdid himself with the elegant design. If it had been built in Scotland, it would have been equipped with turbines. Instead, the engines were a set of four-cylinder triple-expansion engines capable of 4,500 horsepower, designed by A.F. Menzies and built by Wallace under the supervision of J. Browning. The boilers, built by the local Vulcan Iron Works, were 16 feet in diameter and 12 feet long. The construction supervisor was James Cant, and the consulting engineer was William Howie. A new three-storey joiner's shop was built at the yards to facilitate construction.

Top: The Princess Louise *under construction.* 5576

The launching took place August 29, 1921. Ensuing festivities were held in the mould loft, which "was made gay with bunting, flags and flowers, and long tables groaned under weight of good cheer." This was the best-attended launch of any in the history of Vancouver shipbuilding, and those present paid glowing tribute to the accomplishment. D.C. Coleman, vice-president of the CPR, in the August 30, 1921, *Province* described the ship as the first "built in the Americas which will compare in design and finish with the best product of the great yards in the British Isles." The ship itself was resplendent in garb of red, black, yellow and white.

But the day belonged to Andy Wallace as he surveyed his proudest accomplishment with a few well-chosen words.

It has been the ambition of my life to do what nobody else has done. There are one or two other things to do before I leave this map. The building of *Louise* was a great undertaking for a small firm such as ours. Switching from tramp steamers to passenger liners is a feat of which I doubt the yards in the Old Country are capable. We have built this ship, and we hope to build a ship as big as the *Empress of Asia*.

Its great flaring bow gave it a large forward deck, designed so many could stand outside and view the wonders of northern scenery. A few months later, when trials were held, it averaged an impressive 17-plus knots. The operation was completely vibration free. James Pettigrew, the chief engineer, described the engines as "a masterpiece." There "never was a trial trip better." Its first commander was Captain Andrew Slater.

Although described by some as a bit awkward to handle, the *Princess Louise* had a long and profitable career cruising the West Coast. For most of its life it worked the Alaska tourist run, but during many winters ran the night triangle run (Victoria–Seattle–Vancouver). During World War II it joined the US Army Transport Service, plying the route from Seattle to Excursion Inlet in Alaska. Apart from a collision with the *Princess Marguerite* near Active Pass in 1930, it was accident free.

Premier Duff Pattullo often paced the deck of the *Princess Louise* as he made his way to his Prince Rupert riding. In the July 1963 issue of *Harbour and Shipping*, Allan Fraser, general cashier for the Vancouver office of the White Pass and Yukon Railway, recalled, "The *Louise* was really a home to us, and the scene of many a good old party at the close of river navigation in the north." In 1952 it was with-

Opposite and above: Created for gracious living: interior views of the Princess Louise. 27-2518, 27-2527, 27-2521

drawn from the Alaska service because of declining demand and refitted for cruise purposes to replace the *Princess Kathleen*.

When the *Louise* was taken out of service in 1962, its spare engine parts had still not been used. It was sold to the Princess Louise Corporation of Los Angeles on April 28, 1966, and was towed south minus engine and propeller by the tug *La Pointe*. In Wilmington it was converted to a floating restaurant that operated at Berth 236, Terminal Island, Long Beach, California. Much of the ship was restored as nearly as possible to its original appearance, with the portholes and wood panels left intact. The bridge deck with the captain's cabin, officers' quarters and radio shack was also left intact as an authentic marine museum. In the first two years 1.4 million visitors came aboard for lunch, dinner, cocktails or a tour, making it the busiest restaurant in the United States. In 1979 it was moved to Berth 94 in the Port of Los Angeles, near the World Cruise Center.

But even *Princesses* finally lose their buoyancy. On January 15, 1989, it was withdrawn from service, des-tined for the scrapyard. On October 30, 1989, it went over on its side while docked at Terminal Island, San Pedro, California, sinking 23 feet to the harbour floor. Vancouver's TriNav Shipping attempted to salvage it, but that turned out to be too expensive. On June 20, 1990, it left on its last voyage, but before reaching its final burial ground on the seaward side of Catalina Island, it could no longer be kept afloat and sank in 600 feet of water in the San Pedro channel.

In spite of the quality of the *Princess Louise* and its suitability for West Coast use, the CPR took most of its future business back to British yards. The CPR management had strong British connections, and many of the shareholders were British. Shipbuilding and trade were tools of empire for Britain; British shipbuilding only declined when the empire that it was built to maintain dissolved. There were economic reasons as well. Demand inflated prices in Britain in the years immediately following the war, which made it possible for Wallace and other Canadian shipyards to compete at this time. As demand decreased and the British prices dropped, Wallace lost his edge.

Above: The Princess Louise *on the job. Andy Wallace, inset.* 27-2538

The Long Walk to a Dry Dock

It was one of the more unusual incentives ever offered to join a new country. When BC joined Confederation in 1871, the Canadian government promised Victoria a dry dock, although it was not completed until 1887. Vancouver soon outstripped Victoria in both population and as a shipping centre, so it also needed a dry dock to repair and maintain the ocean-going vessels that used its harbour in increasing numbers. The only debate was over whether it should be a graving dock (dug out of land) or a floating dry dock. In 1882 the federal government passed an act offering a subsidy of 3.5 percent yearly for 25 years on the estimated cost of a dry dock, and in the early 1890s Premier John Robson discussed building a dry dock in Moodyville.

North Vancouver's July 30, 1909, *Express* contained a report by Donald Cameron, district engineer, concerning the feasibility of a dry dock for vessels up to 600 feet in length. If expanded to its full capability of 975 feet, this would exceed the capacity of any dry dock yet built anywhere. He estimated the cost for a graving dock as $875,000 and a floating dock at $1.25 million. On April 19, 1910, the same paper reported that Alderman Alexander Smith said he was representing an English concern that was planning to build a floating dry dock for $1 million to $1.75 million.

More solidly based were the plans of the Imperial Car and Shipbuilding and Dry Dock Company, which had a signed subsidy agreement with the federal government for a dry dock and shipbuilding plant at Roche Point, North Vancouver. Banner headlines in the July 8, 1910, *Express* heralded "An Immense Industry for the North Shore." The company purchased over 600 acres and two miles of waterfront, and the writer looked forward sanguinely to "the building up of a vast industrial concern which has probably no equal upon the Pacific coast." But while a sawmill was built, other development did not happen. On April 8, 1913, the company's land holdings were sold to Dominion Trust, acting as trustee for another company. At this time the sawmill was idle.

The local newspaper became an ardent booster of ever more grandiose schemes. On February 16, 1912,

Above: Dry dock construction, July 10, 1923. 27-49

it proclaimed plans for a million-dollar construction project on DL 265 west of Lonsdale Avenue. This combined constructing bulkheads and dredging the seaward side to create a waterfront with a depth of 30 feet at low tide. This was in fact done and became known as "Fell Fill," although the accompanying dry dock did not materialize. The next year the local MP, Robert Rogers, touted this area as a site for a floating dock; federal money, however, flowed less freely than the political rhetoric.

In 1914 the preferred site shifted back to Moodyville, closer to where the Second Narrows bridge is today. Plans by Dominion Shipbuilding Engineering and Drydock Company called for a 1,000-foot graving dock, 100 feet wide at the gates, which would run along 1,400 feet of waterfront west of Lynn Creek and employ 7,000 men. This would be big enough to accommodate the largest vessel at that time afloat and cost an amazing $6 million. Cranes capable of lifting 100 tons would be a part of the

Top: Pontoons for the dry dock under construction on the marine railway. 27-52

project. The June 2, 1914, *North Shore Press* protested—perhaps too strenuously—that this "is not a scheme for selling stock in the open market." In October 1914 about 300 men were employed in preliminary construction, but without a federal subsidy and with the coming of war the project faltered—although as late as January 1917 optimistic reports boasted that the dock would be in operation within a year.

Amalgamated Engineering next emerged as the front-runner in the dry dock sweepstakes, with the North Vancouver city council voting 4-3 on January 28, 1916, to submit a bylaw giving the company tax-exempt status and free water for 35 years and guaranteeing the principal only of $750,000 of the company's bonds. Its proposals called for an immense 1,150-foot-long graving dock on the foreshore of DL 265, starting immediately west of Fell Fill and running from 1,500 to 1,700 feet between Fell and McKay Avenue. A marine railway capable of taking boats up to 3,000 tons was also planned.

A merger of Amalgamated Engineering with Wallace Shipyards made business sense. The former owned a federal subsidy guaranteeing 4 percent interest on $5.5 million for the construction of a first-class graving dock on Burrard Inlet. It needed Wallace Shipyards' developed infrastructure, while Wallace could use Amalgamated Engineering's access to capital. But plans again failed to develop—in his history of BC shipyards, G.W. Taylor suggests it was because of a clash of personalities between Wallace and the owner of Amalgamated.

As the war drew to an end, the worldwide shortage of tonnage heightened the anxiety caused by the lack of adequate repair facilities. In the September 26, 1919, *North Shore Press*, one writer estimated that Vancouver was losing $60,000 to $90,000 a month in business and wages. Regional tensions were exacerbated when shortly after the war the Champlain Dry Dock opened at Lauzon, Quebec. Built at a cost of $3.36 million, it was the largest in North America.

Alfred Wallace saw the building of a dry dock as crucial to the favourable positioning of his company.

On September 30, 1919, he hired William Henry Logan Jr. to design the dock, and on October 8 of the same year, as if to prove his determination, he changed Wallace Shipyards' legal name to Wallace Drydocks Limited.

In October 1919 Wallace, Coughlan's and Pacific Construction Company each filed plans for a dry dock. The latter two proposed graving docks; Wallace proposed a modest 650-foot-long floating dock with 15,000 tons capacity and a cost estimated at $2.5 million. Not long after, Raymond Concrete Pile Company of Montreal also applied for a subsidy for a graving dock. By this time many might agree with the writer in the December 1918 issue of *Harbour and Shipping* that "If the length of the dock is the same as the length of time spent arguing about it, it would be the biggest drydock in the world." On February 21, 1920, the federal government approved Coughlan's application for a dry dock 750 feet long and 110 feet wide, to cost $3.75 million, with a subsidy of 4 percent. Wallace's application lost out, partly because the government preferred a graving dock.

On July 10, 1920, Arthur Meighen became prime minister (Sir Robert Borden had resigned), and local MP H.H. Stevens became minister of trade and commerce. Coughlan signed a contract with the government on October 27 for a graving dock, but in November *Canadian Railway and Marine World* suggested that as Coughlan did not see enough work ahead to warrant the expenditure, it planned to join forces with Wallace Shipyards. Coughlan's precarious financial situation was an added incentive. The company had an expensive mortgaged lot on the waterfront, had paid a large sum for graving dock plans and had paid out considerable sums for political influence.

On September 17, 1921, Wallace and Coughlan signed an agreement to build a dry dock, and Burrard Dry Dock was incorporated on October 6. They chose the name "Burrard" because the new dock would be built on the north shore of Burrard Inlet and it would be more readily recognizable by customers from

distant parts. The dry dock, according to this agreement, would be the floating dock Wallace wanted, rather than the graving dock promoted by Coughlan. The former could be built more cheaply and speedily, which made it more attractive to investors. If more capacity were needed, it could be increased by simply adding more sections, and a floating dock could, if necessary, be moved. This gave Wallace the flexibility for growth that suited his approach to shipbuilding. The main disadvantage was that it could not handle large ships as conveniently and safely as a graving dock, and maintenance was much more costly.

On December 2, 1921, Burrard entered into an agreement with the federal public works department to build a floating dry dock within two years, the cost set at $2.5 million. Wallace paid Coughlan $199,000 for its work to this point.

Coincidentally, the agreement was signed just four days before a federal election. The dry dock project helped Meighen win local votes, but elsewhere he did poorly and Liberal William Lyon Mackenzie King replaced him as prime minister. In Vancouver the

three Meighen candidates, H.H. Stevens, J.A. Clark and Leon Ladner, were elected. Immediately after the election W.S. Fielding, the new minister of finance, brought in fiscal restraint with a vengeance. He issued orders to public works minister Hewitt Bostock to cease all projects that were not imperative. On December 30, 1921, work on the new dry dock was ordered suspended, and on May 13, 1922, a telegram from the new minister of public works, J.H. King, stated that the government had definitely decided against the construction of a dry dock in North Vancouver.

Vancouver's Board of Trade, the Vancouver Merchants' Exchange and other organizations reacted swiftly and vigorously. They pointed out the obvious necessity for a dry dock when nearby Seattle, Bremerton and Prince Rupert all had excellent facilities. At the same time, the new government dry dock in Esquimalt was being given the go-ahead, even though the smaller 1887 dry dock was still in use. Esquimalt's new dock was the second largest in the Empire and the third largest in the world, with a

Top: The Prince John *in the 1925 dry dock, flanked by the* Progressive, *built by Wallace Shipyards in 1906, and an unidentified tug.* 27-3095

length of 1,150 feet and a width at top of 149 feet.

Some locals suggested towing Prince Rupert's dry dock down to the Lower Mainland. Its 20,000-ton capacity was sufficient, and in the early 1920s it was seeing little use—servicing only the Canadian Government Merchant Marine ships, which could in any case be serviced much more cheaply closer to their shipping routes. But while in the world of logic and economics this made sense, in the world of politics it would be dynamite. The dry dock stayed in Prince Rupert, and it seemed that North Vancouver's years of hope and planning might be wasted.

On March 28, 1923, the government had a change of heart. R.E. Beattie, Vancouver's harbour commissioner, had made a trip to Ottawa the previous month and his views of proposed port development in Vancouver had received a favourable hearing. No doubt this influenced the dry dock decision. The new dock was now a go.

Government subsidies at a rate of 4 percent on the calculated cost of $2.5 million meant Burrard received annual payments of $112,500. At the same time a sinking fund was created to cover the cost of renewal of the pontoons. Each year for 35 years, $2,385.92 was deducted from the $112,500 subsidy.

Compounded annually at 3 percent this would accumulate $231,200 at the end of 50 years, the expected life of the pontoons.

W.T. Donnelly of New York prepared plans for the dock, with harbour engineer W.D. Swan of Montreal designing the piers and shops; Messrs. Hodgson, King and Marble drafted the plans and H.W. Read was construction engineer. Wallace's old friend George Doidge superintended construction.

The equally long-awaited Second Narrows bridge was started in November 1923; the dry dock gave added credibility to North Vancouver's need for a rail and road link with its larger neighbour.

The dry dock was built in two sections and registered as two vessels: the first 260 feet in length, and the second 300 feet. The pontoons, which formed the bottom of the dock, were built of wood, while the wing walls, or side portions, were steel. The first section had six pontoons, and the second seven; each was 44 feet long, 126 feet wide and 14.5 feet deep, constructed entirely of heavy timber. The outside surfaces of the pontoons were coated with arsenical tar, covered with tarred felt and sheathed with creosoted lumber for protection against the teredo worm. The pumping plant for floating and submerging the dock

Above: The marine railway's hauling engine, 1927. 27-65

consisted of 18-inch centrifugal pumps, one on each side of each pontoon, electrically driven and operated from a central control station.

By March 18, 1924, the first four pontoons were completed and assembled. The first ship to be successfully lifted out of the water was Union Steamship's 2,200-ton *Camosun*. This had been the first ship docked on the marine ways of Wallace Shipyards when the cradle was completed more than 15 years before.

In August 1925 the final pontoon was launched. The completed dock had a lifting capacity of 15,000 tons and was 556.5 feet in length, 126 feet in breadth and 14.5 feet deep, containing approximately 5 million feet of BC fir and 2,500 tons of steel. At the end of each pier was a derrick capable of lifting 100 tons and operated by two electric motors. These were built by Cowan Sheldon and Company of Carlisle, England, with erection carried out by Hodgson, King and Marble.

Top: The pipe shop on Pier No. 3, 1920s. 27-174
Above: Interior of the machine shop, about 1922. 27-85

The Honourable Dr. J.H. King, minister of public works, officiated at the opening on August 11. His earlier attempts to kill the project were, if not forgotten, at least not raised on this auspicious occasion. Sir Henry Thornton, president of the Canadian National Railway, was among 2,000 guests in attendance, and the Canadian Government Merchant Marine's *Canadian Planter* was honoured as the first ship in the completed dock. A banquet commemorating the opening was held a few weeks later; with characteristic panache Alfred Wallace stated that it was his intent to have two dry docks in operation on the North Shore. No doubt he wished to at least match Victoria.

The new dry dock could accommodate all but the very largest ships (namely the *Empress of Australia*, *Empress of Canada* and *Aorangi*), although it was about half the length of the new government graving dock in Esquimalt. Prospects for future business in North Vancouver were excellent—six steamers were waiting for a berth. The August 28, 1926, *Vancouver Morning Star* stated that in the dry dock's first full year of operation, 149 vessels were attended to, 30 of which would not have been able to use the port if the dry dock had not existed. It was in use for all except 30 days of the first year, with 250 men employed when in full operation.

As part of the general upscaling of operations, Burrard Dry Dock made substantial renovations of the physical plant, including building a machine shop. A blacksmith shop in the eastern part of the yard was connected by a railroad track, and a new general stores building included a pipe and sheet metal shop. Much of the land used was reclaimed using earth that had been dredged up for the dry dock. A concrete pier, 700 feet long and fitted with a fixed 100-ton capacity crane, formed an anchor for the dry dock on the east side and provided a berth for deep sea ships on the west. A steel bridge connected the pier to the shore.

Top: Plate furnace in the angle shop, about 1925. 27-182

The cost for these renovations alone was $950,000, exceeding the permits issued for any one year since the incorporation of the City of North Vancouver in 1907. Total cost, including wharves, buildings and equipment, came to $3.75 million. The company sold both the 1,500- and 600-ton marine railways, as the new dry dock could be broken up into two sections, with each used to dock a smaller ship. The expense and difficulty of separating and rejoining the dock meant that it was more practical to have a separate, smaller marine railway, so in September 1927 a new marine railway was put in operation. This accommodated smaller ships up to 3,000 tons and 250 feet in length.

Burrard Dry Dock was now a well-equipped shipyard with excellent facilities for all phases of ship construction and repair. The shops were spacious and—for their time—bright and pleasant places to work.

The recently opened Panama Canal cut thousands of miles off trips to Vancouver from Europe and the North American east coast. As a result, use of the Vancouver port increased dramatically during the early 1920s. The number of visits by ocean-going vessels rose from 336 in 1920 to 1,009 in 1924. As most of an average dry dock's operating time is devoted to vessels requiring maintenance rather than those that have sustained damage, this increase in traffic was timely for the dock's success.

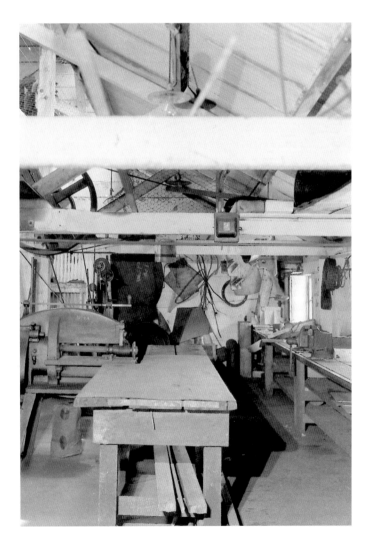 

Left: The sheet metal shop above the pipe shop, circa 1920s. 27-249
Right: The joiners' shop. 27-292

Duelling Ferries

As the North Shore developed, the City of North Vancouver needed another ferry for service between North Vancouver and Vancouver to add to the two already built by Alfred Wallace's company. With the *Princess Louise* completed, and no large new construction projects to take its place, Wallace needed the business. The *Province* of June 27, 1922, reported that North Vancouver city council received two proposals, one from Burrard Dry Dock and the other from Napier, Miller Limited of Glasgow, Scotland. Napier's bid was $200,925, and Burrard's $249,000.

With no duty on ships imported from Britain, local yards had difficulty competing with the larger, more established British yards. Wages were another reason for different estimates, as Wallace himself pointed out in a publicly distributed flyer. Workers at his yard averaged 67.5 cents an hour, while those on the Clyde averaged 33 cents. But the BC wages stayed in BC, with spending going into the local economy and taxes to the local government. City council had to decide if it was worth the additional cost to keep the business and jobs at home. At stake were jobs for 200 men.

Burrard amended its tender to $198,000, only $4,500 more than the figure that Napier, Miller had finally decided sufficient to build the ship. Complicating the choice was the fact that these ships were not identical. The Napier plan called for a double bottom and some other features that may have been designed more for the long sea journey than local service. Doubts were raised as to whether or not it would comply with Canadian regulations.

Charges that William Howie of Burrard had offered Napier a bribe of £2,000 to abandon its bid fuelled the local controversy. The *Sun* of October 24, 1924, contained letters produced by Mrs. MacDonald, Napier, Miller's Vancouver representative, which indicate there was indeed a suggestion of money changing hands, variously reported at anywhere from £2,000 to £6,000. Howie's side of the story was that Mr. Miller had suggested that for a payment of £2,000 to cover expenses to date, the company would abandon the contract. This offer, stated Howie, had been countermanded by Napier. Alfred Wallace denied any knowledge of the whole transaction.

Although it appeared that no money was ultimately paid, the allegations did not help Wallace. When North Vancouver council met to decide who would get the contract, 400 irate ratepayers descended on the meeting. And when Napier, Miller was given the contract on October 26, 1922, it seemed that would end the story. But then new costs and questions of the suitability of the planned ferry, especially the boilers, for service on Burrard Inlet, as well as the possible effects of the Second Narrows bridge, swayed public sentiment. Dugald Donaghy defeated George Morden for the mayoralty in January 1923 and the new mayor and council appear to have been much less pro-ferry. In a plebiscite held in February 1923, the proposed ferry was rejected by a decisive count of 511 to 248.

Leaner and Meaner

The war and post-war years had been good for Wallace and his company. His venture into steel shipbuilding had paid off handsomely, with the success of the *Princess Louise* conjuring up dreams that an *Empress*, a true ocean-going liner, might one day be built at Burrard. The new dry dock reinforced Wallace's dominant role on the Canadian West Coast, but as freight rates fell and the tonnage lost during World War I was replaced, the Canadian shipbuilding business entered a prolonged downturn. As early as 1924 a report from a committee of the Montreal Trades and Labor Council, quoted in the June 14 *Monde Ouvrier*, put the case for shipbuilders bluntly.

~

Hundreds of ships are arriving and departing from our sea port daily carrying our imports and exports and, with the exception of the Canadian Government Merchant Marine boats, not one of these ships were built in Canada, this being done at home port…The result is obvious; the grass is growing over our shipyards and our mechanics and seamen are forced to leave the country in search for employment in other countries.

The problem, the writer suggested, lay in the government's policy of allowing British ships to enter the coastwise trade without any customs duties on ships or supplies. As a result, Canada had fallen from third among shipbuilding nations in 1883 to about eighteenth or nineteenth at this point. In March 1925, *Harbour and Shipping* reported Vancouver shipbuilders' objections to the purchase of Hong Kong-built vessels—many yachts were ordered from these yards. The builders put forward a series of recommendations suggesting that the government take a much more active role in directing subsidies to where they would enable the Canadian shipbuilding industry to compete. In a letter to R.B. Bennett's federal cabinet, much of which was quoted in the August 29, 1930, *North Shore Press*, Clarence Wallace pointed out that from 1922 to 1929, Canadians purchased 411 ships abroad for $97 million. He wanted some of the action to stay at home.

But the cost was too formidable. In 1927 the federal government called for bids for six ships to be built for the West Indies trade. As reported in the September 20, 1927, *North Shore Press*, Burrard, along with a number of other Canadian companies, put in its bid but the job went to Britain's Cammell, Laird and Company for $3.85 million. The lowest Canadian bid came from Canadian Vickers of Montreal for $6.28 million.

Equipping a Canadian navy could have infused life into shipbuilding, but Mackenzie King, prime minister throughout much of this time, was wary of defence commitments and generally worked to distance the Canadian government from the more defence-minded decisions made in London. The few warships purchased were built in Britain, and the government cited cost and the inability of local shipyards to undertake complicated naval construction as the reasons it did not turn to Canadian yards. In 1922 the United Kingdom spent 17 times as much per capita on naval defence as Canada did. In the early 1930s Canada's total navy consisted of only four destroyers (*Vancouver*, *Champlain*, *Skeena* and *Saguenay*) intended for coastal defence.

The May 6, 1928, *Province* reported on a memorandum that eastern Canadian shipbuilding interests presented to Ottawa, pressing for concessions. The memo pointed out that the United States imposed a 50 percent duty on all repairs of American ships in non-American yards and that the coast business remained open to any British ships, or to any foreign ship, on payment of a licence fee of 25 percent of the value of the vessel. Unless protective legislation was enacted, they warned, the Canadian industry could collapse. Thousands of mechanics and workmen formerly employed in Canadian shipyards had been forced to seek work elsewhere.

Throughout the world, shipbuilding's boom years of the 1920s gave way to the Depression of the 1930s. In northeast England unemployment reached as high as 70 percent, and in the United States 49 shipyards disappeared between 1920 and 1936.

Clarence Wallace saw the building of the Pacific Great Eastern Railway to Prince George as crucial to Burrard's future. As reported in the September 20, 1927, *Vancouver Sun*, if Peace River trade, especially grain, were moved through Vancouver, ships would be needed and Burrard would build them. It would be another quarter century before the railroad was completed, however, delaying any economic benefit it might have provided.

For now, Burrard even had trouble competing with Canadian yards. The City of North Vancouver finally did have to tender for another Burrard Inlet ferry as a result of problems when ships knocked the Second Narrows bridge out of commission. The March 10, 1931, *Vancouver Star* reported that Boeing Aircraft and Shipbuilding Company (Vancouver), Walkem Shipyards and Burrard submitted bids, and Boeing's bid for what would become *North Vancouver Ferry No. 4* was accepted, even though its projected speed of 8.25 knots was less than the stipulated 9 knots. The Boeing bid's big appeal was cost—$46,135 compared to Burrard's $61,209.

Burrard could no longer be counted on as a source of jobs or taxes for the North Vancouver community. It posted a loss for every year between 1925 and 1936 except 1927—its total loss for these years was over $536,000. In 1932, its most horrendous year, it lost $117,095.29.

While the Second Narrows bridge brought some repair business to Burrard—the yard dealt with a number of ships that were swept into the bridge by the vicious tide—the long periods of isolation caused by damage to the only rail and road link to Vancouver far outweighed the advantage of a few repair contracts. The disruption of communications had a devastating economic effect on the North Shore, which was aggravated by the deepening Depression. The profligate borrowing in the early years of the century led to payments the municipalities could no longer afford. The many North Vancouver residents on relief also added to the financial burdens, as social assistance was at this time a municipal responsibility. Both the city and district went into receivership in 1933.

In these difficult times Burrard Dry Dock still managed to win a number of new construction

Above: The treacherous currents that swirled around the first Second Narrows bridge (built in 1925) led to a number of spectacular accidents. In April 1928 the Norwich City *cut through the eastern driveway of the bridge, causing major damage. Burrard did temporary repairs for $10,000, but permanent repairs were left for its home base in England.* 27-3067

WHEN I FIRST started working in Burrard Dry Dock with the steel gang, they had a four hour minimum, but all of the work was repair work and it was the usual thing that when the damaged material had been cut away, they would lift some type of template or pattern, and the frames would be bent first. So the old specialist in that job, the frame bender, knew very well that he only had a few hours or a few days work, so he'd make the work stretch out. And it was a common thing to see him standing over the bar that had been bent and if the boss came around, he would spit on the bar, to show that he was watching the heat to see whether the spit sizzled on the bar. If it did, the bar was too hot. All of this was a little bit of pantomime to convince the boss that they were working as fast as possible. In fact, the frame benders and the riveters, and bolters-up and everyone else usually tried their damnedest to stretch the work out, because jobs were few and far between.

Bernie Keely in *A History of Shipbuilding in British Columbia*, pp. 48–49

contracts, which, with a steady repair business, helped keep it afloat. The scow *Tarzan II*, built for BC's Sydney E. Junkins Company from 300,000 feet of BC fir, was launched August 21, 1924. As described in the September 1924 *Harbour and Shipping*, it was built to carry pile-driving machinery, consisting of two Scotch marine oil-burning boilers, a generating and lighting plant, several hoisting engines, a 90-foot-high steel leader and two 30-ton derricks.

Oil drilling and exploration also increased with the need for energy in a developing society. The *Marvolite* was a relatively small 131-ton oil tanker completed in 1926 for the Imperial Oil Company at a cost of $80,000 for bulk service between Tacoma and Skagway. Barges of a similar size were built for the Union Oil Company.

As the Depression took hold in BC, contracts for new ships were even fewer and farther between. An exception was the steel ferry *Agassiz*, built in 1931 for the provincial government for service across the Fraser River between Agassiz and Rosedale. Designed by Thomas Halliday with propellers fore and aft, it

Top: In April 1930 the Losmar, *on its way from Dollarton, struck the concrete pier at the south end of the Second Narrows bridge, tearing it from its mooring. Extensive bow damage was repaired promptly at Burrard. The bridge, on the other hand, remained unrepaired for several years.* 27-3019

was powered by twin six-cylinder diesel engines and cost $60,000. The ferry could carry about 20 automobiles, with enclosed accommodation for some additional passengers.

St. Roch: Creation of a Legend

One of Burrard's few big contracts in the late 1920s became the yard's most famous ship. Assistant Commissioner Stuart Wood, who had commanded the RCMP Herschel Island detachment from 1919 to 1924, conceived the idea of a small ship to serve the needs of northern detachments. The idea took hold, with a design prepared by Charles Druguid, naval constructor of the department of marine in Ottawa. This became the *St. Roch*, which, next to the *Bluenose*, is perhaps the most storied ship built in Canada.

Burrard had not built a shaped wooden vessel since the "Mabel Brown" schooners, so the company called on Arthur Moscrop, long experienced in building wooden ships, to be the shipwright. The detail plans were prepared by Vancouver naval architect Thomas Halliday, who had spent 20 years with the John Thorneycroft Company of Southampton. Halliday's examination of Roald Amundsen's Maud inspired him to create a round, egg-shaped hull. Douglas fir from local sawmills was used to build a hull nearly two feet thick with 1.5-inch-thick sheathing of Australian gumwood, the only wood known to resist the grinding effects of ice; the forward ironbark 1.5-inch planking was protected by sheets of quarter-inch steel. Massive horizontal beams almost a foot thick braced the hull.

Small and stubby—at 90 feet it was the same length as Columbus's *Santa Maria*—the boat had accommodation for 13 officers and men, although at

Above: The St. Roch *under construction in 1928 at Berth No. 1, Pier No. 2 East.* 27-2457

Henry Larsen, "she was the crankiest and most awkward ship" he'd ever set foot in; yet the two bonded deeply through their years of mutual struggle in the icebound North. In 1944 Larsen stated that after spending 10 of its 16 winters in the Arctic ice, only half a dozen planks needed to be replaced. When the *St. Roch* was caught in ice, its design enabled it to ride over the ice instead of being crushed. One time the ship popped out of the encroaching ice to rock on an ice floe.

Bill White, one of the original crew members, recalls, "At the time the RCMP was the Canadian government's only official presence in the North. There was no local government, no game wardens, no social workers, no military—the RCMP did it all." Especially during World War II, the *St. Roch* also helped establish Canadian sovereignty in the Arctic. Among its duties,

times as many as 19 shared the cramped quarters. With a top speed of eight knots, it was built for surviving ice at the expense of both speed and comfort. In the words of long-time skipper, Staff Sergeant

Top: The St. Roch *on its trial run after its first voyage and refit at Burrard Dry Dock, circa 1930.* 4806
Above: On an ice floe next to the St. Roch, *east of Point Barrow, Alaska, are, left to right: Constable and Master Henry Larsen, Constable Jack Foster, Constable Joe Olsen and Constable Terry Parsloe.* 4803

it carried supplies to other detachments, transported patients to the hospital and students to the school in Aklavik, and generally served as a goodwill ambassador between the Canadian government and the people of the North, selflessly assisting in the slow erosion of Native society. It was the last—the *Beaver* being the first—of the small steamers that brought the mixed benefits of civilization to the coastal communities of British North America, accessible at this time in no other way. It was also among the last of the ships that confronted the Arctic with a minimum of technology or external support.

Captain William Hugh Gillen, a former whaler and sealing captain, took the *St. Roch* north to Herschel Island. Then, to his surprise, Norwegian-born Henry Larsen, an RCMP constable, was appointed commander. Larsen remained with the ship throughout its active life. In 1940–1942 he captained the *St. Roch* on the first trip through the Northwest Passage from west to east. When its return trip through the Northwest Passage was followed by a 1950 return to Halifax via the Panama Canal, the *St. Roch* became the first ship to circumnavigate the North American continent. Larsen became the foremost Arctic navigator of his time, the last of the great Arctic explorers. He was immensely skilled, able to sense when a passage in the ice was safe and when entrance could result in disaster. He died in Vancouver on October 29, 1964.

The *St. Roch* was equipped with sails, and traditionalist Larsen liked to use them wherever possible. Crew member Bill White was less enthusiastic.

Top: The St. Roch *east of Point Barrow, Alaska, circa 1928.* 4804

The *Roch* with her bathtub lines was no *Bluenose* and it took a good eye to see any difference either in her speed or her stability between when her sails were up and when they weren't, but the difference in the amount of work involved was obvious. With bare masts all you had to do was hold to the course, but under sail you needed men out on deck to fight the rigging and the steersman had to really work the ship.

A steel shoe was added to its bow in 1939 to help push through ice, and in Halifax in 1944 it was given a new deckhouse, a more powerful 300-horsepower engine and a ketch rig in place of a schooner rig. It sailed west through the Northwest Passage in a remarkable 86 days, arriving in Vancouver October 16. Larsen recalled that one of the greatest difficulties of the trip was navigating through fog—and also that for a month he never took his clothes off.

But times were changing fast, and larger and less austere ships were becoming the norm. On October 19, 1948, the *St. Roch* was taken out of service and laid up at the naval dockyard in Esquimalt. In 1950 it voyaged to Halifax through the Panama Canal, but then in 1954 was sold to the City of Vancouver for $5,000 and came home to its birthplace. For a time it

languished as politicians and others debated its future, but then Wilmot Cliff of M.R. Cliff Tugboat Company; Jack MacDonald, general manager of Burrard Shipyard; and Tom Howarth, secretary of Burrard Dry Dock combined their financial resources to make its restoration possible.

The ship was pulled ashore on a cradle at Kitsilano Beach in 1958, and Vancouver Shipyards, then located in Coal Harbour, removed the 1944 deckhouse, restoring it approximately to its 1928 appearance. In 1966, now enclosed in an A-frame structure, it was painstakingly restored again, this time to its 1944 state. The *St. Roch* was declared a National Historic Monument in 1962 and was opened to the public on October 12, 1974. It remains the centrepiece of the Vancouver Maritime Museum.

Top: *The* St. Roch *with all sails set, circa 1928.* 27-2459

Above: *M.J. "Joe" Olsen on board the* St. Roch *at the Vancouver Maritime Museum in 1984. He was a member of the crew on the ship's first voyage in 1928–1929.* 5627

J.H. Carlisle

Fire had always been a problem on the waterfront, lined as it was with wooden wharves and sawdust burners spewing sparks day and night. Wallace had seen his shipyard damaged by two fires, Coughlan Shipyards suffered a major fire shortly after World War I, and a fire wiped out McNair's North Shore lumber mill in 1923. Vancouver was long overdue for a fire boat.

The September 1928 *Harbour and Shipping* reported that since 1908 Vancouver's fire chief, J.H. Carlisle, had been urging the city council to purchase a fire boat to protect the waterfront, but the city council and harbour board continually avoided responsibility for fire protection. In September 1925 veteran shipping man C. Gardner Johnson and William Howe, engineering expert, placed a proposition before the Vancouver City Council calling for the appropriation of $250,000 for a fire boat. While council did not act on this proposal, in October 1927 Arthur Bennett, who had previously prepared plans

(which had been rejected) to convert a 110-foot American sub-chaser to a fire boat, now submitted plans that met with a positive response. Vancouver agreed to pay for the boat and its upkeep, recovering the cost by charging waterfront businesses a levy based on the reductions in fire insurance rates they paid. The city did $72,000 worth of dredging at this time to make the mills accessible.

Burrard launched the new fire boat August 14, 1928. It was named the *J.H. Carlisle* for Vancouver's fire chief of 42 years. A compact vessel of 47 tons, it was equipped with a 150-horsepower Sterling gasoline engine and pumping equipment that included two 300-horsepower, eight-cylinder Sterling engines and DeLaval 6,000-gallon-per-minute centrifugal pumps. These had 10-inch suction and 8-inch discharge pipes. The ship could go under wharves, where creosoted pilings can burn intensely, weakening the wharf above. It was capable of directing a 2.5-inch stream of water 300 feet vertically or nearly 500 feet horizontally. On its trials it developed an acceptable speed of 9.39 knots; cost was a reasonable $52,440.

Top: The new fire boat, J.H. Carlisle, *ready to go. The "Mabel Brown" type schooner* Malahat *is in the background.*
27-2446

Strictly for use at mills on False Creek (not Burrard Inlet), the boat was held at No. 16 Firehall in False Creek. Captain G.J. McInnes, its first commander, stayed on the job until his retirement in 1963, while the ship carried on another eight years, providing good service for a total of 43 years until its retirement in 1971. Since 1988 its owners have been Wayne Palley, a fisherman, and Denise Arcand, a postal clerk, both living at Port Edward, BC.

By this time industry had left False Creek, making fire boats, if not redundant, at least less crucial. *Vancouver Fire Boat No. 2* was laid up in January 1989, although it was later sold to the Port of San Francisco, where it was still active in 2000. In 1991 tenders were called for five fast-response boats for Burrard Inlet. Celtic Shipyard of Vancouver built these.

HMCS *Comox*

As the 1930s drew to a close, the lowering clouds of impending war flashed a potentially silver lining for West Coast shipbuilders. Memories of government manna occasioned by World War I were still alive, and the shipyards began to ready themselves like jockeys at the starting gate, waiting for news of contracts to be won. Captain Percy Nelles, who became chief of naval staff in 1934, ardently promoted building up the navy, especially minesweepers. He argued that in the event of a war, Canada would pay a high price in sunk merchant ships if there were no navy to protect them. The Munich crisis triggered a doubling of Canada's naval budget in 1936. In the same year Ian Mackenzie, minister of national defence, indicated that the government wanted to increase its navy from four to six destroyers and was also interested in minesweepers.

The building of the Basset class minesweeper *Comox* was the first trickle in what would become a flood of contracts for Burrard Dry Dock, as well as other shipyards. It was one of four ordered by the Royal Canadian Navy, the others being built at Yarrows, Esquimalt; Collingwood Shipyards of Collingwood, Ontario; and Morton Engineering and Dry Dock Company of Quebec City. The *Comox* was the first minesweeper and first warship completed in BC, and after the *Naden*, built by Wallace Shipyards in 1913, the second naval vessel built in the province.

Top: The J.H. Carlisle *shows its stuff.* 27-2449

The $352,000 price tag was $84,000 more than for those ships built in eastern yards, but the government justified the additional cost on the basis of higher pay and transportation costs in BC. This was the first naval work awarded the West Coast outside the naval yards in Victoria and Yarrows, which did much of the naval repair work between 1910 and 1920, and the first contract awarded by the Canadian navy to construct warships in western Canada.

A crowd of several thousand viewed the launch of the *Comox* on August 9, 1938, and Ian MacKenzie lauded the ship as evidence of Canada's awakening awareness of its responsibilities as a seafaring nation. Equipped with anti-aircraft guns, a four-inch gun and minesweeping equipment, it was fitted for, but not with, depth charges. Its engines, constructed at Sorel, Quebec, provided a speed of 14 knots for its tasks of ensuring BC's coast was free of mines and helping out as a fire boat in Vancouver's harbour.

In spite of the rapidly deteriorating political situation, the Canadian government was reluctant to commit further new resources to naval construction. When Canada declared war on Germany, not a single ship was under construction for the Canadian navy.

Top: *The minesweeper* Comox *underway.* 27-2439

Above: *The minesweeper* Comox *under construction at Berth No. 1, Pier No. 2 East.* 27-2426

The *Fifer*: Elegant Beauty

Before the war brought a frenzy of assembly-line construction, the *Fifer* provided an interlude of fine craftsmanship. After many years at sea, Captain William Crawford, president of Empire Stevedoring Company, was planning a luxurious retirement cruising back home via Hawaii and India. A native of Fifeshire, Scotland, he commissioned Robert Allan to design a yacht that would maximize his pleasure. On February 1, 1939, Crawford signed a $300,000 agreement with Burrard, and the *Fifer* was launched November 11 of that year to the skirl of bagpipes. In the apt words of the journalist writing for the November 13 *Vancouver News Herald*, it was "As trim yet as powerful a pleasure craft as ever slipped down the ways from a coast building yard." Two 250-horsepower engines gave it a top speed of 13 knots and a cruising range of 3,000 miles at 10.5 knots. First-class construction included watertight bulkheads and an all-steel hull, with teak decks and wheelhouse.

But World War II had started and the navy had other plans, taking over the *Fifer* and installing machine guns on its upper decks, then sending it out to patrol local waters in search of Japanese submarines. Captain Crawford's dreams of luxurious cruising remained unrealized; he died before the war was over. When peace came, R.M. Andrews of the Maquinna Investment Company bought the yacht to commute from his home at Twin Isles, Gulf of Georgia, to Vancouver.

In 1948 San Francisco sports personality Edward Lowe took over the *Fifer* and voyaged from Mexico to Alaska. In 1955, after a short period of ownership by then lieutenant-governor Clarence Wallace, who used it as his viceregal yacht, it was sold to the Powell River Company, and in 1962 it returned home once more to

Above: The elegant Fifer, *launched November 11, 1939.* 27-2417

Clarence Wallace. It was still going strong in 1986 under the ownership of celebrity lawyer Melvin Belli, still fit, in the opinion of its captain John Manning, to sail around the world. It is now owned by Mr. and Mrs. T. Pellarin of Belmont, California.

At various times the *Fifer* carried lord mayors of London, movie stars such as Gracie Fields, and various members of the royal family, including Prince Philip. Five staterooms provided every amenity, and it had a "large, luxuriously-appointed, teak-panelled, public room with a gently curving, forward bulkhead dominated by 12 armour-plate windows set into bronze and surrounded by hand-rubbed teak…furnished with writing desk, book-cases, chesterfields and easy chairs and even a marble-embellished fireplace."

An Era Ends

Alfred Wallace reaped some rewards in his last few years from the intense activity of his earlier decades. Yachting and the accompanying social life were among the compensations for his years of hard work. When the flamboyant entrepreneur Gustav Constantin Alvo Von Alvensleben hurriedly left Canada after World War I broke out, A. Melville Dollar purchased his unfinished yacht from Hoffar's Motor Boat Company. Walithy Limited of Vancouver completed construction in 1917 and named it the *Walithy*. Wallace purchased the yacht and his family owned it until 1939. Renamed the *Odalisque* in 1938, it has been owned by William Gibson from 1947 to the present and it is still, in David Wallace's words, "in absolutely gorgeous condition."

In 1926 Alfred Wallace moved from the downtown West End to country living on undeveloped land in south Vancouver. At 1250 West 54th Avenue he built a large home on five acres, its name, "Devonia," a tribute to his English heritage. At that time Granville Street was still a dirt road from 25th Avenue south.

Alfred's more sedentary later years led to his packing on added pounds. His grandson David recalls visiting the house as a young boy and watching family friend Earl McColl put Alfred's shoes on. Grandpa Alfred was too large to reach his feet.

Eliza Wallace died February 3, 1927, after being bedridden for two years; on September 24 of the same year Alfred married Mrs. Sarah Bone Chellis, who had been his wife's nurse. Sons Clarence and Hubert were irate at what they saw as a gold digger moving in on their father. They refused to attend the wedding and never had a pleasant relationship with their stepmother. While she lived on until early 1946, her husband died on New Year's Day, 1929, in "Devonia" after a brief illness. Alfred Wallace left a respectable estate valued at $169,731, although he was hardly wealthy even by the standards of his day. His estate ranks as the 29th largest left by Vancouver businessmen who died before 1940. The March 8, 1929, *Province* reports

Above: The Fifer *first tastes salt water.* 27-2420

that Sarah Wallace's annuity on Alfred's death was valued at $74,372.

Clarence took over the house, cut down most of the 600 walnut trees his father had planted and set up a stable so he and his sons could indulge their love of equestrian activities. He had become secretary-treasurer of Burrard Dry Dock in 1921, taking an increasingly active role in the company since the completion of the dry dock, especially after his father went into semi-retirement in 1926 because of ill health. Clarence officially replaced Alfred on January 15, 1929, and Hubert was elected vice-president.

What made Alfred Wallace so successful, with a flourishing company, when so many others either failed or moved out of shipbuilding into less unpredictable enterprises? His wholehearted commitment to the repair and building of ships was certainly a part of the story, but essentially his approach to business was conservative. He took risks, but they were always calculated risks—he never made extravagant promises, but those promises he made, he kept. He never embarked on large projects unless he knew the money would be forthcoming, and he became known for his combination of reliability and practical solutions to complex problems. In the words of long-time Burrard employee J.D. Kinvig, "He followed a creed of hard work stimulated by a great respect for the perfection of detail, a tremendous enthusiasm, and a firm belief in the future." He drove his men hard, but drove himself harder.

He was a tough but generous boss. During the 1913 depression a boilermaker applied for work, but there was none. "Mr. Wallace couldn't give him anything to do, but he told the man to list his grocery and meat needs for the week, and then signed the bill for them." Like his son Clarence, he knew how to create a workplace to which the workers would be bound by loyalty.

"Nerve" characterized many of his endeavours—it enabled him to win the bid for the *Princess Louise* and many other prestigious contracts, to take on other projects that had never been done in this province, and to ignore those who shook their heads and said it couldn't be done. He surrounded himself with dedicated men—men whom he treated well and in return demanded they give 110 percent effort for the company. Many of these workers stayed with the company throughout their working lives. His second wife described his assets as "Terrific energy, immense driving power, an idealist but a practical one, an understanding of human nature with its faults and failings."

His enthusiastic participation in an amateur yacht race, described in the *North Shore Press* "Dry Dock and Harbour" edition of July 1925, exemplifies his fiercely competitive nature and refusal to let his life be controlled by hard facts:

A stiff breeze was blowing and in the ardor of the race, running neck and neck with his closest competitor, Mr. Wallace and his companion clapped on so much sail that a sudden gust of wind caused their boat to run under with the result that he and his companion were precipitated into the water in front of the Hastings Sawmills and had to be fished out in a rowboat. Mr. Wallace always contended that he had the race won had his boat not taken a crazy notion to shorten the distance by attempting to cut off the arc caused by the curvature of the earth.

CHAPTER 4

Paths of Glory:
1939–1946

My gunner died in my arms today,
I feel his warm blood yet;
Your neighbour's dying boy gave out
A scream I can't forget,
On my right a tank was hit;
A flash and then a fire;
The stench of burning flesh,
Still rises from the pyre.
What did you do today, my friend,
To help us with this task?

From Lt. Dean Shatlain's "What Did You Do
Today," published in the *Wallace Shipbuilder*.
During World War I Shatlain amputated his
own foot with a jackknife and thought he was
dying when he wrote this poem. He survived.

Let us not be deluded into the belief
that the importance of sea-power has
declined. In all the great wars of the past,
in 1914–18 as in the Napoleonic wars,
it was sea-power which finally brought
about the downfall of the Continental
power.

From *Harbour and Shipping,*
October 1942, p. 348

In the 1880s Canada had ranked third among shipbuilding countries. During World War II it once again achieved that position, launching 354 10,000-ton (dwt) supply ships,* 281 escort ships, 206 minesweepers, 254 tugs, 3,302 landing craft and many other vessels of various types. West Coast yards including North Van Ship Repairs, West Coast Shipbuilders, Yarrows, Victoria Machinery Depot and Prince Rupert Drydock accounted for 255 of the 10,000-tonners; Burrard Dry Dock built 109 of these in its two yards. War's mass destruction created a bonanza for shipbuilding, with up to 14,000 men and women engaged at Burrard for the war effort. In comparison, the largest yards in eastern Canada, Canadian Vickers and United Shipyards, had maximum employment of 12,000 and 9,000 respectively, although Vickers was also involved in a great deal of war-related activity other than shipbuilding. The entrepreneurial initiative and obsessive energy of Clarence Wallace and his employees made Burrard the pre-eminent Canadian shipyard for turning out the 10,000-ton workhorse maintenance ships.

Canadian shipyards had run down since the end of World War I. Few vessels of any size had been built and facilities were limited, with technological

---

* The number of 10,000-ton ships built by Canada during the war has been cited variously. The number here is based on Robert Halford's count of 321 Fort and Park merchant ships, 12 RN stores ships, and 21 RN maintenance ships. See page 263 of his book *The Unknown Navy*, and also Gilbert Tucker's *The Naval Service in Canada*, Volume II, which cites the same total.

capabilities far behind those yards in other countries (such as England and Scotland) that had continued to build ships on a regular basis. Most of the few skilled workers who remained were older men who had worked on ships during World War I. Only 200 men were employed at Burrard in 1939, and only about 2,000 skilled shipbuilders were available in Canada.

Neither was Canada's navy ready for war. At the end of August 1939 the Royal Canadian Navy (RCN) consisted of six River class destroyers, four minesweepers, a training ship, a training schooner and a trawler—hardly the type of force to strike fear in the heart of the enemy. When war was declared, no new naval construction was underway. The Canadian government needed to make a much greater commitment if its navy was to be more than a token force.

Great Britain declared war on Germany September 3, 1939, and Canada entered the conflict September 10. Immediately the country was galvanized into action, although the previous footdragging meant a lot of catching up was needed. Prime Minister Mackenzie King named C.D. Howe chair of the War Supply Board (till that point Howe

had been minister of transport), with David B. Carswell his director of shipbuilding. The chief of naval staff presented a naval shipbuilding program to the Cabinet on September 18; it was approved within 24 hours, reflecting the sense of extreme crisis. In the first nine weeks of war, German submarines sank 106 Allied ships. Ultimately, 2,603 Allied ships were lost to U-boat action during World War II.

Shipbuilding was crucial to the war effort in the days before air transport was common. A soldier required an estimated 10 tons of support, and a mechanized soldier 100 tons. While Britain had a well-developed shipbuilding industry, it could not supply enough ships, especially when hampered by blackouts and enemy bombing raids.

Corvettes: "Cheap but Nasties"

After the 1938 Munich crisis, the British Admiralty, convinced that war was inevitable, wanted a ship that could be built quickly in yards with limited facilities. During World War I, William Reed of Smith's Dock Company at Southbank had designed the Z class

Top: Quitting time, 1944. At a time when wearing caps was the norm, the different types say much about a person's origin and class. The dunchers worn by the men at the lower left indicate their British working-class background. The fedoras worn by many others suggest North American roots. 27-678

whaler for anti-submarine work. Now he drew up plans based on a whaling ship the company had recently built, the *Southern Pride*, lengthening it by 30 feet, replacing the one water-tube boiler with two Scotch marine boilers, which were more readily available, and making provision for watertight subdivision and the addition of armaments. He dubbed this ship "Patrol Vessel, Whaler Type," although "Corvette" was soon accepted as a catchier name, inherited from the days of sail when a corvette was a war vessel with a flush deck and one tier of guns, ranking below the frigate. Like a whaler, the corvette's acceleration and manoeuvrability facilitated pursuit of its prey.

The standard corvette was 190 feet by 33 feet by 13.5 feet and weighed 950 tons. It was powered by four-cylinder triple expansion engines with a top speed of 16 knots. The original design was for a complement of 47 officers and men, but in operations they always had more. They initially had one four-inch gun forward and a single two-pounder aft, both of World War I vintage. Their main armament was depth charges, dropped off the stern or fired over the side, although often their most effective form of attack on U-boats was simply to ram them, as Roman galleys had attacked their enemies.

Corvettes have been described as "a miserable ship to sail on and to fight in" or, in Winston Churchill's words, "cheap, but nasties." "The vessel was not fast enough to catch a U-boat on the surface, and was originally equipped with obsolete Asdic [an early form of sonar] and a magnetic compass totally unsuitable for [anti-]submarine work." Poor ventilation caused condensation and a permanently damp condition. On the plus side, their buoyancy made them comparatively immune to damage due to stress caused by weather.

The Canadian War Supply Board reported that both corvettes and minesweepers could be built using the same facilities (although not concurrently), and on February 7, 1940, the Privy Council authorized the construction of 64 Flower class corvettes at Canadian shipyards, 54 for the Royal Canadian Navy and 10 for

Above: The corvette Wetaskiwin, *launched July 18, 1940.* 27-2414

the Royal Navy. Canadian yards would eventually build a total of 122. Burrard received contracts for four corvettes at $605,000 each—*Wetaskiwin*, *Trail*, *Agassiz* and *Chilliwack*—which boosted the yard's employment to 750. The cost for each ship was up to $70,000 higher than the prices in eastern yards, with transportation and higher wages counting for the difference. Burrard also built the 2,500-horsepower (ihp) engines, the first to be built in the machine shop since those for the *Princess Louise*. Burrard was the only yard other than Canadian Vickers and Collingwood to build its own engines. These were the only engines built by Burrard, or in BC, during the war.

Workers laid the keel for the first, the *Wetaskiwin*, in April 1940 and completed the contract late that year. It soon proved its worth by rescuing 15 men from the torpedoed freighter *Bold Venture* and 22 from the tanker *Basfonn* in November 1941. On July 31, 1942, it collaborated with the *Skeena* in dispatching a U-boat 700 miles off Newfoundland. The *Wetaskiwin* was formally known as the *Queen of Hearts* after its insignia of a queen of hearts playing card, but more popularly by the punningly appropriate name *Wet-ass-Queen*, with a logo showing a queen sitting in a puddle. It was sold to Venezuela following the war.

On March 11, 1944, the *Chilliwack* collaborated in dispatching *U744*, earning a commendation from the secretary of the naval board in Ottawa on June 2, 1944. "Throughout the action, the performance of HMCS *Chilliwack* reflected great credit not only on her officers and crew but also on her builders." Like all of Burrard's corvettes, it survived the war.

The *Trail* was scrapped in Canada in August 1950. The *Agassiz* joined the Newfoundland escort force in early 1941, and after a number of trips underwent a major refit in January 1943 at Liverpool, Nova Scotia. While scrapped in 1946, it lives on in the book *The Flower Class Corvette Agassiz: Anatomy of the Ship*, by BC authors John McKay and John Harland.

Bangor Minesweepers

More naval construction followed in 1940. Burrard built six of 18 steam-driven Bangor class mine-

---

Top: The Bangor minesweeper Bellechase, *launched October 20, 1941.* 27-2402

sweepers ordered by the Canadian government for $620,000 each. These were based on the Halcyon class minesweeper but were cut down in size and with many of the fittings removed. The *Wasaga, Bellechase, Minas, Quinte, Chedabucto* and *Miramichi* were 171-foot twin-screwed vessels powered by two three-cylinder triple expansion engines built in eastern Canada. They were larger and, at 16.5 knots, faster than the earlier British Basset class minesweepers (like the *Comox*). Armaments consisted of one four-inch or smaller gun and Oropesa minesweeping gear. Neighbouring North Van Ship Repairs also launched six minesweepers, its only naval contract.

Like the corvettes, these were not the most pleasant ships to sail on. They were extremely wet forward in a sea, and living conditions were congested. Tactically they suffered the drawback of short range. Many of the faults were corrected in the later Algerine class, built at Port Arthur Shipyards and in Toronto. While the minesweepers were intended as convoy escorts, the corvettes performed more adequately in this role.

North Sands: 10,000 Tons and What Do You Get?

But more, much more, was needed to combat the German war machine. With the fall of France in June 1940, Allied losses to U-boats, which could now use French ports, mounted dramatically. By the end of 1940 the merchant navy of Great Britain had been reduced by almost one-third. North America, at this point not subject to enemy attack, provided vital support.

In September 1940 the British Admiralty organized a mission headed by R.C. Thompson, managing director of J.L. Thompson and Sons, and Harry Hunter of Newcastle's Swan Hunter yard, and including representatives of Lloyd's and the Admiralty, to assess the shipbuilding potential in the United States and Canada. In BC the group visited the four major yards: Burrard Dry Dock and North Van Ship Repairs

in Vancouver, and Yarrows and Victoria Machinery Depot in Victoria. They found the yards small and not equipped to build sophisticated ships. But—as in World War I—they would have to do. While the western yards made substantial contributions with naval vessels, their main efforts, with the exception of Yarrows, which continued with naval construction, soon focussed on building maintenance ships.

In late 1940 and early 1941, Great Britain placed orders through Canada's minister of munitions and supply for 26 10,000-ton ships, to be built by Davie Shipbuilding and Repairing Company of Lauzon, Quebec; Canadian Vickers of Montreal; and Burrard Dry Dock. Burrard's agreement, signed on January 8, 1941, was for six ships for $1,856,500 each. Two more were added in early February, for a total of $14,847,000. These were to "be of good, staunch and substantial construction and of the best materials and workmanship, shall be seaworthy, shall be built under special survey of Lloyd's Register of Shipping and shall be classed 100A1 or highest class." All machinery was to be manufactured in Canada or the US, with preference given to Canadian sources. These flush-deck ships were 416 feet BP (between perpendiculars) or 441 feet overall, with a beam of 57 feet, and had a deadweight tonnage of 9,300, although they were normally referred to as 10,000-tonners—wartime regulations allowed deeper loading.

The "North Sands" design by Joseph L. Thompson and Sons of the North Sands yard in Sunderland, England, suited mass production by industries not accustomed to the finer points of shipbuilding. No large cranes were needed, although this meant that prefabrication of larger sections was not an option. The triple expansion steam engines and coal-fired Scotch marine boilers were rugged and simple, comparatively easy to build, repair and maintain. New York naval architects Gibbs and Cox produced specifications for the hull and machinery based on the parent ship, the "Empire Liberty" type. Maritime historian Gordon Newell describes the American version of this basic design, the Liberty ship, as—

evolved from the stark design of the Sunderland-built tramps of the British Merchant Navy by Naval Architect William Francis Gibbs. Although lineal descendants of Glencannon's legendary *Inchcliffe Castle*, and designed for construction through the assembly techniques employed in assembling the Hog Islanders and other boxlike "cargo tanks" of World War I, the Liberty ships were a vast improvement over previous emergency designs. Their 420-foot hulls were provided with sheer and camber, avoiding the angular lines of the old Shipping Board vessels and making them better sea-boats. Raked stems and cruiser sterns combined with compact superstructure gave them, when well down to their marks, an almost yachtlike appearance in comparison to the remarkably ugly craft of the first war.

Compare, for example, HMS *Hartland Point*, with its raked stem and pronounced sheer, to the straight stem and lines of the World War I *War Storm* (shown in Chapter 2).

In its parallel program the United States built 2,710 Liberty ships. This was the greatest single ship fleet the world had ever known.

Most Canadian shipyard workers were completely inexperienced, so it was necessary to break down the huge task of building a ship into a multitude of component activities, each of which could be learned quickly. Workers were assigned one activity, which they repeated many times a day, becoming proficient at that task even though they might have little or no knowledge of shipbuilding generally. To help train the workers, Burrard hired a number of skilled personnel from British yards. This stratified approach to the job fostered a multiplicity of crafts and unions that in the post-war world vastly complicated the task of efficient planning and made labour negotiations and productivity a nightmare.

In March 1941 C.D. Howe asked Vancouver industrialist H.R. MacMillan to study Canada's ability to build even more freighters. In April MacMillan met with Clarence Wallace to discuss the construction of 10,000-ton ships. Wallace, never one to back down from a challenge, committed his yards to build an additional 30 ships of the North Sands type. Eastern builders were skeptical of Wallace's prices and delivery dates, but MacMillan agreed to give Burrard a contract for the 30 ships for a total of over $60 million. Burrard not only completed the ships on time, but also for less than the amount contracted. From the *Fort St. James* in April 1941 to the *Mohawk Park* in June 1943, Burrard completed 50 North Sands ships in 26 months. The same approach that had led to Alfred Wallace's immense success mass-producing fishing boats in the False Creek yards half a century earlier now worked for his son.

Burrard, like other shipyards working on the 10,000-ton ships, did not build all parts of the ships. Instead, much of the material was assembled from other companies, with 95 percent of the materials used by Canadian shipyards coming from Canadian manufacturers. William Kennedy and Sons of Owen Sound, Ontario, built all the 18.5-foot-diameter

Above: The maintenance ship Hartland Point. 27-2302

propellers. The 135-ton, 2,500-horsepower (ihp) steam reciprocating engines were built by Canadian Vickers and Canadian Allis-Chalmers, both of Montreal, and John Inglis Company of Toronto. Scotch marine boilers were from Dominion Bridge Company in Montreal and Vancouver, John Inglis, and Vancouver Iron Works. Syd Jopling recalls that Burrard didn't have a big enough slab to build or bend the frames for the larger ships, so this work was also contracted out to Dominion Bridge.

While the massive increase in workers needed for this intense activity caused growing pains, production at Burrard improved greatly after a difficult time in early 1942 when government and some management insisted on piecework for riveters and continuous production seven days a week, 24 hours a day, to increase the number of ships that could be produced. The unions argued that insufficient and antiquated equipment and poor organization hampered their work and accused management of wrapping itself in the flag as an excuse to erode collective agreements and increase the company's profits. But both sides shared a genuine desire to win the war, and by April 1942 the unions agreed to piecework and a seven-day week.

The keel for Burrard's first North Sands ship, the *Fort St. James*, was laid April 23, 1941; it was launched October 15 and delivered January 29, 1942, with the launching ceremony broadcast to all Canada over the CBC. Once completed, the *Fort St. James* was turned over to the British ministry of shipping on March 7, 1942, which in turn passed it over to an English

Above: The construction of the *Fort St. James, the first North Sands ship built by Burrard, from early stages to completion.* 27-2371, 27-2354, 27-2395, 27-2397

STAN MARK was the best rivet heater. When I was holder-on for Lush Campbell and Billy Powell, we all wanted Stan for our rivet heater. You know, a good heater is important. You have to have the rivets right. Bigger rivets for engine beds have to be heated more than rivets for bulkheads, and shell rivets of an inch in size have to be heated a little more than smaller rivets for light bulkheads. Stan very seldom gave us a bad rivet. This made it a lot easier on both the riveter and the holder-on. It took all of us to do the job.

Hec Smith in *A History of Shipbuilding in British Columbia*, p. 41

shipping line, Ellerman's Wilson Line. This was the second 10,000-ton ship launched in Canada (the first was the *Fort Ville Marie*, built in eastern Canada) and the first large steel ship built by any shipyard on the Canadian Pacific coast for 20 years. While the waters still roiled from its launch, a derrick swung a new keel into place for the next hull. The race was on.

The 10,000-ton supply ships soon made a difference. Each "could hold 6,270 tons of bacon, ham, cheese, flour and canned goods, enough to feed 225,000 persons in Britain for a whole week; 2,150 tons of steel bars and slabs; enough Bren gun carriers, tanks and motorcycles to equip a battalion of infantry, 1,900 tons of aircraft bombs; sufficient lumber and nails for 90 four-room cottages; 2 complete bombers and the aluminum required to build 310 medium

Top: Riveters, circa 1943. 27-795

bomber aircraft." The ships kept the vital supplies for the military forces flowing.

The Canadian hulls, built in established yards, were 90 percent riveted, requiring about 383,000

ONE OF Burrard's first welders was Mark Falconvitch, who started work with the yard in late 1914 using an AC welding machine. Other early welders were George Hampton and Davey Simpson. Later Falconvitch employed electric welding and saw it gradually gain acceptance in the marine community. During World War II he created a tiny 84-by-300-inch park that symbolized his vision of industrial progress. Called "Age and Industry" and located at the south side of the welding shop, it portrayed the history of culture from the Stone Age to the present day using statues, shrubs, flowers and plaques. Falconvitch retired from his position as welding foreman in November 1949 and died in 1960.

Wallace Shipbuilder, July 1944

SLIM EDISON and I drove side by side, and he drove 1,088 rivets and I drove 1,066 on a shell bottom in one day, and that [was] the record. And I drove the record on the shell—drove 1,688 one-inch rivets on the shear strake on the sledging. So I'm telling you this, because shipbuilding started to slow down and we got together, Jack MacDonald and I and a few more in South Burrard there and we got the ball rolling on this: We said, "Look, guys are being laid off, and we're still driving 700, 800 or 900 rivets a day, piece work here." So we started it off by cutting the quotas down. We put ourselves on a quota—you couldn't drive more than so many rivets a day.

Sam Jenkins in *A History of Shipbuilding in British Columbia*, p. 86

rivets for each ship. In contrast, the American yards, building from scratch, were able to use welding, which was the state-of-the-art construction method. To convert Canadian yards to all-welded construction would have meant unaffordable delays. While riveting added extra weight and was slower than the prefabrication that welding made possible in Henry Kaiser's mammoth American yards, it was simpler and made quality control more effective.

As the war progressed, Burrard increased its use of welding (by 1945 the yard employed 1,200 welders and burners). John Lockhart directed the installation of a union melt welding machine in the South Yard, on the Vancouver side of Burrard Inlet. This could do two feet of half-inch weld in a minute and was used for all flats, such as decks, bulkheads and tank tops. The first large-scale hull welding at Burrard involved the American Liberty ship *James Otis*, which had been damaged by grounding rather than any structural failure of welding.

In *A Vancouver Boyhood*, Robin Williams recaptures the mingled excitement and fear, no doubt felt by many, when as a green 17-year-old he worked as a rivet-passer during the summer of 1941 at Burrard's neighbour, North Van Ship Repairs.

⌒

Jim took a swig of water out of a canvas bag, ran over with another white hot rivet, then explained my job. He held up a cone-shaped metal scoop the size of a rugby ball with a handle halfway down. "This is your bucket. When I toss a rivet, you catch it in this bucket, grab it with these short tongs, run over as fast as you can and stick it into the hole next to the one Hank just pounded in…I'll toss a few slow 'til you get used to it, but then we've gotta speed up or we'll never make our quota." He paused a second for a breath, then said, "And for Chris'sake, try not to miss 'em…a guy down below ain't too tame if he gets a white hot rivet down his neck."…

My upper leg muscles quivered with strain but I was still too scared to stand up straight, and I didn't dare look over the side, just concentrated on getting from here to there and praying to God I was doing it right. Hank kept banging them in, so I guessed things were going all right. But I didn't know how long I could keep it up. I was tired as the dickens and the nausea in my stomach told me I was running out of energy…

From then until the whistle blew for lunch it was back and forth dumb and numb as a pit pony. I was past the point of feeling hunger, or the pain in my legs. Or thinking. Or fearing. I had become an unfeeling, unthinking gear in the shipbuilding machine. It took just half a day, and like a malleable fresh rivet out of Jim's barrel, I was pounded into shape, turned into an obedient shipyard worker.

Plant Development

In 1940 Burrard constructed Berth No. 2 for the corvette and minesweeper contracts, as well as a sawmill/joiner shop/pattern loft and a pipe shop. When it won contracts for 10,000-ton ships in January 1941, more and different building facilities were needed. The company purchased the Evans, Coleman and Evans property on the east end of the North Yard to provide more space. This acquisition included St. Georges Avenue below Esplanade and the property and water lots 400 feet east of St. Georges. Four new building berths were added, with the original two (including the new No. 2 berth) filled in and covered with shops. The company also added four long piers, four fixed five-ton cranes between each of the two pairs of building berths, and two five-ton-capacity travelling cranes on two of the piers. The old covered construction shed used for the *War Dog* (shown in the photo of this ship under construction in Chapter 2) was moved to become the west gantry.

A new copper and sheet metal shop and a pipe shop were constructed, and the machine shop was extended 60 feet north. The old joiner shop was demolished and a second plate shop with a mould loft on the second floor erected in its place. A steel fabricating shop was erected at the east end of the yard. These extensions, costing $3.5 million, tripled the size of the plant.

Still more space was needed, and the site that Wallace had acquired in 1921 from Coughlan on Burrard Inlet's south shore was a logical location for additional facilities. Northern Construction Company started work in April 1941 on a shipbuilding plant here that would be equipped to construct four 10,000-ton ships at one time on the 400 feet of water frontage. Squatters' shacks on the property to the west of the Burns and Co. plant were razed.

Hugh Lewis was appointed manager, later succeeded by the more experienced John Dalrymple. The Burrard (Vancouver) Dry Dock Company was

JOHN LOCKHART is one of the legends of Burrard and of shipbuilding generally on the West Coast. Born in 1864, he apprenticed in the yards of S. and H. Morton in Leith, Scotland. After a distinguished career in Scotland and Ireland, he left for the United States in 1900 as general manager of a company building torpedo and other vessels. He came to Vancouver in 1916 as general manager of John Coughlan & Sons, and when it closed worked as a surveyor for the ship classification company Bureau Veritas. In 1926 he joined Burrard Dry Dock, and although when World War II started he was well past the age when most men retire and confined to a wheelchair by a stroke that paralyzed his left arm and right leg, he performed invaluable service as director of the Burrard Dry Dock (Vancouver) plant. His secret? "Smoke ten pipes full o' baccy every day." He died in March 1947 and his ashes were scattered over Burrard Inlet.

Vancouver Province, September 14, 1942, and January 9, 1945; *Vancouver Sun*, January 3, 1946

incorporated with an authorized capital of $250,000, and by September 1, 1941, four shipbuilding berths had been constructed, complete with 10 five-ton derricks. Two large fabricating plate shops, along with compressor houses, stores, buildings, lunchrooms, canteens and offices were built. The South Yard "completed all steel work on the hull, installed shafting, propeller and rudder, all bilge and ballast; air and sounding pipes, fuel pipes, heating coils; auxiliaries and all deck machinery and piping. The North Yard installed the engine and boilers and completed the outfitting." Eventually 4,500 workers were employed in the South Yard, giving Burrard a total of eight berths for building ships, four in each of the North and South yards.

There were management changes in the North Yard around this time. Burrard hired Bill Wardle from Canadian Vickers in February 1942 to be general manager, a position that logically would have gone to Hubert Wallace. However, Clarence's younger brother was notoriously unreliable, even though he was intimately acquainted with all aspects of shipyard work. His drinking interfered with his work too much for him to be given this responsibility.

The South Yard's first hull, the *Fort Qu'Appelle*, was launched January 24, 1942. Many others followed. This yard built 55 10,000-ton hulls, as well as four China Coasters. After the war the South Yard closed and the equipment was transferred to Burrard's North Yard or sold to Yarrows.

Victory Ships

As the war progressed and the tide started to turn in the Allies' favour, Canadian builders improved the 10,000-ton ships to make them more economical to operate. The result was the Victory ship. Canadian Victory ships were only slightly improved models of the North Sands, unlike the American versions, whose increased power and speed prepared them for post-war needs. While North Sands ships had three Scotch marine boilers and were coal-fired, Victory ships' two

Right: Applying the first coat of grease for the launching of the Dunlop Park *in 1943. After this coat has hardened and set, a coat of slip grease, more slippery and softer, is put on top of it. The sliding ways are then placed on top of this. From left to right: Jack Livingston, Hubert Hyde, Frank Hayes and Tom Paterson.* 27-348

oil-fired water-tube boilers saved fuel and the cost of additional firemen. The oil-burning machinery required an increase in piping in the double bottom and machinery space, and heating coils were needed to heat the oil so it could be pumped more easily. Other differences were minor. The North Sands ships had two lifeboats on the captain's bridge and two on the boat deck, while the Victory ships had all their lifeboats on the boat deck. The North Sands ships had a bunker hatch aft of the funnel through which coal was loaded—this hatch was not necessary on Victory ships.

The keel for Burrard's first Victory ship, the *Fort Columbia*, was laid March 18, 1943, and the ship delivered July 12, 1943. Between the *Fort Columbia* and the *Coronation Park* on November 1, 1944,

Top: The Victory ship Westend Park, *the 300th Canadian-built cargo ship.* 27-2309

AS YOU went into the yard, there was a big target up in the air that showed you the number of vessels that had been built on such and such a day, and the number of sinkings that had taken place on that day in the Atlantic. And at one time the sinkings were greater than the new vessels that were being turned out. Then finally they reached a sort of level, and then the turning point, where there were more vessels being built than being sunk. Then we knew we were on our way to winning the war from the shipbuilding point of view.

Jack Lawson in *A History of Shipbuilding in British Columbia*, p. 75

Burrard laid keels for 34 Victory ships. Because of concern that oil might not be available, 31 of the later Victory ships (six by Burrard), often referred to as Canadian types, were constructed with both oil tanks and coal bunkers so they could burn either fuel. Their lifeboats had also reverted to the same position as on the North Sands ships.

In the summer of 1943 Burrard received a contract from the British ministry of transport to convert eight Victory-type ships to victualling or stores-issuing ships, whose task was to supply naval units in the Pacific. Converted between November 1943 and December 1944, each had 111,480 cubic feet of refrigerated space between decks.

Beginning in June 1944 Burrard constructed 10 maintenance ships to take care of repairs to the

Above: The south side of the electrical shop in July 1945, showing Val Attwood, Peggy Milstead and Sue Ferguson making straps for electric cable. Gladys Conway, farther down, is drilling fixtures. To the right, Jonas Wallin and Betty Trythall are busy at switchboard work and Jean McKay punches straps on the punch machine. 27-77

machines and equipment of the fighting units. Each was equipped with four additional electric generators powered by diesel engines built by Vivian Engine Works of Vancouver. These supplied power for the welding equipment, air compressors, air-conditioning units and refrigeration. Five refrigeration chambers between decks had a capacity of 9,900 cubic feet. At $2 million each, these were slightly more expensive than the North Sands and Victory supply ships because of their elaborate repair equipment. Each ship had a complement of 350 officers and men, including machinists and engineer staffs trained in marine ship work.

RATIONING LIMITED drinking, but he [Red Ross] would go around and talk to some young girl helper or something and ask, "What are you doing with your ration book? Have you got any coupons left for this week or this month?" And he'd talk her into giving him the coupons. You'd get about a bottle a week, or a bottle a month. There were all kinds of tricks in those days. When you took a liquor permit into the liquor store they would stamp it so you couldn't bring it back tomorrow and get another one. So they'd often put a thin coat of wax on the liquor permit, and when they stamped it you could go outside and scrape it off and put some more on.

Tom Knox, foreman at Burrard Dry Dock

Above: The north side of the electrical shop in July 1945, where armature winding and motor repairs are done. From left to right: Dave Coward, Ralph Pithart, Henry Brewar, George Mason, Percy Ruffle, Alex Russell, Ellen Hutson, John Wallace, Gus Hassell and Tommy Laurie. 27-75

Top left: The yard in its heyday, about 1944, looking north past North Vancouver to the mountains. 02-16B

Top right: Wartime construction at Pier No. 5, looking up St. Georges Avenue. 27-169

Above: A busy yard. Girdle Ness, Dodman Point *and* Fife Ness *are under construction in the summer of 1945.*

The Girdle Ness *later became the trials ship for the Sea Slug missile system used in the 1982 Falklands War.* 27-2289

Women in the Yards

As the summer of 1942 drew to a close, many of the teachers and students who had worked at Burrard for the summer returned to school, leaving gaps in the workforce. Many men were called up into active service, further decreasing the labour pool. The labour shortage led to some men being assigned the work of passer boys, normally reserved for teenagers. The men were paid at a higher rate than the boys who, understandably upset, staged a number of work stoppages in their quest for fair treatment and soon formed their own union to protect their jobs. In the meantime, a plan by which high-school boys would be released from school on alternate days to work in the shipyards met with a cool reception—only 21 boys in Vancouver high schools indicated a willingness to participate in the plan. More workers were needed to fill the gap, and women were the obvious choice.

Bill Wardle, Burrard's general manager, was adamantly opposed to hiring women, but Clarence Wallace, unlike his father during World War I, realized there was no alternative if they were to fulfill their contracts. Burrard became the first shipyard in Canada to employ women in significant numbers. Doris McEwan (age 22), hired by the South Yard in August 1942, was the first

A foolish girl was Letty Lat
She would not wear a safety hat.
A four-inch gash is in her dome,
A hearse has taken Letty home.

Women's First Aid, North Yard, in *Wallace Shipbuilder*, March 1944

woman welder in Canada and the first woman admitted to the Boilermakers' Union. By September, 10 women were employed in the South Yard: three welders, five plate markers, one electrician and one pipefitter's helper. Their supervisor was Nije Wier, her unique first name composed of the initials of her four aunts: Nan, Isabel, Jean and Elizabeth.

The North Yard hired its first group of 11 women September 30, 1942—they worked in the pipe and sheet metal shop. Under the watchful eye of their supervisor Grace McGaw, who had previously been in charge of women at the Sea Island aviation plant, women worked at a variety of jobs including plate markers, carpenters' helpers, derrick signallers, store helpers, hammer drivers, bolt threaders and numerous other positions previously reserved for men. A few worked as tracers in the hull department, tracing ships' plans on linen. Their generally smaller size and greater flexibility made them valuable for working in tight quarters. By November, 149 women were employed, and some of them had been promoted out of the passer-girl group to be bolters-up. The first two bolters-up (who helped bolt the plates of the ships into place, with the bolts taken out as the plates were riveted) were Phyllis Nugent (19 years old) and Lorraine Deegan (18).

In March 1943 the company opened a new building across Esplanade

---

Above: Burrard Dry Dock employees Phyllis Plume (left) and Maria Bouvier, circa 1945. 9613

from the main office entrance with "Women Only" marking the door. A lunchroom, nurse's room, offices, locker rooms and washrooms gave women employees a sense of belonging, temporary though this would be. In early August, South Burrard also completed a women's building with accommodations for 250 women a shift; by the spring of 1944 some 1,000 women were working at Burrard. This number decreased to 625 by late August, although the number of men was also declining.

Lives of women workers were circumscribed by numerous rules. While some, such as regulations on hair and the wearing of jewellery, were motivated by safety, other strictures attempted to control social interaction with men. The pace of hiring was to a large extent governed by the construction of separate facilities for women. They were not only expected to eat in separate quarters, but were also required to enter and leave by different gates. Socializing did, of course, inevitably take place. Robert Downing, who worked as a steamfitter's helper for a short time in 1943, recalls, "I've seen a fitter and a lady disappear into a water tank. What went on was their business." Doug Kinvig recounts another incident:

One woman was hired to sweep the lower decks in a carrier, but the charge hand often found her sweeping up the flight deck. After chasing her below a number of times, he finally asked her, "Why are you so often on the flight deck?" Her reply was, "My husband is working in the plate shop and from the flight deck I have a good view of the plate shop and so can keep a good view of my husband and the other women working there."

Above: Five women shop stewards in the Burrard canteen in 1942. Nancy Buker is second from right. 8073

While women made an important contribution to the shipyards, their numbers remained relatively small and with a few exceptions they were confined to "lighter" occupations, freeing men for those that were "heavier." Riveted construction meant heavy rivet guns—no women were hired for this job. While Kaiser's yards, which used many more welders, employed as many as 30 percent women, Canadian West Coast yards did not exceed 7 percent. Rightly or wrongly, most employers thought that women lacked the strength to perform the more physical jobs with the competence of their male counterparts.

Women who were hired were generally young and single—married women with children were the last to be sought. It was always tacitly assumed that this was a temporary measure and that when war ended the men would get their jobs back and the women would return to the home. And this was what in fact happened. The war did not bring permanent changes in women's status. It was 1981 before Burrard next hired a woman welder—Amanda Kirby.

> WE WERE told we could go down to see our ship launched. When I saw that ship slide down the ways, I was so proud. I felt that I had helped to build it. I wanted so much to help win the war against the fascists. I wanted my son and everybody else's sons, fathers, brothers and other men to come home from the war and we'd have peace again. I thought what a senseless thing war is.
>
> Alice Kruzic in *A History of Shipbuilding in British Columbia*, p. 105

Top: Women workers at Burrard in August 1945. 1421

A Job Well Done

Although they had to be built at speed, the 10,000-ton ships were also constructed with the care essential for those whose lives depended on their efficient operation. In one stretch, 13 of Burrard's Victory ships passed inspection without a single defect. Between July 1943 and October 1944, 32 out of 38 Victory ships built by Burrard received a clean bill on their first inspection.

These ships were built for specific wartime use, but many lived a much longer and productive life. Most did not survive the 1960s, more because they were too small and slow to compete economically than because they were no longer seaworthy. However, a few endured. The *Fort Brisebois* escaped the shipbreakers until 1992. HMCS *Cape Breton*, ex-HMS *Flamborough Head*, was towed home to Burrard's former dry dock in North Vancouver in April 1999, its rusted hulk a sad reminder of its past glory. Here, only a few metres from where it was built, it was prepared for its final resting place as a Canadian merchant navy memorial artificial reef near Gabriola Island. Its stern has been cut off and is being retained to grace a proposed new waterfront museum in North Vancouver. HMS *Rame Head* is still afloat, but awaits scrapping in Portsmouth, England.

In a 1942 estimate, the Canadian program was responsible for 47 percent of ocean-going ships completed by the UK and all Commonwealth countries. The experience and efficiency gained by building numerous similar ships enabled Canada to turn them out at a relatively low cost. The average cost of $1,700,000 for a 10,000-ton ship in Canada's program compared favourably to $1,780,000 in the US Liberty ship program. The American ships cost more because US wages were higher. Burrard and the other West Coast yards contributed to Canada's edge over the US. The *Vancouver Province* reported on February 23, 1944, that the cost of a 10,000-ton ship in Canada's eastern yards was $2,046,000, while on the West Coast

Our Ship

The Hull lay poised in her cradle,
Her skids had their greasy coat;
They'd given her a name to bear to fame
And murmured a prayer for God to spare
And keep her safely afloat.

With bated breath we watched her
As she started from her berth,
Gathering speed, like a well reined steed,
Straight down the ways and out from the maze
Of her timbered cocoon girth.

Then she curtsied to the water
And we cheered her as she came.
Forgotten the rain, the grind and the strain,
The gas and smoke from the burning coke,
The heat from the searing flame.

The hissing sparks from the burners,
The glare of the welder's quill,
The clash and squeal of the tortured steel,
The crescendo run of the rivet gun,
The groans of the reaming drill.

As brothers we stood together;
Our feuds were a thing of the past.
With taunting jokes and friendly smokes
Our hopes and fears had died in the cheers,
Our Hull was a Ship at last.

Cecil Perkins, North Yard plater, in *Wallace Shipbuilder*, August 1945

it was only $1,422,000. However, in the more experienced (and lower paid) British yards, the cost per ship of this type was less than half that in North America. As the editorial writer in the *Vancouver Sun* stated with satisfaction on July 23, 1946:

Using half the capital of Quebec shipyards the shipyards of British Columbia employed more men, paid more in salaries, spent less on power and materials and yet turned out more and better ships…The coast shipyards led the Dominion, putting out products valued at $155,636,195 from materials costing $41,906,924 and power $1,190,242. The capital employed totalled $49,570,908.

The success of the West Coast yards in general, and the Burrard yard in particular, owed something to the mild winters, which made year-round construction possible. Greater competition for skilled labour existed in the war industries of the east, whereas in BC the relatively high wages attracted skilled tradesmen from throughout western Canada to work in the yards.

But that takes away nothing from Burrard's achievement. In the *Vancouver Sun* of February 28, 1944, C.D. Howe described Burrard as "one of the best yards in the Dominion…From the outset they could turn out ships at lower costs and greater speed than other yards." Most of Burrard's ships were actually built below the cost of the contract, so the

BURRARD LAUNCHED the *Fort Simcoe* November 10, 1943. It was completed January 26, 1944, and after a world tour under the flag of the Canadian Shipping Company, it arrived back in Burrard Inlet on February 21, 1945, as the *Green Hill Park*. On March 6, shortly before noon, while at Pier BC loading drums of sodium chlorate with 100 men aboard, a series of four explosions in No. 3 hold killed eight men and injured 19. Nearly 30 years later, an article on the incident in the November 1973 issue of *Harbour and Shipping* reported that thousands of windows were shattered and buildings were rocked a mile away, while "red hot rivets shot about like shrapnel." Fifteen minutes after the blast, debris was still falling to the ground and some was later recovered from as far away as Lumberman's Arch in Stanley Park, a mile away. The cargo of mustard pickles plastered the surrounding area. Only prompt action prevented a much higher death toll; the Royal Canadian Navy tug HMCS *Glendevon* drew alongside four times to take off survivors. The tug *R.F.M.* and a navy vessel *Squamish* also provided crucial assistance.

Its sides cracked and superstructure weakened, the *Green Hill Park* was beached on Siwash Rock. After being

towed to Ballantyne Pier on March 13 so its cargo could be unloaded, the ship was moved to the North Shore between Imperial Oil's dock and Evans Coleman Evans. Justice Sidney Smith presided over an inquiry that concluded the explosion was caused by improper storage of explosive material and by a lighted match dropped into whiskey spilled on the floor. No charges were laid, but five persons were censured. This remains the worst disaster in the history of the Vancouver waterfront.

The Green Hill Park *beached near Siwash Rock (above) in Stanley Park and back at Burrard being rebuilt (opposite).*
27-2332, 27-2335

Many years later, *Province* columnist Chuck Davis received a letter from a man who claimed that in 1957, one of the men on the *Green Hill Park* had told him the supposedly true story of what happened that fateful day. In his February 3, 1980, column, Davis wrote that the two men were in hospital at the time, and the teller of the story died shortly after. Behind the ship's main cargo of explosive sodium chlorate, ran the account, were some barrels of liquor. The longshoremen soon found these and helped themselves to a little extra for the night ahead. One man, already not seeing too clearly after a few drinks, struck a match to light his way. The resulting explosion when the fumes ignited killed him immediately, but "Joe," who was nearby, escaped with only a few bruises to tell the story and live for another 12 years.

The blasted hulk was sold for $160,000 in July 1945 to S. Paranthyiotis of New York, representing Brazilian interests. Pacific Salvage Company floated it off the North Vancouver shore under the guidance of William Jordan; the hefty bill of $50,000 was at length negotiated down to $32,500. Burrard's cost for repairs amounted to approximately $500,000 for the hull. The $200,000 contract for the superstructure was later also awarded to Burrard.

By June 1946 it was ready for the sea again, risen from the ashes as *Phaeax II* and once more receiving Lloyd's A1 rating. In late June 1952 it was back at Ogden Point in Victoria for a business call. One of its officers was quoted in the June 25, 1952, *Vancouver Sun* saying it was as "sound a ship as you'll find afloat." It was sold to Greek interests in 1956, renamed the *Lagos Michigan,* and later sold to Italians and operated under the Panamanian flag. In 1967 it ended its career with a Formosan shipbreaker.

ONE TIME I was there and a fellow came in with a great steel suitcase and he says, "Mr. Murray here?" And I said, "No, he's gone to lunch." And he said, "Oh well, I'm going to leave this here." And he put it beside my desk. Murray came back and he said, "Oh, has what's his name been here with our money?" Money? "Yeah," he said, "he's got the payroll." Everybody was paid in cash those days. And the money was brought over from Vancouver in the North Vancouver ferry by this clown. And he opened up the suitcase and it was just a big travelling suitcase full of money. We're talking a hundred thousand bucks or more. Leaving it with me. Not a very safe procedure.

David Wallace, general manager of Burrard Dry Dock

contracts were renegotiated and the government received the excess. Burrard "produced more tonnage in a twelve-month period than did any other similar industry in the British Empire." The City of North Vancouver, in receivership since 1933, came out of receivership in 1944 largely because of the contributions of this industry.

At the same time the company made a healthy if not outrageous profit. A memo dated November 27, 1942, from Wartime Merchant Shipping indicates the payment for the North Sands type was $50,000 per ship over the audited cost. The arrangement for the Victory ships was more complicated, but generally came to a similar figure. This, however, was before taxes. The company's best year was 1941, with a net profit before taxes of $2,204,504.92, but an after-tax profit of only $493,004.92.

In May 1945 the council of the Vancouver Board of Trade made Clarence Wallace a member of the Order of the Vancouver Gold Key at a ceremony marking the delivery of the 100th 10,000-ton freighter during a luncheon at the Hotel Vancouver. Not to be outdone, the North Vancouver Board of Trade arranged a dinner at the Olympic Club, where North Vancouver's mayor Jack Loutet presented to Clarence Wallace a bronze plaque engraved "Opus Artificen Trobat—A Workman Is Known by the Quality of His Work."

The company's drive to win the war had a personal edge: all four of Clarence Wallace's sons were in uniform. They had joined the air force because they felt the navy was too stuffy and conservative. Clarence's eldest son, Blake, was shot down and killed over the English Channel on October 27, 1941. Philip later crash-landed and broke his back. David Wallace says that Philip's officers tried three times to send him home, but he was flying again within six months. He was shot down over Cannes four days after D-Day and parachuted to safety, although he broke his ankle and was captured by the Germans. Richard was in the Sicily invasion, then was shot down over Albania by flak while strafing the beaches. He was imprisoned in Stalag Luft III for 18 months. Youngest son David enlisted in April 1942, but an oversupply of pilots led to his being trained as an air bomber. He languished for the remainder of the war as an instructor at the No. 8 Bombing and Gunnery Station in Lethbridge. In August 1944 the Jericho Air Station's playing field was dedicated to Clarence Wallace's sons for their selfless dedication to the war effort.

CLARENCE WALLACE, our Burrard president is very much in the local sports news! He and his clever little black mare, Topsy, won the saddle bending race at the West Vancouver Lion's Gymkhana at Ambleside on July 29 [1944]. Twisting in and out on a gallop through close-placed poles is a feat that calls for real nerve and good horsemanship. Mr. Wallace displayed both in all three heats.

Wallace Shipbuilder, August 1944

Conversion of Aircraft Carriers at LaPointe Pier

Allied experience with convoys in the North Atlantic had made it clear that air escort was essential. The military had found that the most successful way to prevent U-boats from shadowing convoys was to use aircraft to patrol, keeping the U-boats submerged. As they could not keep up with the convoys when submerged, the U-boats fell behind and lost contact.

In March 1943 the British Admiralty started talking with Burrard about converting aircraft carriers to suit the Admiralty's requirements, and by May the two parties had agreed on Burrard's role. At first the company planned to do the work in the North Yard, but its berthing facilities were inadequate, so Burrard leased LaPointe Pier on Burrard Inlet from the National Harbours Board and developed it. This was a less-than-ideal location as it was designed for handling grain cargoes, but the yard was equipped as well as possible in a very short time.

The original plan was for Burrard to convert 14 carriers that were being built in the Kaiser yard at Vancouver, Washington. These would be delivered at the rate of one a month, with two to be delivered in October. Burrard estimated this would require a maximum of 700 workers. J.D. Kinvig was hired as supervisor, with the first ship to arrive August 1, 1943. Kinvig worked with Hubert Wallace, although the latter's habit of disappearing for several days at a time without warning in search of convivial company created problems. Bert Scott replaced Hubert late in 1943.

On June 18, 1943, it was announced that instead

Above: At work on an aircraft-carrier conversion in the dry dock. 27-2780

of the Kaiser-built carriers, which the US Navy would retain, the company would convert 23 Smiter class carriers from the Seattle-Tacoma Shipbuilding Corporation in Tacoma. This demanded some quick modifications in the berthing of the ships and the positions of the cranes, as there were slight differences in the designs of the two classes of carrier.

The first ship, the *Ameer*, arrived on July 18, two weeks earlier than the original schedule, and the yard was not ready to go. The offices were just completed, but the stores were only half finished, with very little equipment installed in the workshops. Electric power was available at only one transformer station. Three more ships arrived before the middle of August, so instead of one ship the first month, as originally agreed, four had arrived. At some points it was necessary to work on as many as six ships at one time, though when the first ships came in there was power only at two berths (it was later extended to four berths).

Work went more slowly than expected, especially on the earlier ships. Working drawings, which were originally supposed to accompany each ship, had to be done by Burrard. Electricians were scarce. In addition, when the ships left Tacoma they were fully stored, which meant that in order to get at certain compartments the stores had to be removed. A number of naval ratings living aboard further complicated work.

In the first seven ships, the turbine rotors had to be modified, which took at least four weeks and slowed the work; in later ships US shipbuilders did this job. All required dry docking. The first seven were done at the North Yard, which not only seriously interfered with their repair program, but also damaged the dry dock. Very heavy amidships, these were at the extreme limit of the dock's capacity. Later ships were dry docked at Esquimalt after all other work had been completed.

The majority of the workers were inexperienced, which led to some rough workmanship in the earlier

ships, although this improved considerably. The times for the work lessened as procedures became more organized and the workers more efficient. The slowest time was for the *Begum* (114 days) and the fastest for the *Arbiter*, *Rajah* and *Smiter* (45 each).

Why convert new ships? Strange as it seemed, even at the time, it was considered more practical to alter the ships to suit the techniques of signalling and handling practised by Canadian and British crews rather than retrain the crews.

The changes went beyond a simple adaptation. Flight decks were lengthened (although at less than 500 feet they required all of a pilot's skill), alterations made to the catapult machines for ejecting planes, new landing lights installed, the ships ballasted to give greater stability for the extra number of planes carried, and all electrical fittings raised 10 feet above the hangar deck as a safety precaution. Firefighting capabilities were augmented, extra ventilation installed, and torpedo and bombing arrangements and ammunition storage altered to accommodate both British and American types. Asdic was installed for tracking submarines, and steam lines were added to de-ice the ship. All were powered by turbines from the Allis-Chalmers company of Milwaukee, which gave a speed of 16 knots. The carriers had a full displacement tonnage of 15,160 and could carry up to 20 planes.

At its peak in early November 1943 the LaPointe Pier yard employed 2,040 workers, not including subcontractors, converting 19 carriers between July 1943 and July 1944. The US leased these ships to the British Admiralty, although the Canadian government debated whether or not it should acquire any for the RCN and establish a fleet air arm. Canada and Britain finally agreed that two carriers, the *Nabob* and the *Puncher*, would have British planes and air crew and a Canadian naval crew, although differences in pay and accommodation in the two navies made this arrangement unsatisfactory.

The *Nabob* was commanded by Mackenzie King's nephew, whose resounding name, Captain Horatio

Nelson Lay, did not prevent his ship running aground in January 1944 on Roberts Bank. It was freed after four days of effort, fortunately undamaged. In February 1944 it took aboard the Royal Navy's 852 Squadron of Avengers at San Francisco, and the next month was at sea with a load of Mustang fighters. In August it was in Norwegian waters on an aerial mining operation, but on August 22, at the end of an operation to attack the *Tirpitz*, a torpedo from *U354* in the Barents Sea caused a 50- by 20-foot gash. Fortunately the *Nabob* was able to limp to the Royal Navy base at Scapa Flow in northern Scotland. Although condemned by the British Admiralty and destined for the scrapheap, post-war buyers rebuilt and re-engined the *Nabob*, selling it to the German shipping company North German Lloyd in 1952 for use as a training ship for German cadet officers. It made a commercial call in Vancouver in 1960 and in 1975 was still afloat under the flag of Panama as the *Glory*, owned in Taiwan.

The *Puncher* left Norfolk, Virginia, in July 1944 for Casablanca with a cargo of 40 US army aircraft. It left Scapa in February 1945 to take part in a strike against German shipping in Norwegian coastal waters, followed by two similar operations, and then was converted to a troop carrier to return Canadian servicemen from Europe. In January 1946 it was handed back to the US Navy at Norfolk and converted again for merchant service a few years later. Most of the carriers were returned to the US after the war and converted to merchant ships.

Conversion of the *Princes*

During the late 1930s, the Royal Canadian Navy developed designs to convert the three newest Canadian National (CN) steamers—*Prince Robert*, *Prince David* and *Prince Henry*—to warships in the event of war. The British Admiralty deposited armament in Canada and agreed to allow the RCN to use

Above: The Prince Robert *being converted to an armed merchant cruiser at Pier No. 3 in 1940.* 27-3102

12 of the six-inch guns to equip the CN's *Prince* ships as armed merchant cruisers. The ships' speed and range gave them great potential value as naval auxiliaries. The Canadian government purchased the *Prince Robert* and *Prince David* for over $1.4 million and bought the former CN ferry *Prince Henry*, which in 1938 had been sold to the Clarke Steamship Company of Montreal and renamed *North Star*, for over $800,000.

Work began on the *Prince Robert* and *Prince David* on November 26, 1939, and on the *Prince Henry* early in 1940. Plans were drawn up by Messrs. Lambert, German and Milne, with the *Prince David* assigned to Halifax Shipyards, the *Prince Henry* to Canadian Vickers and the *Prince Robert* to Burrard Dry Dock. Burrard's contract, assigned on February 9, 1940, for $755,300, was completed by the end of

July of that year, although the final cost was much higher.

Each ship received four six-inch and two three-inch guns, some light anti-aircraft guns and a number of depth charges in chutes at the stern. The top two decks were removed, as well as one of the three funnels, and a cruiser-style superstructure and bridge fitted. Until late in the war they were the Canadian navy's most powerful units, but the lack of range and fire-control of their armament—the six-inch guns from the King Edward class battleships had been cast at the beginning of the century and their three-inch guns were from light cruisers vintage 1916–1918— hampered their effectiveness. In addition their rapid and jerky roll was a disadvantage both for the accuracy of their artillery and from the point of view of comfort.

Top: The Prince Robert *converted to an auxiliary anti-aircraft cruiser in 1943.* 27-3107

Still, in five years of war they cost the Germans 18,000 tons of shipping. On September 25, 1940, the *Prince Robert* surprised and captured the 9,000-ton German merchantman *Weser* near Manzanillo, Mexico. The *Weser* was registered as a Canadian ship, renamed *Vancouver Island* and later sunk by a German torpedo. In 1941 the *Prince Henry* captured the crews of the scuttled German ships *Munchen* and *Hermonthis*.

As the war entered another phase, different craft were needed. The invasion of Europe meant increased demand for landing craft. With this in mind, the *Prince David* and *Prince Henry* returned to the West Coast and in 1943 were reconverted by Burrard to infantry landing craft, with eight Canadian-style plywood invasion barges slung from each of their sides. Their heavy armament was replaced with four four-inch guns, two single Bofors, and ten Oerlikons. Each could accommodate about 550 army personnel. Cost for the *Prince David*, completed by November 30, 1943, was $751,067.41. After their second conversion, the *Prince Henry* and *Prince David* served at the Normandy invasion, the southern France assault and the freeing of Greece.

The *Prince David*, refitted at Esquimalt in 1945 for operations in Southeast Asia, was sold to Britain's Charlton Steam Shipping Company in 1948 and scrapped in 1951 at the Giants Grave shipbreaking yard. The *Prince Henry* served in the Royal Navy as an accommodation ship at Wilhelmshaven. Later it was taken over by the British ministry of transport and renamed *Empire Parkeston*. In 1952 it was sold to Italian interests and taken to the Italian shipbreakers at Spezia in 1962.

In early 1943 the *Prince Robert* was reconverted by Burrard to an auxiliary anti-aircraft cruiser. With five twin four-inch guns, eight two-pounder pom-poms and 12 Oerlikons it spent a year as anti-aircraft escort to United Kingdom–Mediterranean convoys before becoming one of the ships that brought released prisoners home from Hong Kong. Along with the *Prince David*, it was sold to the Charlton Steam

Shipping Company in 1948, later becoming the Italian cruise ship *Lucania* before a 1962 rendezvous with the Italian shipbreakers in Spezia.

Other Conversions

Other ships needed to be adapted as wartime needs evolved rapidly. The Russian cargo ships *Krasnovaritsz* and *Karl Lubkin* arrived at Burrard for reconditioning in March 1942, the work funded under the American Lend-Lease Act. In June of the same year another Russian ship, the *Klarizilko*, arrived for repairs and to have ice stiffening installed. It would have disrupted the Kaiser yard's assembly-line approach to make these changes.

Eventually 28 ships, mainly Liberty vessels, went from the US to Russia on Lend-Lease. Cracks showed up in the hulls of the Liberty vessels in cold water and threatened their seaworthiness. For about $200,000 a ship at America's expense, Burrard stiffened the hulls and installed gunwale bars before they left for their new home.

Kaiser may have had the edge in terms of turning out ships in the shortest time, but the welding procedures used caused unexpected stress build-up through contraction and expansion. Major cracks

I WORKED for Burrard Dry Dock [as a photographer] after the war, showing how Liberty ships cracked in the middle. My job was to make that crack look like the Grand Canyon, so that when we sent a photograph to the owners they would say, "My god, fix it!" Turbine blades would get a crack you could barely see. I would photograph it to make it look like the Grand Canyon. Sometimes engines would be damaged in transit from Scotland. This was far more important than taking progress photos.

Jack Cash, Burrard Dry Dock official photographer

appeared in 95 of the American-built hulls (about 3 percent), with five splitting in half. The *John P. Gaines* broke in two on November 25, 1944, during a storm in Alaskan waters. The *Alexander Baronoff* met a similar fate the same month off the Aleutians, making maritime history when the forward section broke off, drifted in a half circle and rammed the after part, becoming one of the few ships ever to collide with itself. A T2 tanker split in half at the outfitting berth prior to delivery. Some Canadian shipbuilders felt this was vindication for riveting, although it was more a reflection on the haste of wartime welding.

The Party's Over

In September 1944 the British Admiralty placed orders for 71 transport ferries designed to carry tanks, armoured vehicles, trucks and personnel. Burrard received a contract for nine, each to cost about $2 million. These were snub-nosed, flat-bottomed ships fitted with bow-opening doors and without the graceful lines of the Victory ship. Practically without superstructure, the bridge and accommodation, as well as the engine room, were located aft. Their longitudinal system of framing, as opposed to transverse framing, was new to Burrard and a relatively recent innovation on the West Coast. In this method of construction the framing ran lengthwise rather than across the breadth of the ship.

With Japan's capitulation in August 1945, however, Ottawa ordered construction stopped, affecting over 1,200 workers at Burrard. In October, just as the transport ferries under construction were to be torched, six of the fifteen—one from Burrard's South Yard—were purchased from the War Assets Corporation by Straits Towing and Salvage Company of Vancouver and by Island Tug and Barge Company of Victoria for conversion to log carriers, each to have a capacity of 700,000 feet of logs. Only two conversions were actually completed, with a third becoming a rail barge. The rest were scrapped or never laid down.

From a high of 42 ships in 1943, Burrard launched 27 in 1944 and 17 in 1945. Layoffs at Burrard, begun in August 1943, continued. While the decline was not steady, and severe shortages occurred at times in some trades, the trend from this time on was for fewer ships and fewer employees. In February 1944, 16,000 worked in all the West Coast yards, down from 24,000 a year earlier. The launch-time per hull was extended from 60 to 80 days in September 1943, then to 100 days as the U-boat menace decreased. One of the four berths at each of the North and South yards was closed in August 1944.

Immense transportation resources would be needed to rebuild England and other ravaged countries, and the Canadian Seamen's Union and a number of people in the government favoured the re-establishment of a merchant marine. But memories of the merchant marine's financial drain after World War I were too raw in the minds of others, particularly members of the newly formed Canadian Maritime Commission, whose chair, J.V. Clyne, was strongly opposed to any policies that would lead to a

---

AFTER THE WAR everybody was working hard, and you'd decide we've got to start cutting down now because it was the last of the contracts, and so they had to let people go. So they would let 300 or 400 people go, and the production would go up. And they'd let 200 or 300 more go, and production would go up again. Everybody decided to fight for their job by this time. This was before unemployment insurance. He's going to try and stay on the job as long as possible. He'll work hard to make a good front for the boss, so he won't be laid off for a couple more weeks.

George Matthews, foreman at Burrard Dry Dock

BY THE END of 1944, David Wallace's service as an instructor for the Canadian air force came to an end. He was officially discharged February 7, 1945, and returned to work at Burrard. Bill Wardle arranged a special four-year apprenticeship for him titled "Steel and Iron Shipbuilding and Engineering." Starting in January 1945 Wallace went from department to department to understand the operations of the company—ideal training for a future manager. He threw himself wholeheartedly into the work, often with near-disastrous results. In the electrical department he dropped his screwdriver over three 4,000-volt fuses. He was so badly burned his eyes sank out of sight. "My face was absolutely shredded. Blood dripping and all like raw beef steak." He was back at work in 14 days, much against medical advice. Even then, he remembers, "If you touched my face, it would bleed."

After his apprenticeship was finished on January 8, 1949, he spent a year with the large American firm of Sun Ship in Chester to gain further experience.

David Wallace's certificate of apprenticeship.

major financial commitment by the government.

The 10,000-ton ships were a source of immediate cash for the government, which had set up the War Assets Corporation to oversee the disposal or redeployment of some $2 billion worth of now redundant vessels and equipment from the war. At one-quarter to one-third their original cost, the price was attractive, and as quickly as Canadian buyers could be found, the ships were sold off.

In 1948, Canadian owners were allowed to sell the ships to foreign buyers as it became clear that most of them were too slow and small to be suitable for Canadian trade. Canadian owners were originally supposed to replace them with Canadian-built ships, but because of the high price of Canadian construction this generally did not happen. Canadian goods continued to travel in ships built in other countries.

In 1944, 18 steel shipbuilders had formed the Canadian Shipbuilding and Ship Repairing Association to find ways to soften the inevitable decrease in shipbuilding. While they recognized that the level of shipbuilding could not be maintained at its wartime pitch, many also realized that to maintain even a modest industry, some consideration would have to be given to the high costs of labour and materials in Canada. A brief presented by the shipbuilders to Ottawa on August 30, 1944, outlined 10 recommendations. Key among these were the reservation of coastal shipping for Canadian ships, the encouragement of Canadian shipowners engaged in foreign trade to build and register their ships in Canada, and the passing of laws requiring that all Canadian naval and fishing vessels be built in Canada. Ottawa did not respond favourably at this time.

The war and the changing demands of shipbuilding had also transformed North Vancouver. On February 28, 1941, the federal government established Wartime Housing Ltd., which built an eight-room school and 683 houses in the city.

Extensive as this housing was, it could not begin to accommodate the vast numbers of workers needed for wartime shipbuilding. Before the war, most of Burrard's employees had lived on the North Shore and much of Burrard's construction had been for Lower Mainland customers. This fostered close connections with the community. But beginning in the 1940s, most employees lived on the other side of the inlet, and they were working on large contracts for the federal or provincial governments. While the sense of community among the shipyard employees remained strong, the company's connection to North Vancouver decreased.

CHAPTER 5

Peacetime Retrenchment:
1946–1960

She starts—she moves—she seems to feel
The thrill of life along her keel!
And, spurning with her foot the ground,
With one exulting, joyous bound,
She leaps into the ocean's arms!

From Henry Wadsworth Longfellow's "The
Building of the Ship"

The Pace Slows

Except for the recession of 1958–1962, the 15 years after the war were good ones economically for most British Columbians. While shipbuilding was increasingly an international game, and Japan, Britain, Sweden and other countries had a depth of skill and tradition that was hard to match, Canadian yards remained relatively busy. The BC ferry fleet expanded rapidly and most other shipbuilding revenue on the West Coast now came from federal government contracts. During the war the government had established itself as the major source for new construction, and government departments now built their ships at home rather than in England as had been the case prior to the war.

Britain was in these years by far the world's major shipbuilder. In 1946 the world's total registered tonnage constructed was 2,127,421, with Britain accounting for 1,133,245 tons, or over half. Canada, with 71,898 tons, was a distant fourth after Britain, the US and Sweden, and would soon fall far behind many other countries. Japan, third behind Britain and France in 1950, soon became a world player.

Federal contracts buried the germinating seeds of future problems. Rollie Webb notes that during these years the workforce at Burrard "became very stratified with little real communication crossing the boundaries, and throughout the post-war generation, productivity of the whole organization decreased." Many still believed in British expertise, and the company filled senior positions by importing men from England or Scotland rather than by promoting from within. No one addressed the difficult subjects of high overhead, stationary middle management and inefficient union work practices.

During the war, the labour unions had become much more powerful and were able to establish closed shops—in which union membership was made a condition of employment. Even decreased employment after the war did not diminish the fervour for what many saw as a class struggle. A number of the local labour leaders, such as Bill White and William Stewart, had strong Communist affiliations, which tended to make them more militant and involved in broader political issues. For example, the August 19, 1947, *Vancouver Sun* reported that picket lines declared a Dutch ship "hot" because of Dutch action in Indonesia. The combination of militant union leaders and generally conservative business leaders also produced an atmosphere of confrontation, which led to a rocky relationship over the next few decades.

A shortage of domestic steel hampered the shipbuilding industry during this time, as Canadian foundries were reluctant to incur the great expense of creating a capacity for what might be a temporary demand. Even more detrimental were the relatively high labour costs in Canada, particularly on the West Coast. Only the United States had higher costs, and it had a system of subsidies. Canadian shipbuilders persistently lobbied Ottawa for subsidies (with some success) and requirements that ships plying Canadian coastal waters be built in Canadian shipyards (with no success). Largely because of higher wages, BC's share of new tonnage fell from just under half that of the eastern yards in 1945 to less than 20 percent in 1949.

Burrard Dry Dock and the municipal politicians continued their dance in the post-war years, with Burrard pushing the council for property tax concessions and the politicians lending their lobbying efforts for more contracts. For example, the *North Shore Press* on February 25, 1949, described a meeting between North Vancouver mayor Frank Goldsworthy and Fisheries Minister R.W. Mayhew in which the former argued the need for shipbuilding contracts to solve North Vancouver's unemployment problems.

Shipbuilding was the number one industry on the North Shore, and city council appreciated its contribution to the economic well-being of the area, but also tried to maximize the city's revenue from taxes. Burrard's appeal of the assessment of its dry docks was reported in the *Vancouver Province* of January 21, 1955. This was the first time the docks had been assessed for taxes. Burrard argued that because the docks were registered as ships, they should not be assessed, but it lost the appeal.

Although the war was over, the federal government promised it would not cancel any more planned projects, including the 15 China Coaster vessels (six of them at Burrard), some of which were already under construction. These small 1,340-ton freighters were designed for war freighting in the Pacific theatre, but were adaptable—and hence sellable—to any coastal service. Of traditional steel riveted construction, some were propelled by steam and the rest by diesel. Four were built at the South Yard and two at the North.

On completion they were taken over by the War Assets Corporation, which acted as a broker. In March

Above: The China Coaster Luzon, *launched February 26, 1946, delivered May 1, 1946.* 27-2276

1946 it sold six—three from Burrard and three from Pacific Drydock (formerly North Van Ship Repairs). Three went to Clark Steamships of Montreal and three to De la Rama Steamship Company of Manila for $300,000 to $400,000 each. The final seven were sold in May to China for about $2.5 million, and Burrard received a contract to convert four of these to accommodate more passengers.

The company continued to do well financially in the immediate post-war years. Burrard's operating profit rose from $1,341,251 in 1947 to $3,789,929 in 1948, although it fell to $585,289 for 1949.

The *Canadian Constructor*

To ease the transition from intense wartime activity to the slower pace of peacetime, late in the war the federal government ordered three freighters through

Wartime Shipbuilding, one each from Burrard Dry Dock, Davie Shipbuilding and Canadian Vickers of Montreal. Like the "Canadian" series of freighters constructed at the end of World War I, these were in part a federal job assistance program for returning servicemen. Burrard's $2.5-million contract for its first peacetime ship in six years called for a 16-knot freighter, with detailed plans and specifications drawn up by Cox and Stevens of New York.

The *Canadian Constructor* was not only the biggest ocean-going freighter yet to be constructed in BC, but was also the first to be diesel powered. Its four-cylinder opposed-piston diesel engines, a Doxford design built by Canadian Vickers, could generate 6,000 horsepower, turning an 18-foot bronze propeller. Diesel-driven generators that provided electricity for lighting, deck machinery and refrigeration, as well as state-of-the-art wheelhouse and navigation

Top: At Berth No. 2, Pier No. 4 West, the Canadian Constructor, *launched April 3, 1946, appears part of the North Vancouver urban landscape.* 27-2252

equipment, made it the last word in modern freighters.

In February 1947 it was put through its trials, with its maiden voyage planned February 20 for the Atlantic coast via the Panama Canal, where it would ply the West Indies trade route for Canadian National Steamships under the command of D.C. Wallace (no relation to Clarence). Its North Vancouver construction swelled civic pride, as reported in the *North Shore Press* of February 14, 1947.

~

North Vancouver-built, she steamed out of the harbor, gleaming white and a thing of beauty. As she cleared the Lions' Gate bridge, the telegraph rang "full speed ahead." Six thousand horsepower twisted the massive screw, the rolling bow wave became a plume of white water—the Motor Vessel *Canadian Constructor* was outward bound eating up the sea miles at 16 knots.

It stayed on the Montreal–West Indies run until a seamen's strike led to CN abandoning the service in 1957. The September 1983 issue of *Harbour and Shipping* states that in 1958 it was sold to the Cuban government and renamed *Ciudad de Montreal*, although because of the Cuban revolution it did not leave for Havana until 1962.

French Colliers: Wallace Wins One for the Home Side

While Canadian government contracts for Canadian shipbuilders in the immediate post-war years were scarce, war-torn Europe needed rebuilding, and federal loans to foreign governments aided European reconstruction while bringing benefits to Canadian suppliers. France received $240 million with the proviso that it purchase Canadian goods, ships being among them.

While this was good news for the Canadian industry as a whole, Canadian yards still had to compete against each other for the contracts. Wages in the West Coast yards were undeniably higher than in the east, which—Burrard's management took every opportunity to point out—increased the cost of the ships. On the other hand, the workers argued that the main problem was the higher cost of transportation,

Above: A classic shot—the Canadian Constructor *steams under the Lions Gate bridge.* 27-2270

especially of steel. And in the West Coast's favour, the relatively balmy winters meant outdoor work could be done year-round, somewhat countering the disadvantages of high wages and transportation costs.

In 1946 the French government let a lucrative contract for 15 colliers, to be used primarily to transport coal from the eastern United States for use on the French railroads. The Canadian Export Board acted as agents for the French Supply Council in Canada, representing the provisional government of the French Republic. Not many gave the western yards even an outside chance, so it was a major but welcome surprise when Clarence Wallace phoned yard officials from Montreal on January 15, 1946, to announce that his company had landed contracts to build 11 of the 15 colliers. The rest went to Davie Shipbuilding in Quebec. Seven of the ships were between 5,300 and 5,700 tons; the other four, 3,630. As part of the post-

Top: The collier Vaires *under construction.* 27-224

Right: Nestled amidst the construction infrastructure, the collier Tergnier *takes shape.* 27-2209

war loan to France, Yarrows received a contract for four lighthouse tenders, and Dominion Bridge a contract for four river barges.

On January 17, 1946, the editorial writer for the *Vancouver News Herald* eloquently expressed the buoyant chauvinism that has always characterized the West Coast:

~

Altogether, Mr. Wallace has given a shining demonstration of the spirit and the confidence in ourselves essential if we are to make what we should of our postwar opportunities. He is to be commended for the material results he has obtained and most of all for the example he has set.

The first collier, the 3,630-ton *Vaires*, was delivered to Commander Rebaud in January 1948. It boasted a propeller that at 22,000 pounds was the largest ever cast in western Canada; it took workers two weeks to mould the 17-foot blades from a single pattern. The colliers were both riveted and welded; the latter method was used for such features as plate butts, tank panels and bulkhead panels. Engines for the larger colliers were Inglis-Parson steam turbines manufactured by John Inglis Company of Toronto,

while those for the smaller ships were Vickers-Skinner Unaflow engines by Canadian Vickers in Montreal. Boilers for both types came from Vancouver Iron Works. The French did outline drawings for the ships, but Burrard draftsmen prepared the detailed drawings.

Construction, especially of the first ships, was slower than originally contracted for, necessitating a memorandum of agreement dated February 16, 1948, which amended the delivery dates of the smaller colliers. Original contract price for each of these was $1,175,000. A total of 1,590 late days for the five ships cost Burrard $238,500, although an escalator clause to cover increased wages netted the company $1,001,687.50. In a sense Burrard was ahead in the game, although the extra money for the salaries covered only increased costs.

This contract, which provided about 2,000 jobs over two years, had come none too soon. In December 1945, as work on the China Coasters wound down, 20 to 50 men a day were being laid off, and by Christmas 1,000 were gone. By early 1946, employment was down to 2,400. To add to Burrard's woes, a fire swept through a building housing tool stores, locker rooms and a rigging loft, causing a loss of about $100,000. The South Yard, no longer buoyed

Top: The completed collier Venissieux. 27-2200

by wartime contracts, closed down at the end of January 1946. The collier contract was an exception—generally Burrard did not participate in the post-war boom that brought a flood of contracts to other yards, especially those in Britain. Canadian Vickers got a contract for 12 ships for Brazil, but Burrard's hopes for overseas contracts with China and Holland did not materialize.

The CPR, which might have been expected to support the yards of its home country, contracted with Fairfields in Scotland for its next two liners. CP's arguments were that insurance money for lost shipping was in sterling, which had to be spent in Britain, and that Britain needed the exchange this purchase would bring. Regardless, many resented a Canadian company, which was still receiving good service from the Burrard-built *Princess Louise*, giving the local yards a cold shoulder. Colonial attitudes die hard.

So how could Burrard build the colliers at a competitive price and the 10,000-ton maintenance ships at a lower cost than the eastern Canadian yards when it found it difficult to compete on other contracts? It appears that while Burrard's higher wages made it difficult to compete for one-off jobs, its efficient operations enabled it to cut costs when building a number of ships of the same type. Unfortunately, contracts like this were few and far between in the post-war years.

HOW COULD they [Canadian shipyards] compete? There was in the machine shop and the engine fitting section I would think maybe four or five men who were not Scots or were not English. In other words they were people who learned their trade in England and they were really expert. That continued during my time there [1935–1948]. Outside my father, he was probably the only one you could call a Canadian, or born in Canada.

Bob Logan, Burrard Dry Dock employee

A Few Old Ships Made New Again

With the onset of peace, warships needed to be converted to other uses. Not only were their assignments different, but in a post-war world more power was needed to carry heavier loads greater distances. In 1947 Burrard was awarded one of three Castle class corvette conversions for Union Steamship Company—the other two went to West Coast Shipbuilders. These British-built vessels were considerably larger, at 1,838 tons, and generally better outfitted than the Flower class corvettes. The job provided work at Burrard for about 200 men for four months.

Union Steamship had purchased the ships at a bargain basement price of $75,000 each, but the cost of upgrading ballooned from an expected $500,000 each to $750,000. These would not rank among Burrard's greatest successes. Bow rudders installed to make the ships more manoeuvrable proved useless and were sealed after their first dry docking. They used more fuel and carried less cargo than the other Union ships, while a low funnel often spewed soot over the decks and burned the lifeboat covers.

Burrard's corvette, HMCS *St. Thomas*, became the Union Steamship's *Camosun* (III), then briefly the *Chilcotin* before it was sold to the Alaska Cruise Lines in 1958 and renamed the *Yukon Star*. Like the other corvette conversions, this ship entered the tourist trade in the Queen Charlotte Islands and on other northern BC runs. It could accommodate 100 first-class passengers, with a spacious lounge for dancing, movies and other entertainment. Originally Alaska Cruise Lines planned year-round service, but a lack of business during the winter decreased this to seasonal. *Yukon Star* was eventually towed to Tacoma and broken up for scrap in 1974.

In 1946 Burrard converted the *Waitemata* from an unfinished maintenance ship to a passenger-cargo vessel for Union Steamship Company of New Zealand to serve on the Vancouver–Australasia run. In the early 1950s the company completed a number of other conversions. The *Western Challenger*, a former twin-screw YMS hull was converted for Nelson

Brothers Fisheries, which used it for towing fish barges. The *Chief Maquinna* was converted for Nanaimo Towing from a ferry to a pleasure craft and general utility ship. In 1955 the tug *Sea Monarch* was repowered for Dolmage Towing Company. Built in 1927 as the motor patrol boat *Nemcha*, it had been sold after the war and used as a private yacht. Burrard changed it from double to single screw, installing an 800-horsepower (break horsepower or bhp) Enterprise diesel engine. And in May 1954 Burrard was awarded the $2.75 million contract to convert the HMCS *Beacon Hill*. Built at Yarrows in 1944, it was one of 21 Canadian River class frigates converted to Prestonian class ocean escort vessels. "Squid" mortars replaced depth charges, and the radar and accommodations were updated.

Buying Out the Competition: Purchase of Yarrows and Pacific Drydock

After the war there wasn't enough work to keep all the West Coast yards going, and Burrard pursued a policy of buying out its main rivals to reduce the competition and ensure its own survival.

Yarrows had been active in Victoria since 1914, when Alfred Yarrow left the United Kingdom to purchase the British Columbia Marine Railway. In 1946 Sir Alfred Yarrow's son Norman, though only 54, was ready to call it a day. His only son had been killed in a car accident in 1938 and his daughter was not interested in the company, so the incentive for carrying on had disappeared. The Wallaces acquired Yarrows in March 1946, with the transfer taking place April 12. The total purchase price was about $3 million.

Yarrows had two yards: the original plant and one owned by War Assets Corporation that had been built to handle wartime naval construction. Burrard acquired both, although it sold the No. 2 yard to Manning Timber Products in July 1948. Yarrows was an efficient yard, with a long history of ship repairing and shipbuilding, complementing Burrard's operations. Its purchase gave Burrard access to the Esquimalt dry dock, still the largest in the north Pacific, and a total of four shipbuilding ways. After the purchase, E.W. Izard, Alfred Yarrow's original colleague, continued as general manager of the yard, while Clarence's younger brother Hubert became the managing director. Hubert's son John became general manager when Izard retired in 1956.

Yarrows' first major contract under its new owners was the 5,000-ton, $3-million, 322-passenger *Prince George* for CN Steamships, the largest commercial passenger vessel built to this time in western Canada. The yard operated for some years as a separate corporate entity with its own management team. Only Burrard's secretary-treasurer (a position equivalent to chief financial officer) was responsible for both companies. From 1956 to 1967 Norman Brown held this job. Bidding was done in a co-operative spirit, avoiding direct competition for any given job. Extensive sharing of work occurred, with contracts moved back and forth. In 1957 Burrard and its subsidiaries were brought under one corporate entity, and over the next 20 years, with changes in management, integration of administration and operations achieved greater efficiency. On January 1, 1979, Burrard and Yarrows formed Burrard Yarrows Corporation. From this time on it functioned as one company with two operating divisions.

Above: Hubert Wallace in 1952, as managing director of Yarrows. 27-542

Burrard's main North Shore competitor during the war had been North Van Ship Repairs, which since 1925 had operated out of the nearby waterfront property west of Lonsdale, graced in earlier years by Pete Larson's Hotel North Vancouver. During World War II North Van Ship Repairs had employed as many as 9,500 workers, completing 63 ships for the war effort. It had two floating dry docks and two operational building berths, but business was insufficient to keep two North Shore yards profitable. The owner, A.C. Burdick, was 77 and not interested in carrying on, so on May 2, 1951, Burrard acquired the company, known since 1945 as Pacific Drydock, for $900,000.

David Wallace says that they were not allowed in the yard until after the payment was made, and they were surprised to find a 120-foot company yacht (the *Odalesque*) and a dozen Chryslers for use by the fore-

men. David believes the Burdick son was more interested in an affluent lifestyle than the business.

When Clarence Wallace bought the yard he intended to close it down. But his brother Hubert convinced him that it would be useful to keep it open. The existence of four major yards on the West Coast—Burrard, Yarrows, Victoria Machinery Depot and Pacific Drydock—would, he argued, convince the government in Ottawa that more contracts for shipbuilding were needed. Burrard's general manager Bill Wardle was strongly opposed, but as Clarence was busy with his duties as lieutenant-governor, Hubert got his way. He spent $80,000 on a new covered building berth for four wooden barges ordered by Straits Towing, much to the chagrin of David Wallace, Bill Hudson, and many other members of the management team. It took two and a half years of wasted

Top: An aerial view of Esquimalt Harbour, looking northeast. The naval dockyard is in the foreground, the government dry dock in the left background. The Yarrows shipyard is on the right, opposite the dry dock. 27-3769

profits before the yard was closed in November 1953, though the company recovered the cost of closing the yard in one year. Hubert was not pleased.

Moveable equipment was relocated to Burrard and Yarrows. The two floating dry docks were moved to the Burrard yard, and part of the property was leased to a number of tenants. In 1966 all except the northwest triangle was sold to Island Tug and Barge for $550,000. The balance, consisting of the main office and the stores building, was sold to Stork Werkspoor Pacific for $90,000.

Naval Engagements

When the last of the French colliers was launched towards the end of 1948, no new shipbuilding contracts were on the horizon. In mid-1948 Burrard employed 1,700 workers, but Clarence Wallace stated that after the colliers were finished they would be lucky to have work for 400. The November 1948 issue of *Harbour and Shipping* noted that new construction in Canadian yards had dropped 38 percent since March.

Top: An aerial view of Pacific Drydock after it was taken over by Burrard Dry Dock. 27-3559

During the Depression the federal government had implemented social programs such as family allowance, while the shipbuilding program in World War II had reinforced the notion that the feds had both the power and responsibility to use shipbuilding as a tool for social engineering. In the post-war world the federal government, accepting this enhanced role, often used shipbuilding contracts as a means to keep the yards active and Canadian workers employed.

Shipbuilding contracts were also important for national security. At the end of World War I, Britain's naval supremacy had been unchallenged, which meant new naval construction in Canada was assigned a low priority. But the end of World War II told a different story. The unknown extent of the Russian threat, especially the submarine menace, caused greater anxiety. The two world wars had shown that it took time to gear shipbuilding up for the needs of war and now, in a nuclear world, immediate response was imperative.

The Canadian Shipbuilding and Ship Repairing Association had developed into a more effective lobby group, pointing out how important the industry was to the economy and possibly the future security of the country. The Canadian Maritime Commission, formed in 1947, also exerted influence. Its second report, published in 1949, recommended against a Canadian-built merchant marine, but argued that a case could be made for a small ocean-going naval fleet to protect national security.

The May 19, 1950, *Sun* reported that Clarence Wallace joined with other spokesmen for Canada's shipbuilding industry to take their case to Transport Minister Lionel Chevrier. Wallace argued that Canada's coastal shipping trade should be reserved for ships built in Canada and operated by Canadian owners (as was done in the US). Edouard Simard, vice-president of Marine Industries in Sorel, Quebec, pointed out that Canadian coastal trade was the only form of internal transport open to carriers from outside the country.

The government did nothing to restrict coastal shipping,* but heedful of its commitments to NATO and the politics of the Cold War, the feds initiated a major shipbuilding program that would maintain strategically located shipyards across Canada, creating and maintaining a workforce of skilled technicians. Burrard's first naval contract was for a 125.5-foot "gate vessel," built to defend against submarine attacks by, among other methods, laying protective submarine nets or chains across the openings of harbours that required protection.

---

* A quarter century later, in 1976, the federal government did finally introduce Bill C61, which limited coastal trading to Canadian flag vessels. But the bill was opposed by resource industries and some provinces, including BC, which believed the cost of intercoastal shipping through the Panama Canal would increase—even though little trade of this sort existed—and the restraint on national railway rates would be lost. Bill C61 died.

Right: HMCS Porte Quebec, *a gate vessel used for handling anti-submarine nets, launched August 28, 1951, from the same shed that was used for the* War Dog *(see photo in Chapter 2).* 27-2059

The *Porte Quebec*'s August 1951 launch was the first of a naval ship on the West Coast since the war. For four and a half years it was engaged in submarine defence and research on navigation and oceanography, mostly in BC coastal waters. The July 1978 *Harbour and Shipping* reported that in 1967 it was recommissioned at HMC Dockyard, Esquimalt, to train naval reserve officers and men. In 1995, in the twilight of its career, it was still operating out of Esquimalt.

The major breakthrough for Burrard and other yards in Montreal, Sorel, Quebec City, Halifax and Victoria came with the government's decision to build 14 anti-submarine, St. Laurent class destroyer escorts, the result of a 1948 commitment by Canada to contribute to NATO in anti-submarine warfare. Burrard received the contracts for four of these, originally

costed at $8 million each, although difficulties in getting materials, inexperience in building ships incorporating the most sophisticated technology, and frequent design changes by Ottawa greatly escalated the cost. Bill Hudson, at this time secretary-treasurer and later CEO of Burrard, recalls the difficulties and frustrations of these contracts. "In one instance, as I recall, a destroyer escort of the Restigouche class was on the building berth for a year without anything being done to it. They hadn't designed the gun on the forward decks, so that had to stay there for a year. They would produce the drawings as they went along."

In naval heritage these were successors to the wartime corvettes and frigates. Designed by Captain A.H. Baker and the naval staff in Ottawa, they were the first warships designed in Canada; machinery was

Above: Blacksmiths in 1958 are, left to right: Bill Shepherd, Keith Myles, Bob Fleming, Pete Blondoff, Jim McEwen, Tom Watt and Gil Cavill. In front of them are pins and shackles and two lift forks. 27-13

also made in this country. The use of a considerable amount of aluminum instead of heavier steel for the superstructure meant they could carry more equipment. Their speed (in excess of 20 knots) and British sonar and American radar equipped them to hunt subs, while their low profile made their observation by enemy craft more difficult. Armament included four three-inch and two 40-millimetre guns, along with either two Limbo anti-submarine mortar mounts or "Squid" mortars aft. Their 300 motors and motor generators consumed enough energy for a town of 10,000; complex systems required a large crew of 250 men and 20 officers.

Burrard laid the keel for its first destroyer escort, HMCS *Skeena*, on June 1, 1951, and the job provided steady work for 300 to 350 men over two years. To facilitate its construction, Burrard built a massive

Top: R. Macy, Clint Eadie and Len West furnace a plate in the west gantry in 1957. 27-257
Above: The machine shop after a facelift in 1958. 27-90

concrete pier between the two major berths and erected two 50-ton travelling Colby cranes on the pier. David Wallace recalls that up to then they had been building ships with five-ton fixed wooden cranes, as they were not allowed to use steel for construction of cranes during the war. This had greatly affected the size of units they could prefabricate, slowing the speed of construction. Along with the new cranes, the use of welding rather than riveting also made it possible to use large units—in the *Skeena*'s case there were 75 prefabricated sections weighing from 5 to 27 tons. The company built a unit construction shop (also known as the erection shop), completed in 1952, where workers fabricated these large steel structures. This shop was 350 feet long, 50 feet wide between columns and 50 feet high from floor to crane rail. With its two 30-ton travelling bridge cranes, it cost $520,000. When Pacific Drydock was

Top: Welders received eye protection before their helpers. Ed Esakin, sheet metal apprentice, avoids looking down while Pete Lalonde welds in 1957. 27-254

Above: Activity in the copper shop, May 1957. Workers from left to right are: Ernie Shenbach, Bert Philips, Don Archibald, Glenn Archibald, Harry Phillips and Ray Hutchinson. 27-178

closed in late 1953, its two dry docks, several cranes and various machine shop equipment were relocated to Burrard, doing much to improve its capacity.

The *Skeena* was the largest warship constructed on the Canadian Pacific coast to this time and was planned in such a way that in the event of war, similar hulls could be built in large numbers—as had been the case with the 10,000-ton ships in World War II (although the cost for the destroyer escorts was over 10 times higher). These new ships were equipped for the whole range of attacks the Russians could throw their way. As the *Vancouver News Herald* reported on March 28, 1957:

The ship can be sealed against atomic, biological or chemical attack with provision for re-circulation of air within the ship through the air-conditioning plants. Personnel who have been exposed can be decontaminated in either of two compartments, one located forward and one aft.

The *Skeena* was the fifth of the St. Laurent destroyer escorts to join the Royal Canadian Navy and the first to be commissioned on the West Coast. Its launch on August 19, 1952, was a major event in the shipping world—although delays in its complicated outfitting meant it was not accepted by the Royal Canadian Navy until March 30, 1957. Most of these lengthy and costly delays were the responsibility of the federal bureaucracy, as thousands of changes in design details and specifications flowed from Ottawa to the West Coast yard in an attempt to keep pace with the latest developments in naval architecture and electronics.

Top: Burrard employee Jack Goode captures the frustration often felt with the federal bureaucracy.
Above: The commissioning ceremony held for the Skeena, *March 30, 1957.* 27-2101

In the short run this cost-plus contract worked to Burrard's advantage. Each additional change resulted in more man-hours, with the company then sending its bill to Ottawa. But as there was virtually no control over escalating costs, this was an inefficient way to build a ship. And while it resulted in high-quality work, it developed a habit of perfectionism that was often inappropriate in commercial work, where clients prefer a rougher but cheaper job.

Construction of HMCS *Fraser*, originally awarded to Yarrows, was transferred to Burrard because berths at the Victoria yard were not big enough. It was launched February 19, 1953, and towed to Yarrows April 9, 1953, for completion. After a lengthy outfitting, during which its cost ballooned to $23 million, its commissioning took place June 28, 1957. Man-hours were still 350,000 less than for the *Skeena*, a discrepancy management had difficulty explaining. Although the *Fraser* benefited from being the "follow" ship, it was hard to justify the much higher number of hours for the *Skeena*.

The other two anti-submarine vessels built by Burrard, the *Kootenay* and *Columbia*, were of the Restigouche class. Again, many changes delayed construction. In one instance a change in the location of fire pumps necessitated ripping out considerable work already done. Both ships were commissioned in 1959. Of the 14 destroyer escorts built for the Canadian navy, the *Columbia* required the fewest man-hours—although its overall cost of $25 million was not the cheapest.

The *Kootenay* served with the Atlantic fleet until October 23, 1969, when an explosion in the engine room forced its return to Halifax under tow. At this time it was converted to an Improved Restigouche class destroyer. It was recommissioned June 7, 1972, and returned to the Atlantic fleet, later returning and joining the Maritime Forces Pacific Fleet.

In January 1956 the government announced another round of contracts involving $60 million for 12 new vessels: seven destroyer escorts, two lighters, two modified Norton class tugs and one loop layer.

Top: The unclad Fraser *proceeding under tow of Pacific Salvage tugs* Salvage King *and* Squamish Queen *to Yarrows in Victoria for fitting out, April 9, 1953.* 27-2072

British Columbia was allotted three escort vessels and one crane lighter, with Burrard getting one of the escort vessels.

Burrard's contract for the *Yukon*, its fifth and last destroyer escort, belonging to the Repeat-Restigouche or Mackenzie class, was finally awarded in October 1958. The keel was not laid until a year later, and it was not commissioned until May 25, 1963. It was the first ship built under a new target incentive program, in which the shipbuilder was paid on the basis of a target cost (2,207,000 man-hours). The builder received 40 percent of the savings if the vessel was produced for less. Burrard completed the *Yukon* in 1,447,000 man-hours, a saving of 760,000 hours. The contract totalled $9,881,368, saving the government $2,834,602 off the original estimate. This encouraged much greater efficiency than the previous cost-plus system. By way of comparison, the *Skeena* took 2,744,000 man-hours, the *Kootenay* 2,451,000 and the *Columbia* 2,315,000.

A December 7, 1965, memo from the Audit Services Branch to S. Walton, accountant at Burrard Dry Dock, illustrates the government auditors' at times niggling attempts to bring costs under control.

~

Page 3 of the Agreement between Burrard Dry Dock Ltd. and Camus Services Ltd.…states that coffee and doughnuts or equivalent will be served twice daily for 25c per man per day. Would you please determine the reasons for both a) the charge at double the stipulated rate for the regular two coffee servings, and b) the supplying of an additional serving at no charge.

Mr. Walton's response remains unrecorded.

A decade later the high-tech destroyer escort marvels of the 1950s were yesterday's ships and in need of updated equipment. The *St. Laurent*, completed seven years previously for $15 million, was the first to enter Burrard for a refit, a nine-month job completed in August 1963. The ship's entire afterdeck was

Above: The Columbia *cuts a gleaming swath through the dark waters.* 27-2041

converted to a helicopter landing platform, and its electronic gear brought up to date. The *Saguenay* followed for similar reconstruction at a projected cost of $2.8 million, and the *Antigonish*, a Yarrows hull built in 1944, was refitted in March 1965. Variable depth sonar, fin stabilizers and Sea King helicopters were added, while the men's mess deck and recreation area was enlarged.

The federal government spent enormous sums to build and refit the destroyer escorts. In 1962 a quarter of the federal budget, $1.6 billion was going to defence, as the threat of Russian attack in the context of such events as the Cuban Missile Crisis was a strong political motivator. But missile-equipped Russian nuclear submarines could do 40 knots, while the destroyer escorts had a top speed of under 30. Submarines could now strike at a great distance from the relative security of the deep ocean or from under the polar ice cap. The navy admitted that in the new world of high tech the $30-million destroyers were obsolete even before they were launched—but then so was all new construction. If Canada was to be a world player in the armament game, greater financial

commitment was necessary. But such was not in keeping with its national bent. Canada's path since this time has been to allow responsibility for defence and its expenses to shift to other countries, especially the United States. Our expenditures on naval resources have in recent years been minimal.

Department of Transport Contracts

Copious amounts of federal money also flowed from the department of transport. In March 1949 the department awarded Yarrows an $896,000 contract to build a lighthouse supply ship and buoy tender vessel. This contract was transferred to Burrard and became the first Burrard ship of all steel-welded construction. It incorporated the latest navigational and electronic equipment including direction-finder, echo-sounding device, gyroscopic compass and radar. Twin 10-cylinder Vivian diesel engines could generate a combined 1,000 horsepower, while one-foot bilge keels running the entire length of the ship below the waterline acted as stabilizers.

This ship was launched January 12, 1950, as the

Above: The Alexander Mackenzie, *complete and ready for service.* 27-2131

CCGS *Alexander Mackenzie*, sponsored by Mrs. Ian Mackenzie, widow of the late senator and former cabinet minister Ian Mackenzie, with Norman MacKay as its first commander. After outfitting, it was based at Prince Rupert, where it serviced departmental lighthouses, buoys and other aids to navigation from Cape Scott to the head of Portland Canal, including the Queen Charlotte Islands. It was also available for rescue work. A similar ship, the CCGS *Sir James Douglas*, built five years later, replaced the 35-ton lighthouse tender *Berens*, built by Victoria Motor Boat Company in 1921.

Discovery of oil and minerals in the Arctic islands and under the northern continental shelf piqued the interests of many commercial operations. The federal government saw the opening of this region as a way of asserting Canadian sovereignty, as well as generating resource revenue. Icebreakers were an essential component of these plans, as ships from private companies needed help in navigating these mostly icebound waters.

The CCGS *Camsell*, named after Dr. Charles Camsell, an Arctic geologist and explorer, was the first icebreaker built on the Pacific coast and the first of many built by Burrard. Although Yarrows originally won the contract, Burrard constructed the hull because its dimensions were too large for Yarrows' building berths. While the contract was awarded in August 1957, delays in settling design details and obtaining steel meant the keel was not laid until March 18, 1958. Built of fine-grain steel 1 to 1.25 inches thick, the vessel's frames and ribs were 16 inches apart over the midship area and 15 inches apart forward and aft, with the main castings of special nickel-alloy steel.

Top: Boss framing mocked up for the Camsell *by, left to right: foreman loftsman Jim McColl with loftsmen Tom Knox and Doug Wallis.* 27-147

Above: A bow section of the Camsell *is lowered into place.* 27-1895

Four diesel engines manufactured by Fairbanks Morse Canadian Locomotive Company of Kingston gave the *Camsell* a cruising radius of 12,000 miles. The February 19, 1959, *North Vancouver Citizen* reported that it was based in Victoria, serving as a helicopter-equipped icebreaker escort to ships operating in the western Arctic, and also performing lighthouse supply and buoy work. For its 51-person crew's comfort it had three separate messes served from a large, fully electric galley; its first captain was A.F. Dawson. Life for the Arctic patrol had changed a lot since the spartan days of the *St. Roch*, although historic firsts were not over. In 1962 the *Camsell* became the first ship to circumnavigate King William Island.

In 1978 it was holed by ice about 122 miles east of Cambridge Bay, and the engine room was flooded through an eight-foot gash below the waterline. The crew put on a temporary steel patch and the boat was towed back to Victoria by the Canmar tugs *Supplier 3* and *Seaspan Sovereign* for repair at Yarrows. The *Vancouver Province* reported that it took Ottawa 18 months to decide on appropriate action; the work, which took a year, included the removal and rewinding of all auxiliary and main propulsion units, as well as the renovation of the crew accommodations. The bill was $3.6 million—not much less than the original construction cost of $4.4 million.

Burrard won the contract for the icebreaker CCGS *Simon Fraser* on the open market with other Canadian shipyards. Workers laid its keel February 23, 1959, in the same berth the just-completed *Camsell* had vacated. Main castings were made from high-tensile nickel-alloy steel, while twin propellers eight feet, three inches in diameter were made from

Above: The prefabricated bow section of the Simon Fraser. 27-1874

Nikalium, a special copper-nickel alloy, to withstand the severe icebreaking conditions.

Based in Victoria, the *Simon Fraser* was designed for use as a search-and-rescue vessel on the west coast of Vancouver Island, as well as for tending and maintaining the 46 lighthouses and more than 500 spar, cone and bell buoys, and supplying stores to coast guard stations up to the other side of the Arctic Circle. It delivered the mail, including correspondence courses for children of lighthouse keepers. In early 1963 it was transferred to the east coast, where it was stationed in Quebec. Nearly 40 years later, in 2001, it accompanied the RCMP's *Nadon* in a re-creation of the original traverse of the Northwest Passage by the *St. Roch* in 1940–1942.

Log Barges Replace Log Rafts

While Burrard relied mainly on government contracts, it also did a considerable amount of private construction, especially of barges. Until the 1950s the most common way of transporting logs was in log rafts, known as Davis rafts. However, logs in these rafts were subject to teredo worm damage, and it cost a lot to put rafts together and dismantle them. It took 18 men 10 to 14 days to assemble a Davis raft, and 10 men 7 to 10 days to dismantle it. In addition $15,000 of cables, chains, etc., went into the assembly of each raft.

In the early 1920s Captain Walter Wingate bought the steamer *Bingamon* from the British Transport Company in Seattle and had Burrard mount a derrick that ran on rails along the deck for loading and unloading logs. Although this design had mixed success, he followed it with several others. In the late 1920s Captain B.L. Johnston used the masts of a sailing vessel, the *Drumrock*, as derricks to load and off-load logs stowed in the hull, although ships of this type were not generally well suited for carrying logs.

In 1936 the Victoria-built "Mabel Brown" type wooden schooner *Malahat* was drastically altered; a 50-foot hole was carved in the deck to allow the boat to carry logs. With a heavy lift cargo boom, this ship became for a brief time the only self-loading, self-propelled, self-dumping log barge in the world.

After World War II, surplus vessels became available for barge conversions. In 1945 Island Tug bought two transport ferry hulls from West Coast Shipbuilders and Burrard Dry Dock and converted them to log barges, becoming the first company to carry logs on a continuous cargo deck. Sause Brothers Towing of Oregon came up with the idea of flooding one side of the barge to make the logs slide off, discovering that rather than the logs sliding off, the barge shot out from underneath the load.

Burrard incorporated and refined these pioneering developments in 1954 in a $1-million contract for two log barges for Kingcome Navigation. About the same time, Island Tug bought seven shallow-draft tankers from Venezuela to BC for conversion to self-

Right: Powell No. 1 *log barge fully loaded.* 27-2006

dumping barges. Both projects were designed by naval architect Robert Allan to serve as an alternative to Davis and Gibson rafts. These barges could move logs much more quickly—at eight knots compared to two and a half for the rafts—with fewer losses and hence lower insurance. They could also navigate waters that a log raft couldn't. It took four men 25 hours to load the new barges and only 30 minutes to unload them using their unique self-tipping method. When valves were opened at the bow and stern on one side, water rushed in to fill self-flooding tanks with a capacity of 68,000 cubic feet. This tipped the barge sufficiently to shed its load. The barge righted itself and drained the tanks automatically when the load was dumped. Draft when loaded was 14.3 feet but was only 3.9 feet when empty. Each barge could carry 1.5 million board feet; if required they could also be used as bulk oil carriers. The unbroken deck was ideal for

logs, but had other uses as well—before *Powell No. 1* was launched, the BC Lions football team used it as a practice field.

Powell No. 1 was launched June 17, 1954, and workers immediately laid the keel for *Powell No. 2*. These barges were assembled from prefabricated sections weighing up to 37 tons, which reduced the number of sections required from 120 to about 40. The sections could be built under cover, an obvious advantage when no covered berth existed for hulls of this size. Later renamed *Alberni Carrier* and *Powell Carrier*, these barges were the direct antecedent of every log barge on the coast today. Their success led to four more contracts for Burrard in 1957. The yard built the *Straits Cold Decker* and the *Straits Water Skidder* for Straits Towing, and the *Crown Zellerbach No. 5* and *Crown Zellerbach No. 6* for Crown Zellerbach Canada.

Top: The Straits Cold Decker *dumps its load.* 27-1967

The *V.T. 57* and *V.T. 58*, at 1,055 tons each, were the largest steel, all-covered, dry cargo barges ever built in BC. They transported wood and paper products between Ocean Falls and Vancouver for Vancouver Towing. The National Research Council Maritime Division had collaborated in the design of earlier V.T. models. Successful tank-testing of the scale model for the 900-ton *V.T. 44* showed that bigger barges were possible, which led to Burrard's construction of these hulls. The larger models had improved stability.

Other Burrard construction during the 1950s included nine chip scows, an oil scow, a derrick scow and a crane lighter.

Top: The derrick scow Y.C. 250, *launched from Pacific Drydock October 14, 1953, for the department of defence.* 27-2019

Above: The V.T. 57, *in 1956 the largest covered dry cargo barge built in BC.* 27-197

The Industrial Division

As World War II drew to a close and new construction decreased, work in Burrard's machine shop slowed down. At the same time, Vancouver shops doing industrial work were generally fully occupied. Jack Watson, the machine shop foreman, had worked as maintenance boss in BC pulp mills and later as shop superintendent of the Vancouver Engineering Works. He suggested to management that the company set up a separate division that would solicit miscellaneous work from BC industry to compensate for declining shipbuilding. In 1947 this division employed six men, and by 1951 it had grown to about 100, becoming a formalized department in September 1951 under Jack Watson, with its own staff. Clarence Wallace's son Richard joined the division in 1952, becoming its manager in 1956.

The industrial division developed into a small but profitable operation for Burrard. It often found itself on the innovative edge, as BC's rich resources were tapped for ready markets. It operated primarily to do repairs for the forest, mining and petroleum industries in BC's burgeoning post-war economy. At times, as when it manufactured a 30-ton derrick and winch for a barge being built for Crown Zellerbach, the division worked closely with the shipbuilders. But most projects were its own.

One of its first major enterprises was to help equip the Aluminum Company of Canada (Alcan) smelter at Kitimat, part of the mega-project that opened in August 1954. Burrard supplied mining cars

Above: A barge, digestor, dry dock and ship—all built by Burrard. 27-3927

and dollies, four pitch-melting tanks, and steel ribs that supported a 10-mile tunnel, with a diameter of 25 feet, through which the Nechako River was reversed to provide much-needed power.

As the shipbuilders were providing ships for the logging industry, the industrial division also found contracts in the woods. By 1956 Burrard had installed machinery in all pulp and paper mills in BC. And as spar trees of the natural sort became more rare, it fabricated and sold a number of these in the 1950s and 1960s. Because steel spar trees were portable, they saved, according to one user, three days' rigging time with each move. However, the industrial division's greater expense and lower quality compared to its main competitor, Madill in Nanaimo, affected sales. In April 1958 Burrard's share of that market was an unsatisfactory 30 percent.

Top: Putting the finishing touches to a 135-cubic-foot ore car built for Alcan. 27-3949 *Above: Forming tunnel sets for Alcan.* 27-3519

Other equipment produced for the logging industry included hydraulic barkers for mills in Alabama, Texas, New Zealand and elsewhere. These removed bark as part of the process of manufacturing pulp. The division constructed a pilot grinder mill in the mid-1950s for the Pakistan Development Corporation, to be used at the Karnaphuli Paper Mills.

Burrard pioneered much of the new plywood technology. After it started manufacturing plywood presses, only one was imported into BC; previously all had been imported. In 1963 Burrard's Leo Boehm designed and built BC's first hardboard press, a 30-opening, four-foot-by-eight-foot, $220,000 job for the Pacific Veneer Division of Canadian Forest Products. It was installed at Jen's Brothers at Canim Lake, east of 100 Mile House, and led to the division securing similar contracts with other BC companies.

Burrard then ventured into the design and manufacture of hot plywood presses, winning contracts

Top: A 96-foot spar tree, built for Rostadt, ready for travel, 1960. 27-3452

Above: A steel spar tree, built for Crown Zellerbach, ready for use. 27-3447

for presses with Kicking Horse Forest Products (1966) (in competition with Sweden and Japan), Crown Zellerbach (1971) and Kamloops Pulp and Paper (1971). Customers for other large presses included Saskatchewan Forest Products, Merrill and Wagner, Canadian Forest Products and Georgia Pacific. Its main competition was Superior Presses of Portland, Oregon, which had a 15 to 20 percent price advantage, not including duty.

In 1971, under a federal aid program, Burrard exported two plywood presses to Sharikat Jengka, a Malaysian plywood plant designed to clear the jungle and establish plantation areas for palm oil trees. Each

press was worth $100,000. In December 1974 the company shipped two 175-ton plywood hot presses by boat to Manaus, Brazil. Burrard's Bill Dalgleish supervised their installation. Each had 20 openings, one for 4-foot-by-10-foot panels; the other for 45-inch by 8-foot. Closer to home, a 52-opening plywood press costing $169,000 was installed in the North Central Plywood Company mill in Prince George. At 45 feet high this was the largest ever constructed or installed in a Canadian mill; it could produce 52¾-inch or 104⅜-inch plywood sheets every five minutes. Cold presses were also developed from patterns by "Brick" Arnold.

Top: A hydraulic log barker built for H.A. Simons. 27-3941

Pulp-baling presses included two 1,000-ton pressure jobs designed by Leo Boehm and completed for the Intercontinental Pulp Company's Prince George mill in 1967. This project ran considerably over budget, with the labour, originally estimated at $19,630, ending up at $34,000. While other presses were built for Eurocan Pulp and Weyerhaeuser Pulp,

both in Kitimat, Richard Wallace doubted they could compete in this work with Dominion Engineering, which had built between 10 and 20 of these presses.

For the petrochemical industry, Burrard designed and manufactured equipment to separate sulphur from natural gas. In 1952 it filled an order from the Canadian Chemical Company at Edmonton for a

Above: A plywood cold press dwarfs a worker. 27-3533

111-foot-high distillation tower for the production of propylene oxide. This was transported by rail on three flatcars.

In 1969 Burrard acquired Quadra Steel, one of the largest steel warehousing firms in Western Canada. This proved highly profitable—in the bleak year of 1971, when shipbuilding operations lost $42,000, Quadra saved the day with its healthy profit of $1,055,000. On December 2, 1971, the company approved the purchase of a new site for Quadra in Richmond. In September 1977 Quadra was sold to Drummond McCall of Montreal.

In later years, when shipbuilding and repair contracts were scarce, the industrial division was called on to fill the gap. During 1977–1981 it manufactured plywood presses and provided machine shop and full repair services for heavy industry. As former president David Alsop says, "We put a big push to try and capitalize on that industrial experience, marry it to our knowledge of shipbuilding techniques, and try and find a niche for equipment that could be built at tidewater, delivered on a vessel or delivered afloat, and installed adjacent to tidewater." The idea seemed to make sense—and was perhaps the only option—but it had mixed success. BC's traditional resource industries of mining and logging were in decline, and few companies were in a position to make heavy investments in new equipment.

By November 21, 1989, a March 1988 contract with the Port of Tacoma for two post-Panamax container cranes designed by Kone of Finland worth $9.15 million showed a small profit of $89,681. But a

Top: A pulp-baling press. 27-3970

$10.2-million contract signed in June 1988 with the Alaska Industrial Development and Export Authority for the design, fabrication and delivery of a dock conveying system was, in the words of Marine Workers' Union president George MacPherson, a "total disaster." Constructed and installed in modules, this conveying system was used for handling zinc and lead concentrates from Cominco's Red Dog mine in Alaska. As of November 21, 1989, it was $292,539 in the red. MacPherson argues that "it was the kind of job that should have been done in a structural shop and not a shipyard. Shipyards are good at shipbuilding. Structural shops are good at structural shops.

And we proved that quite well in the Red Dog mine. It was a total disaster for everybody."

In Burrard's final years, industrial work became its primary focus. While there was much grandiose talk, with plans for everything from cutting-edge medical technology to maintenance of military tanks, no contracts materialized. The people at Burrard Dry Dock were, after all, shipbuilders. Neither the management nor the workers could be expected to have the skills to suddenly switch directions and still remain profitable, any more than a company that built bridges could easily switch to ships.

Above: Workers are dwarfed by this huge Y for a penstock pipeline. This was delivered to the BC Power Commission for use at the Puntledge River Power Development on Vancouver Island. 27-3994

Lieutenant-Governor Clarence Wallace Captains the Ship of State

To say Clarence Wallace and his company made a significant contribution to the war effort would be a major understatement. That contribution also cemented his place in the provincial establishment. By the 1950s his formidable network included directorships of the Crown Life Assurance Company, Canada Trust Company, Commonwealth International Corporation, British American Oil Company and Cassiar Packing Company. He was also honorary president of the Navy League of Canada, vice-president of the Canadian Ordinance Association, a member of the Industrial Defense Board and honorary colonel of the Duke of Connaught's Own BC Regiment. It was hardly a surprise when in 1950 he was appointed lieutenant-governor of British Columbia.

He infused the office with his blend of friendliness and formality and an insatiable love of social life. He travelled widely throughout BC, spending lavishly on the entertaining that was so much a part of the job. He had his own personal pipe band and also enjoyed early-morning horseback riding, duck hunting and fishing.

The May 3, 1955, *Sun* reports that he was once surprised in his bathtub by some young girls whose curiosity had led them into Government House. He bowed graciously and greeted them, "Good afternoon, ladies." Other ladies and gentlemen he entertained in more formal ways included Queen Elizabeth and Prince Philip; the Archbishop of Canterbury and Mrs. Fisher; Prince Akihito, Crown Prince of Japan; Prince Axel of Denmark; and many of the leading government and entertainment people of his day. He received honours including Commander of the British Empire (CBE) in 1946 and an honorary Doctor of Laws from Queen's University in 1959. In the fall of 1955, shortly before his tenure as lieutenant-governor ended, politicians and others from BC and Alberta attended a testimonial dinner for him at the Hotel Vancouver. He was succeeded by industrialist Frank Ross.

While the lieutenant-governor's office is largely ceremonial, Clarence Wallace's tenure included one occasion for a major decision. In the provincial election of 1952 the surprise results produced 19 seats for the Social Credit and 18 for the CCF—neither party had a majority, although the CCF had more voter support at 34.3 percent as opposed to 30.2 percent for the Social Credit. Who to call on for the next government? Wallace consulted high court judges and even Prime Minister Louis St. Laurent, but no one could offer a clear answer. Finally he called on Social Credit, led by W.A.C. Bennett, partly because he felt the Liberals and Tories would be more likely to support a Social Credit government. And there can be no denying that the Social Credit party was far more in tune with his own political views than was the CCF.

During Wallace's leave of absence, Claude S. Thicke managed the yard. Thicke was appointed

Above: Clarence Wallace about 1950, with a photograph of his father Alfred on the wall. 27-524

executive vice-president in May 1951, and Bill Wardle, who had been general manager during the war, was thoroughly offended at being passed over for this position. Rather than continue, he quit.

Thicke brought to his new position extensive experience as general manager with the Blue Band Navigation Company and later the Hayes Manufacturing Company. When hired by Burrard he was president and owner of the Pacific Truck and Trailer Company, and he retained close contact with this company while he was with Burrard. Thicke oversaw the closure of Pacific Drydock and the development of Burrard's Industrial Division. He was especially interested in anything to do with logging equipment, as Pacific Truck and Trailer built logging trucks. Bill White describes him as "a real tough old rooster, he was just about as direct as a bolt of lightning." He resigned May 31, 1956, when Wallace returned, but remained on the board of directors.

In 1956 J.W. (Bill) Hudson was appointed executive vice-president of both Burrard and Yarrows, and Clarence's youngest son, David Wallace, became general manager of Burrard. That same year, Hubert's son John was appointed general manager of Yarrows.

Hudson and David Wallace worked closely and for a time harmoniously together, running the day-to-day operations of the company, although Clarence's unwillingness to relinquish final control hampered their ability to undertake new initiatives. The two men complemented each other. Hudson was quiet and thoughtful, while Wallace was outgoing and aggressive. Hudson was in charge of all contractual matters, government, commercial, corporate investments, insurance and public relations. David Wallace took care of the practicalities of shipbuilding, including the actual work in the yard, and maintained and developed contacts for ship repair sales.

As Clarence Wallace aged, especially after 1960, he withdrew from active involvement in the firm to pursue his interests in fishing, yachting and his estate at Minnekhada on the eastern outskirts of Vancouver, which he had purchased in 1958. In 1959 he sold the Wallace home "Devonia" to "Sonny" Wosk for $121,500 and moved to an apartment at 700 Chilco near Lost Lagoon. At Minnekhada Lodge he realized his lifelong dream of a country hunting retreat in a setting of style and elegance. Here he continued to entertain local business and political leaders as well as visiting royalty such as Princess Alice of England and Princess Bernhardt of the Netherlands. Duck and pheasant hunting combined with black-tie dinners on his 3,000-acre estate. Local recognition came in 1968 when he was made the City of North Vancouver's 33rd freeman.

CHAPTER 6

Last Years of the Wallaces: 1961–1972

If there is one thing better than the thrill of looking forward, it is the exhilaration that follows the finishing of a long and exacting piece of work.

From Alec Waugh's "On Doing What One Likes"

During the 1960s, the size of new ships increased astronomically; monster tankers satisfied an energy-hungry society and cargo ships responded to increased trade. While doubling the size of a hull increases the building cost by a factor of four, it increases the earning power by a factor of eight. Hulls of 100,000 tons, then 200,000 tons made their oceanic debuts, while 500,000-ton and even 1 million-ton tankers were discussed.

Japan replaced Britain as the world's leader in shipbuilding. In 1968 a shipyard in Yokohama completed the first of six 276,000-ton deadweight tankers, and later that year the 331,825-ton *Universe Ireland* was completed in the same city. While ships traversing the Panama Canal were limited to about 80,000 tons, those travelling the Pacific had few limits beyond the size of the ocean.

Burrard had neither the facilities to build and service these hulls, nor the private or government support to build the necessary facilities. These were years of continued reliance on the uncertain largesse of government contracts and subsidies, with the occasional private contract mainly for barges and scows. High wages and transportation costs continued to inflate the cost of West Coast-built ships compared to those in eastern Canada. An increasingly cost- and vote-conscious government was reluctant to pay anything more than the cheapest price possible. Naval work on the West Coast generally went to the government yard in Esquimalt, and after the launch of the *Saguenay* in 1964, Burrard received no new naval contracts in the 1960s. Substantial profits during the 60s disappeared as the 70s dawned; in 1971 Burrard received no orders for new ships.

BC Ferries Go Provincial

In the spring of 1958, during the centennial of the colony of BC, a strike by the Seafarers' International Union shut down the CPR ferries and severely hampered Black Ball service. In a response that was more consistent with his entrepreneurial character than his free enterprise political philosophy, W.A.C. Bennett assumed control of the Black Ball Line on June 23, 1958, under the Civil Defence Act.

The provincial government decided to establish its own ferry service and immediately called for bids to build two large ferries that would operate between Victoria and the Lower Mainland. These ferries were to be based on the design of the Black Ball's *Coho*. The *Tsawwassen* went to Burrard and the *Sidney* to Victoria Machinery Depot after bidding on the open market with other Canadian, British and Japanese shipyards. Showing it still had the ability to be competitive, especially when it came to ferries, Burrard

undercut a bid from Fairfields of Scotland and was $600,000 under an eastern Canadian bid, although Victoria Machinery Depot had the lowest bid of all. These ferries provided much-needed jobs—250 to 275 for Burrard alone.

Philip Spaulding and Associates of Seattle prepared plans for the *Tsawwassen*, with McLaren and Sons of Vancouver acting as design consultants. Powered by a pair of 3,000-horsepower (bhp) 16-cylinder Mirrlees diesel engines from Mirrlees, Bickerton and Day of Stockport, England, the ferry was capable of 18 knots. It had twin propellers and twin rudders.

The *Tsawwassen* had bow and stern loading doors on the car deck, which meant vehicles did not have to turn around to disembark through the same door by which they boarded. The ferry had a capacity of 106 cars that were lined up in four lanes on each side of a centre casing. Two lanes of traffic could load or unload simultaneously. Licensed to carry 1,000 passengers, it had only four passenger cabins—a sign of changing priorities in modern travel. The *Princess Louise*, in comparison, had 210 beds and 26 single berths.

Burrard laid the *Tsawwassen*'s keel on May 28, 1959, and the ship was launched only six months later on November 28. It began service on the Swartz Bay–Tsawwassen route on June 15, 1960, and underwent a name change, to *Queen of Tsawwassen*, in 1963 to conform to the ferry company's naming system.

The *Tsawwassen* cost $2,541,260. By comparison, the 6,787-ton *Princess of Nanaimo*, built in 1949 for the CPR by Fairfield in Govan, Scotland, to transport 1,500 day passengers and 130 to 150 vehicles, cost $4.5 million. The Canadian-built ferry was actually cheaper on a per passenger/vehicle basis.

This set the pattern for future BC government ferry construction. Unlike the CPR, which persisted in ordering ferries from Britain, BC ferries were built locally. Except for CP's last ferry, the *Princess of Vancouver* (1955), which allowed stern loading and unloading but was not double-ended, all CPR ferries loaded vehicles through side doors, a cumbersome and time-consuming procedure. Not only were BC ferries constructed in ways more suitable to the West Coast and a car-oriented culture, but the fare charged users was also competitive. Until the mid-1970s, travellers paid a very reasonable five dollars for

Top: The Queen of Tsawwassen, *first of the new BC coastal ferries, shortly after launch.* 27-1856

car and driver, with a small additional charge for each passenger.

The government built a two-mile causeway out into the Strait of Georgia at Tsawwassen, with BC Ferry administration buildings and passenger service facilities at its terminus. Constructed with an eye on the private automobile and its user, the new ferries ushered in an age of mass transportation on BC's coastal waters. The Trans-Canada Highway officially opened in the summer of 1962, along with numerous other highways and bridges, as BC's Social Credit government established access to blacktop as an inalienable BC right. Ferries were a natural extension of the highway system—at least that was what W.A.C. Bennett believed—and few would contradict him in these years of lively economic growth. Bennett's highways minister, "Flying Phil" Gaglardi, orchestrated the development of the new ferry system, which was spectacularly successful.

Burrard's second BC ferry contract was for the

Above: The City of Vancouver, *later* Queen of Vancouver, *outward bound past the Lions Gate bridge.* 27-1752

City of Vancouver (later the *Queen of Vancouver*). Tenders were called March 3, 1961, with Burrard submitting the lowest bid of $3,595,460. The launch took place January 16, 1962, and the ship that could accommodate 1,000 passengers and 106 cars took its place on the Tsawwassen–Swartz Bay run.

The *City of Vancouver*'s beam was increased by two feet at the car deck level over the *Tsawwassen*'s, which provided more space for cars and their drivers. The stern doors were also widened by two feet. Added passenger facilities included a passenger elevator, a 144-seat restaurant and more lounge area. The bridge front was extended 28 feet to give better vision over the bow and provide more passenger space behind it. A bow thruster was installed, which with a 500-horsepower propeller could turn the ship 90 degrees in a little over two minutes. Four Rustin-Paxton main engines developed 6,600 horsepower, 11 percent more than the first two ferries. Maintenance could be carried out on a single engine while the vessel was on the run. Along with the new *City of Victoria*, built by Victoria Machinery Depot, the *City of Vancouver*

provided hourly service between Swartz Bay and Tsawwassen.

On September 1, 1961, at the request of the residents of the Gulf Islands, the BC government purchased Gavin Mouat's four-vessel Gulf Island Ferries for $249,823. The government built a new terminal on Saltspring Island in 1962 and rebuilt the terminals on most of the other islands over the next few years. It also ordered a larger vessel to provide service between the mainland and the Gulf Islands. Burrard laid the keel for the *Queen of the Islands* on December 28, 1962, and had it ready for service July 4, 1963.

At $2.1 million, with accommodation for 40 cars and 400 passengers, the 16th ship in the provincial government's fleet was a less-expensive and smaller version of its well-endowed sisters. A special turntable allowed cars to load and unload from the same end and theoretically adapted the ship to the needs of the different island ports, although it was a jigsaw puzzle to load, and "unless loading was done with meticulous precision, she sailed with a pronounced list."

Top: The Queen of the Islands. 27-1600

Haste in the ferry's construction may have been the cause of future problems. The final sea trials were nearly over when a main engine fluid coupling failed. On its inaugural run to Saltspring Island, the engines broke down and it arrived ignominiously under tow by tugs. Subsequently it served on the Gulf Islands–Tsawwassen run and often in the summer months between Powell River and Comox, although mechanical problems persisted throughout its useful life—in 1985 it is noted as being inactive.

BC government ferries now served Vancouver Island, the mainland coast and the islands between. The Black Ball Line was relegated to the run between Victoria and the US. The BC government asked owner Captain Alex M. Peabody to expand his services; he was in agreement but his bankers weren't, so in November 1961 the BC government bought the Black Ball ferries for $6.69 million.

Federal subsidies in the early 1960s facilitated ferry construction, but when the subsidy was reintroduced at 25 percent in early 1966 after a hiatus of a little less than a year, vessels built by provincial governments were excluded. While there was much local railing against the federal government's BC-bashing, the feds no doubt thought prosperous BC quite capable of financing its own ferries. Premier Bennett was more chauvinistic, as the following quote from the January 19, 1966, *Victoria Colonist* indicates: "There might be a little jealousy on Ottawa's part because our ferry fleet is larger than their navy." In any case, a year later the subsidy for provincial construction was reinstated, with some restrictions.

The provincial government's ferry service was a huge success,

with 2.7 million passengers in 1962 and substantial increases in the following years. The ferry system provided 1,200 jobs, with hundreds of others involved in the construction of the ferries and related work. By May 1964 its 19 ships made the BC ferry service the largest in the world. Burrard did not, however, get a proportionate share of the contracts for new construction. Most went to the Victoria Machinery Depot.

Burrard fared better with contracts for ferry expansion. Almost as soon as the ferries were built, they were too small. Restructuring existing ferries was a relatively inexpensive way of creating added carrying capacity. Especially after Burrard purchased Victoria Machinery Depot in 1967, BC Ferry Corporation became the company's best customer. In early 1967 Burrard built extra car-carrying platforms on the *Queen of Vancouver* and *Queen of Esquimalt*,

Right: The Queen of Esquimalt, *cut in half and ready for lengthening.* 27-3139

increasing each ferry's capacity by 32 vehicles, for $296,888 each. Burrard completed similar work on six other BC ferries over the next two years.

A more innovative way to increase a ferry's capacity was to actually slice it in half vertically and insert

an additional section. In January 1969 Burrard submitted the lower of two tenders for the first "stretching." The *Queen of Esquimalt* was the candidate. The United Kingdom's Teddington's National Physical Laboratory ran model tests to determine the final speed of the lengthened hull and discovered, surprisingly, that the added length had a negligible effect on the speed.

After the ship entered dry dock, the cut was made. The forward section was then flooded and the aft section floated off. The new 84-foot centre section was floated into place and attached to the forward section, and the aft section was brought back to be connected. By June 14, 1969, it was back in service, its capacity

Top: The Queen of Esquimalt *with its new midsection.* 27-3152
Above: Construction of the new midsection for the Queen of Esquimalt. 27-3143

increased by 60 cars and 200 people, with a new dining room and expanded cafeteria, at a cost of about $2.25 million—a saving of about $8.5 million over new construction.

The next year the *Queen of Victoria* received a similar facelift, with Burrard outbidding Yarrows for the work by $2.58 million to $2.63 million. Though they operated as separate companies, the two worked closely together. When it came to bidding, the atmosphere was certainly more co-operative than competitive. In February 1971 Burrard won the contract to stretch the *Island Princess*, which was originally built in 1958 by Allied Shipbuilders and ran between Kelsey Bay and Beaver Cove on northern Vancouver Island. While Vancouver Shipyards submitted a slightly lower bid ($904,243 as opposed to $940,726), Burrard's

On August 2, 1970, the Queen of Victoria *left Tsawwassen for Swartz Bay 20 minutes late. The Russian freighter* Sergey Yesenin, *bound for Vancouver, collided with it in Active Pass (top). The freighter sliced deeply into the side of the ferry (right), killing three people. Both vessels made it to port under their own power, with the* Queen of Victoria *limping to Burrard for repairs. A 110-foot-long gouge carved 40 feet deep into the ferry was repaired, with 250 men working three shifts to complete the job in just 26 days. The total cost was $544,803.* 27-3209, 27-3210

work schedule (11 weeks as opposed to 17) won the contract. Burrard's relative efficiency in terms of time was often its main selling point in these years, especially for expansion of ferries, when time out of service meant lost revenue.

Burrard won the contract to stretch the *Queen of Saanich* in August 1971 for slightly over $3 million, but when Vancouver Shipyards bid $2.4 million for a similar job on the *Queen of Victoria*, Burrard was asked to rebid on the *Saanich*. Its new bid of $2.6 million won it the job but cut its profit margin to the bone, although early delivery on March 29, 1972, earned Burrard a contract bonus of $116,000. Later that year the *Queen of Burnaby* was stretched with a new design that increased its capacity to 300 cars, 100

Top and above: The Island Princess *in the process of being converted to a catamaran.* 27-2943, 27-2936

ALFRED WILLS, the son of Alfred Wallace's sister Annie, began his apprenticeship in 1908 at the age of 13 with Robert Jackman and Son in Brixham, the same yard where Alfred Wallace had served his apprenticeship. He started work with Wallace Shipyards in 1924, becoming shipwright and joiner in 1935. He was responsible for both launchings and the docking of ships for repairs, and in 1949 was appointed dockmaster in charge of all dry docking. He retired in 1962 after nearly four decades with Burrard.

Burrard News, January 1963

more than the other stretched ferries. The *Queen of New Westminster* had its physique stretched similarly. Burrard did both the jobs.

Not all ferries were stretched. The *Island Princess* was to be converted to a catamaran style, which gave a high ratio of available deck area to displacement. This was an advantage for a vehicular ferry, increasing its carrying capacity from 32 to 50 cars. The hull was cut into four sections and rejoined with a new 70-ton superstructure. Previously cars using the ferry had been loaded by a boom and sling, a cumbersome and time-consuming operation. Now they were able to drive on and drive off.

Above: The Island Princess *after its conversion to catamaran.* 27-2948

The *Fort Langley* Dredge

The federal department of public works contracted Burrard to build a dredge, the *Fort Langley*, to keep the Fraser River estuary from silting up. It replaced the *Fruhling*, built back in 1907 originally to dredge Germany's Kiel canal, and acquired by Canada in 1919 as war reparations.

Burrard won the contract for the *Fort Langley* in competitive bidding with Yarrows and Victoria Machinery Depot (although none of the eastern yards put in a bid). It had some help from the local community, for which shipbuilding remained an important generator of revenue. F.R. Goldsworthy, mayor of the City of North Vancouver, sent a telegram to the department of public works, urging it to give Burrard the contract. "Winter work urgently needed for ship-

builders. Early consideration of Burrard Drydock's low tender to construct Fraser River hopper dredge would be most helpful at this time."

Gilmore, German and Milne of Montreal prepared the basic design of the dredge. For this project, Burrard worked with IHC, a partnership of six leading Dutch shipbuilders and engineers, which since 1880 had built more than 3,000 floating craft of all types. According to the May 1961 issue of *Harbour and Shipping*, IHC was the only dredge specialist producing its own propulsion units tailored to suit its dredging equipment.

Burrard's original bid of $3,615,919 was the lowest of the three, but was far higher than the government's expected $2.6 million. Bureaucrats at the department of public works accused Burrard of deliberately padding the estimates until general manager

Above: Splashback at the launching of the Fort Langley. *Clarence Wallace gets his champagne, but not in the usual way. David Walker, the minister of public works in the left background, enjoys the scene.* 27-1689

David Wallace went over the figures again and found that the government and its "experts" had not included the main pumps, the main engines, all spare gear, propellers and 12 percent sales tax. For political reasons the government was unwilling to admit its errors publicly, so Burrard sharpened its pencils and slashed everything it could, dropping the cost to $3.2 million. Later the items cut out were quietly added back in by the government as extras. David Walker, minister of public works, apologized to David Wallace for his department's ineptness. In the end, while the whole affair was a mess, Burrard still made a profit.

Meanwhile, many questioned whether a new dredge was needed at all. The *Vancouver Province* engaged in a vigorous campaign, arguing on January 16, 1960, that there were enough private companies to do the required work without the federal government

Top: The Fort Langley *off Point Grey in August 1961.* 27-1695
Above: The Waitomo *made its way to Burrard in late 1960 after grounding on a coral rock at Apia, Samoa. Workers replaced 45 plates in the ship's bottom, with 40,000 rivets driven. Five gangs of riveters were hired to complete the job. Nearly 100 tons of steel were used for shell repairs and another 34 tons on the internals. Left to right are: Eric Lazenby, Tony Pavicic, Jack Forbes, Charlie Irvine, Sven Nielsen, Fred Hill.* 27-3398

stealing their business. In addition, aspects of the dredge's construction, especially the relatively opulent living quarters, came in for a great deal of criticism.

But the ship was built, launched on an unusual single-centre launchway on April 28, 1961, and immediately put to work. Dredging was carried out by two 26-inch suction dragarms that could work to a depth of 50 feet. They could fill a 1,330-cubic-yard hopper in only 36 minutes, with disposal via 12 hydraulically controlled doors on the hopper bottom. The public works department took delivery of the *Fort Langley* on August 23, 1961, and it remained in service until 1995, when it was sold to Viatech Trading.

Federal Subsidies

Shipbuilding in the 1960s was dominated by Japan, Great Britain, Sweden and West Germany, with Japan's aggressive expansion winning it the contracts for about half the world's tonnage.

These were the years of the Japanese miracle. Japan's Nippon Kokan developed an automatic system for painting ships' hulls that was 30 times faster than traditional manual spray painting. The same company pioneered computerized systems for doing initial designs of ships that were 15 to 30 times faster than conventional methods. Japan also developed

Above: During heavy fog in October 1962 the Norwegian freighter Granville *collided with LaPointe Pier while attempting to dock, causing the collapse of a grain gantry and an estimated $500,000 damage to the pier. The ship was locked to the pier by its bow, which was embedded in the concrete footings, and by the weight of the gantry on the forecastle. Eight tugs freed the vessel, but not without damage to the tug* Anna Gore. *Total cost of repairs to the port bow and quarterdeck of the* Granville *was $66,487.* 27-2914

high-tensile steel plate, which reduced the bulk and weight of ships. Between 1958 and 1964 the amount of steel per gross registered ton in Japan decreased by 36 percent.

Canadian shipyards were often on the cutting edge of technical innovation, but they were not leaders in the mass-production technology needed to make them viable internationally. By 1968 Canada had fallen to 16th on the list of shipbuilders, with less than 1 percent of the world tonnage built.

With the naval program winding down, Canadian yards were in trouble. On May 12, 1961 (which just happened to be days before the Esquimalt–Saanich by-election), Transport Minister Leon Balcer announced a generous federal government subsidy of 40 percent of the approved cost of new ship construction from that date until March 1, 1963. The

subsidy would be 35 percent thereafter. There would be a 50 percent subsidy for steel fishing trawlers of not less than 75 feet, provided they replaced a boat being taken out of service. Construction assisted under the regulations had to have a high Canadian content. The government also reserved the Great Lakes domestic shipping business for Canadian ships.

Bill Hudson recalls being "staggered" and totally surprised by this sudden largesse. The move towards a protectionist position generally met with an enthusiastic response from the shipbuilding community, not to mention the shipowners, although Hudson feels in retrospect that it should probably not have applied to coastal vessels, as these were a captive market, necessarily built close to where they would be used. Many tugs and barges soon replaced a large number of obsolete craft. The March 1963 *Harbour and Shipping* reports that by this time, 268 ships had been constructed, were under construction or were planned

under the government subsidy, with a value of $200 million. The subsidy continued, at various levels, until 1985, at which point over 1,000 ships had been built under the program.

Small and medium-sized shipbuilders were the big winners, as fishing and other small vessels were naturally built locally. For larger ships—the market for which Burrard aimed—it was a mixed blessing. In the early years Burrard prospered, receiving a full subsidy for the BC ferry *Queen of the Islands* and a partial one for the *City of Vancouver*, as well as for the passenger/cargo ship *Northland Prince* and a number of barges. In early January 1962 the company employed 1,100 men. A similar number worked at Yarrows, with another 1,000 at Victoria Machinery Depot. Most federal government contracts in the early 1960s were awarded on a regional basis, so the higher West Coast salaries were not a hindrance. By 1965, however, Defence Minister Paul Hellyer began to talk about

Top: In November 1963 Burrard installed side-loading doors and insulated the holds of the Cap Corrientes, *fitting skeleton decks so the ship could carry bananas while allowing chilled air through the cargo. Burner Bob Owen is shown here with shipwright Martin Brommeland. Total cost was $105,855.* 27-2858

awarding contracts on a national basis, with the lowest bidder getting the job. He allowed the West Coast a transition period from 1965 to 1970 to somehow make its yards nationally competitive, but the higher costs on the West Coast were an unavoidable fact—wages remained about a dollar an hour higher than they were in the east. In April 1966 no West Coast shipbuilders bid on a $20-million naval contract, expecting that it was not worth the $80,000 to $100,000 tender cost.

Industry Minister C.M. Drury sent a chill through the hearts of local shipbuilders during a September 1967 visit when he suggested that it might be cheaper for Canada to buy large ships from overseas and that local yards should concentrate on building small ships for the local market. The September 13, 1967, *Province* quotes him as saying: "[I]f West Coast yards can't make the adjustments which will make them competitive, it [is] unsound economically to shore them up with subsidies." In January of that year a $47.5-million contract for two Royal Canadian Navy operational support ships had gone to St. John Shipbuilding and Dry Dock Company in New Brunswick. In April 1968 Marine Industries of Sorel, Quebec, and Davie Shipbuilding of Lauzon, Quebec, received contracts for four helicopter-carrying destroyers worth $220 million to $225 million.

The subsidies for all but the steel fishing trawlers were suspended February 22, 1965; the high level of employment and buoyant economy were given as reasons. In January 1966 a lower subsidy of 25 percent was reinstated, with the Canadian content requirement for new vessels withdrawn. Beginning in 1969 this subsidy was reduced by 2 percent a year until it reached 17 percent in 1972.

Taking Care of Number One

In 1947 Burrard had become a publicly traded company, with 25 percent of the company sold to the public. Up to that point the Wallace family had held all stock. However, Clarence and Hubert felt it was time to get some money out of the company. The stocks were divided into two types: the 750,000 Class B shares that the Wallaces held, which allowed them to control the company, and the 250,000 Class A shares, which were publicly traded.

In 1954 the Wallaces' financial advisor Bill Patrick recommended to Clarence and Hubert that to avoid capital gains and inheritance taxes they should establish a holding company that would be owned by their children. The company, Wallace Enterprises, had 75 percent interest in Burrard Dry Dock in two types of shares: those with a monetary value (Class A) were evenly divided among Clarence and Hubert's six children, while Clarence and Hubert held the Class B voting shares. Though Clarence and Hubert controlled Burrard, they in effect no longer owned the majority of the company.

Burrard Dry Dock's profits during the 1950s and 1960s remained substantial, always in the hundreds of thousands of dollars each year (a net profit of $796,830 for 1961, for example, and $1,052,030 for 1962). In November 1961 the company declared a $4.8-million dividend on its 750,000 Class B shares, all held by the Wallace family ($6.40 a share). The publicly traded Class A shares, meanwhile, received a modest dividend of 75 cents a share on 250,000 shares for a total of $187,500.

The size of the payout to the Wallaces did not ease the course of labour negotiations, especially as management frequently complained about the high cost of the workers' wages. Much discussion of the Wallace windfall took place in the press and elsewhere, including a self-righteous editorial in the November 23 *Province* titled "How Socialists Are Made…," which pointed out that the Wallaces' windfall was largely the result of hefty government contracts. The Wallaces took the attitude that it was nobody's business but their own. However, no one appeared to have an understanding of the financial reasons for issuing such a large dividend until the following appeared in the December 1961 *Ship and Shop* over the byline of the Trade Union Research Bureau.

Since Burrard Dry Dock announced its special $4.8 million dividend on Class B Shares, the daily papers have been speculating about why the Wallace family should choose to pay the high income tax rates on a large volume of dividends in one year, instead of spreading it out over a period of years, and thereby paying lower percentage rates.

The answer, which the financial pundits seem to have missed, is that this particular dividend is non-taxable. The reason is that the Class B stock is held, not by individual members of the Wallace family, but by a corporation called "Wallace Enterprises Ltd." That being the case, the dividends constitute dividends received by one Canadian corporation from another Canadian corporation, and as such are exempt from tax. The only exception is nine qualifying shares, held by the nine directors of the company, who receive a total of $58.50, which will be subject to the tax.

This still leaves the question, why pay it all in one year rather than in annual amounts over a period of years. The answer to this is in the share structure of the company. Class A shares normally receive 45 cents a year in dividends. Class B dividends cannot go over 15 cents a share without increasing the Class A dividends, the limit of the latter being 75 cents. If the extra B dividends were spread out over a period of years, the Class A shareholders would have to receive 75 cents each year. By doing it all at once, they had to pay the Class A equity its extra 30 cents only once—a total of $75,000.

In short this is the only way the Wallaces could help themselves to the surplus without sharing it with the small shareholders.

The Many Lives of the *Northland Prince*

Burrard's first major bonus from the government's 40 percent subsidy plan came in 1962 with a contract for a $3.5-million coastal passenger-freighter for Northland Navigation Company. Although the ship could have been built for $100,000 less in Scotland (even taking the subsidy into account), and $40,000 less in eastern Canada, Captain Harry Terry, who had founded Northland Navigation in 1942, wanted to keep the business at home.

Designed by Vancouver naval architects Jackson, Talbot and Associates, the *Northland Prince* was the first passenger vessel built in BC for private commercial interests since Burrard had built the *Princess Louise* way back in 1921. The keel was laid June 14, 1962, and the ship launched on February 2, 1963; service commenced in June of the following year from

Right: Fabricating the double bottom for the Northland Prince *in the west gantry.* 27-1602

Vancouver to Prince Rupert and Stewart. The 108 berthed and 12 day passengers were all accommodated aft, which gave an unbroken area for cars on the weather deck.

While carrying passengers in its 42 passenger cabins was part of its job, the *Northland Prince* was primarily a cargo ship, transporting freight in special folding containers designed by Northland Shipping Company. Its refrigerated holds had electronic temperature controls for frozen or cooled foodstuffs. This was the first vessel Burrard built with flush hatch covers on the main deck. These allowed the crew to use forklift trucks to load and unload freight.

The boat's manoeuvrability, a main concern in the tight harbours that it often needed to navigate, was enhanced by a bow thruster. Bridge equipment was also designed to facilitate docking, while with only half a turn of the wheel the ship could be put from hard over to hard over in 14 seconds. The 4,200-horsepower (bhp) engines built by Stork Werkspoor of Hengelo, Holland, generated a cruising speed of 17 knots. This was the first diesel ship built on the West Coast to use heavy bunker oil of B or C grade.

The vessel was idled when Northland Navigation withdrew from freight and passenger service to BC outports in 1976. Captain Terry sold his controlling interests to Van Ommeren of Holland. The next year, renamed the *St. Helena*, the ship was sold to Curnow Shipping of Porthleven, Cornwall. After a $2 million refit in Southampton it sailed on a route from Bristol to St. Helena, Ascension and Tristan da Cunha, becoming the only British ship to carry passengers

Above: The Northland Prince *ready for work.* 27-1628

WHEN SAM BURICH was commissioned to do a sculpture of a whale for the Vancouver Aquarium in 1964, he set off with a harpoon to secure a model. On July 16 Burich's group made a direct hit but decided that rather than kill the whale, they would tow it in alive. David Wallace agreed to provide a temporary home, and on July 17 "Moby Doll," supposedly a 15-foot, 4-inch female, entered the small No. 3 dry dock. As its pod of whales followed it into the harbour, they talked back and forth.

Over the next eight days about 10,000 people came down to look at the first long-term captive killer whale. (A previously captured whale had died within 18 hours.) Filmmakers, scientists and others flew in from all over the world.

On July 24 he—the name had turned out to be more clever than accurate—was towed in No. 3 dry dock to a more permanent home at a wharf on the air force base at Spanish Banks. Six weeks later he died, perhaps drowning because low salinity in the water made it too difficult to swim.

Burrard News, September 1964, and interview with David Wallace, general manager at Burrard Dry Dock

between England and Capetown. It was popular with adventurers who enjoyed the thrill of the journey as much as the destination, and was at one time featured in a TV special.

In December 1986 *Harbour and Shipping* reported that in 1982, fitted with a helicopter landing pad, the *St. Helena* was dispatched for service in the Falklands conflict, where it lived another life as a mine countermeasures support craft before resuming service to St. Helena. It was replaced in early 1990 by a larger ship, also called *St. Helena*, with the older ship becoming *St. Helena's Island*. *Harbour and Shipping* continued to track its progress and in October 1990 reported that it had reappeared under a Malta flag of convenience, now renamed *Avalon*, inaugurating a new service on five-week circuits from Durban, South Africa, to the Comoro Islands, Mozambique Coast and the

Seychelles, carrying cargo and up to 64 passengers. It was again renamed, now the *Oceanique*, and finally scrapped in 1996–1997.

Right: *Moby Doll, a 15-foot, 4-inch killer whale, in captivity in Burrard's dry dock after it was harpooned by Vancouver Aquarium staff off Saturna Island.* 27-3980

Coast Guard Contracts

Although it had operated as a part of the department of transport for many years, the Canadian Coast Guard was first officially established under that name in 1962. The department of transport transferred its fleet of 241 vessels to the coast guard's jurisdiction, which was to be "responsible for icebreaking, northern resupply, marine regulations, search and rescue, environmental and emergency response, public harbours and ports, and marine navigational aids." The coast guard also had to maintain the Distant Early Warning (DEW) Line, established in the 1950s to detect Russian attacks. More ships were needed to control fishing and other activities in coastal waters and to establish the sovereignty of Canada's north.

Burrard launched the *Ready*, one of 10 search-and-rescue cutters on order for both coasts and the Great Lakes, May 27, 1963. Based at Victoria and first captained by John Strand, the 90-foot ship was modelled on United States patrol cutters of the same length. It was powered by four heavy-duty 600-horsepower diesels and had the latest in electronic navigational aids. When first in service, its main area of operation was the heavily used lower end of the Strait of Georgia and its duties included picking up survivors, care of the injured, fighting fires and carrying out underwater emergency work such as welding and metal cutting.

In August 1963 the department of transport awarded Burrard the contract for a weather and oceanographic vessel, the CCGS *Vancouver*. Burrard's bid of $8,874,781 was over $2 million lower than the next bid of $10,874,816 from Victoria Machinery Depot, which had been consistently outbidding Burrard for BC Ferry contracts. Burrard wanted this one badly so it could keep crews available for ship repair work. This may have led it to underbid.

Top: The search-and-rescue cutter Ready *is ready.* 27-1666

In any case, the project was beset with problems. To begin with, the designers, G.T.R. Campbell and Company of Montreal, underestimated the total weight by about 600 tons. As a result the whole of the double bottom units were increased to 3/4-inch steel plating, which meant the construction plans had to be redrawn. Nearly 90 design changes from the federal government greatly added to the cost and delayed construction. Burrard's drawing offices, in particular, were placed under a great deal of pressure. The superstructure was changed from steel to aluminum, which the March 12, 1964, *Vancouver Sun* reported was four times as expensive. The actual cost of the ship was $11 million, which at $2 million over the contract price meant it was profitable, but only just.

Partway through construction a general strike further eroded already low morale. When all but the pipefitters returned, management exerted pressure by laying off groups of men. Layoffs bore no relation to whether or not the men were usefully employed, but somehow were supposed to coerce the pipefitters into returning to work. Not surprisingly, morale took a further dip and production suffered.

Its launch on June 29, 1965, caused a stir in the

Above: The Vancouver *begins to take shape.* 27-1526

HULL 327
30. Jan. 1967

assembled crowd when, instead of waiting dutifully for the proper speeches and the champagne christening, the *Vancouver* showed a mind of its own and started to slide down the ways prematurely. The sponsor's attempt to break the bottle on the retreating bow failed. Clarence Wallace, alert to such problems, responded immediately. According to the July 3 *Sun*, "He grabbed Mrs. Laing's [wife of the minister of northern affairs] swing of the bottle on the rebound. He scored a hit but still the bottle remained intact. A split-second try and he made it." Being ripped untimely from the womb was followed by a variety of other problems with everything from radar to generators and circuit breakers. It took a year and a half to get the ship operational, and by July 6, 1966, the total man-hours of 860,790 were substantially up from the estimated 672,474.

The *Vancouver* was followed a year later by CCGS *Quadra*, launched by Burrard on July 4, 1966. This ship was constructed in a much more economical manner because components were delivered in a more timely manner and because the experience with the first ship facilitated construction. David Wallace recalls that when the bids were opened, the department representative turned to him and asked, "Mr. Wallace, have you got the main engines included in this bid?" The competitor, Victoria Machinery Depot, did not think it stood a chance of getting the contract, so had bid much higher.

The *Vancouver* and the *Quadra* were destined to replace the converted naval frigates *Stonetown* and *St. Catharines*, which had been supporting Canada's Weather Station Papa, 900 miles west of the BC coast, since 1950. For this task their navigation equipment

Top: The Quadra *is ready to go.* 27-1523

included two marine radars, Loran, echo depth sounders and course recorders. The main innovation was balloon-tracking radar that could track meteorological balloons up to 100,000 feet, detect storms as far away as 200 miles, and keep track of aircraft within a radius of 70 miles. The 24.4-foot-diameter plastic radome that protected this radar gave the ship a unique appearance. The September 1978 *Harbour and Shipping* reported that while they were designed to carry two service vessels, which would be launched by cranes from an upper deck, neither the vessels nor the cranes were ever fitted as it was feared the extra gear would topple the ships. The ships needed 450 tons of concrete in their hulls to stabilize them.

Operating cost for these two ships was a hefty $2 million a year, but once the bugs were ironed out they were extremely busy giving weather reports. Surface weather conditions were reported every three hours, and every six hours the crew released a weather balloon and tracked its movement by radar for a distance of 40 or 50 miles. Observations were transmitted by radio to Vancouver. The vessels relayed information back to the mainland, which was used to give other planes and ships reports on their speed and positions. And perhaps they had other functions as well. A rumour persists that they gathered information, which was relayed to the CIA. They did indeed have degaussing equipment, designed to repel torpedoes—a strange feature for a weather ship.

The *Quadra* and *Vancouver* were taken out of service on April 1, 1979; satellite observations had by this time made their work redundant. In 2001, after attempts to convert them into cruise ships had gone by the board, they were sold to China for scrap.

Work on these ships was not enough to prevent layoffs; Burrard's workforce dropped from 1,000 in May 1963 to 700 by August 15, although a $3.2-million contract for the *Parizeau* helped keep the pot boiling. Pacific coast yards felt they were often treated unfairly compared to their eastern counterparts—in the fiscal year 1963 they received only $47.9 million or 13.3 percent of the $358.8 million worth of contracts for federally funded ships. Often the western yards

Right: The Quest *dwarfs those assembled for its launch.* 27-1423

were not given enough time and the detailed specifications needed to put together a competitive bid. Local squabbling did not help the problem; Victoria Machinery Depot lobbied hard to steal the $10-million contract for the *Vancouver*. In addition, most western naval work went to Esquimalt's naval dockyard rather than being put out for tender as it was in eastern Canada.

Burrard did win one Royal Canadian Navy contract for the *Quest*, an oceanographic ship and experimental platform for submarine detection. It was touted as a silent ship, especially suitable for marine research, so one can imagine the consternation when it was taken on trials and the propeller sang, in the words of David Wallace, "like an opera singer." Thorough checks revealed nothing wrong, but its current condition made it totally unsuitable for the planned work.

David Wallace, coming as he did from a practical shipbuilding background, had a solution. In his experience, this noise was caused by a resonance within the structure of the propeller. His solution was a good whack with a heavy lead hammer. The government representatives were adamantly opposed, so David Wallace took things into his own hands.

⌐⌐

So that night I went down and saw Scotty on our engine fitting crew and said, "You and I are not having this discussion, but I would be delighted if we went out tomorrow and didn't hear that damn propeller singing." "Davey, I'll take care of it." Went out the next day, not a problem. All hell broke loose. And we were accused of destroying the thing. They insisted that we go back and it be examined and checked carefully from every damn direction. But that completed all our trials and on it went.

Above: The William Denny *doing a 550-ton test lift.* 27-1406

The $8.6-million auxiliary naval vessel could then legitimately be touted as the quietest ship afloat, a necessary characteristic whether for detecting submarines or for the more customary task of delicate marine research. Noise-dampening techniques included acoustic traps in piping systems to reduce fluid-borne noise; specially designed ventilation and air-conditioning systems, unique in surface operating ships; and a quiet propeller.

Bigger Better Barges

Burrard's skill and innovation in the construction of barges led to a variety of orders, greatly bolstered by the federal subsidies. The *Lakelse*, built for Northland Shipping in 1962, included a cargo elevator with a main loading door that could be raised to meet changing tidal and loading conditions. This made it possible to use forklift trucks for loading. The next year the company built *B.A. Steveston* for the British American Company to supply petroleum products for

JIM WILSON arrived in Canada from England in 1911 and started with Burrard in March 1913, cutting rivets from buckets by hand in the old dredge *Mastodon*. He worked at Burrard until April 30, 1962. On his retirement he was assistant foreman of the caulkers, drillers and rivetters. An avid and talented soccer player, he captained Canada's first All-Star International soccer team in its match in Montreal against Scotland.

Burrard News, April 1962

Top: In 1971 the Rothesay Carrier *was the world's largest newsprint barge.* 27-1313

the company's water lease at Steveston. Other hulls of this type included six flat-deck scows for Gulf of Georgia Towing in 1962 and 1963; two flat-deck scows in 1963 and two river cargo barges in 1970 for Harbour Industries; six chip scows for the Vancouver Tugboat Company in 1964–1966, with another added in 1969; a bulk cargo barge for Barclay Industries in 1967; four chip scows for Island Tug and Barge in 1968; a gravel barge for Rivtow Marine in 1968; and a flat-deck cargo barge and three cargo and oil barges for Northern Transportation Company in 1969–1970.

Barges that delivered chemicals to the mills could not bring back the pulp or paper, which meant all barges were travelling empty half the time. To cut down this needless expense, Vancouver Tug Boat Company, with Robert Allan acting as naval architect, designed a barge that would carry chemicals to the mill in tanks and return with pulp in covered holds. Yarrows and Burrard built the first two of these—*Gold River* and *Gold River II*, respectively.

In June 1969 Burrard built a $4,832,470 crane derrick barge for Raymond Concrete Pile Company of Unionville, Ontario. The *William Denny* was fabricated in three sections at Burrard, then towed to Yarrows for assembly in the government dry dock as this was the only facility large enough to assemble a hull of this size. Burrard's need for a new and larger dry dock was becoming increasingly more evident. Back at Burrard the barge was fitted with a 270-foot, 500-ton, diesel electric floating crane that was one of the 10 biggest of its kind in the world, capable of laying 48-inch pipe 200 feet under the water. On location it was anchored by eight 25,000-pound anchors.

Another collaborative effort with Yarrows was the *Island Forester*, which was the world's largest log barge, with a capacity of 5 million board feet. As neither shipyard had berths large enough to do the whole ship, Burrard built the 105-foot bow section and Yarrows the stern, with the two welded at the graving dock in Esquimalt. This was a self-loading, self-dumping barge. Its two diesel-operated cranes with 115-foot booms had a lifting capacity of 55 tons each. The barge's capacity of 20,000 short tons of logs provided enough lumber for the construction of 400 three-bedroom homes. It could dump an entire cargo in 30 minutes; for the first time cargo dumping and water ballast could be operated from a tug by remote control.

The yards managed construction of the *Rothesay Carrier* for MacMillan Bloedel in a similar fashion, with Yarrows again building the stern and Burrard the bow. Robert Allan designed this $2-million newsprint barge, completed in 1971 for service on the east coast between the MacMillan Rothesay mill at Saint John, New Brunswick, and the US Atlantic seaboard. Its 7,200-ton capacity made it at this time the world's largest newsprint barge. A shallow notch in the stern enabled it to be pushed by a tug when it approached river ports such as Baltimore and Philadelphia.

JACK MITCHELL joined Burrard in 1919 as an office boy at seven dollars a week. The *Burrard News* for March 1957 reports that when he was 17 he had a badly ruptured appendix, but thanks to Alfred Wallace, medical specialists and nurses were made available for his recovery. He became an extremely loyal supporter of the company, and his jobs included passing rivets, working in the riveting office, bolting up, electricians' and welders' helper, working with the docking crew and in the mould loft and joiners' shop. His work included laying out planking for the *St. Roch*. In 1966 he became foreman dockmaster, retiring in 1970. For a number of years he made ashtrays, raffling them off at Christmas each year, with the proceeds going to St. Christopher's School; the total he raised was nearly $1,000.

Burrard News, March 1957

Imperial Skeena: First Tanker in 40 Years

It had been over 40 years since Burrard had built a tanker (the *Marvolite* in 1926) when it won the contract for its next, the *Imperial Skeena*, in competitive bidding with the eastern yards. This was a much larger $3.3 million hull for Imperial Oil, built to replace the 30-year-old *Imperial Vancouver*. It was a quarter-scale model of the 300,000-ton tankers, but still the largest built in BC.

The ship had a bulbous bow, which provided increased propulsion efficiency. This design was selected through computer analysis after tests for the appropriate hull form were carried out in the Netherlands at Wageningen—the first time this design method was used in BC. Two independent rudders and a bow thruster increased its manoeuvrability and braking capability in small ports. Twin British Polar engines gave it 3,000 horsepower (bhp)

and a trial speed of 12.5 knots; a semi-automated engine room meant only six officers and six men were needed to operate the ship.

The *Imperial Skeena* was launched on the foggy morning of November 29, 1969, and delivered on April 16 of the next year. It was the first in Canada to be equipped with a five-ton deck crane, which made it possible to carry containers and palletized packaged petroleum products as well as bulk cargo that was stored in 12 main tanks and two smaller tanks. The ship delivered Esso products from the Ioco refinery to various BC ports. Cargo-hose flow booms allowed for speedy offloading of bulk oil products.

A decade later it was still looking good after 400,000 miles. Redesign work by Cove-Dixon and Company increased capacity by 400 barrels, and removal of a heavily built foremast improved visibility, while underwater sonar gear was fitted in 1979.

Above: The Imperial Skeena *with the Lions in the background.* 27-1342

Struggling to Remain Competitive

Burrard Dry Dock needed state-of-the-art equipment to remain at least potentially competitive in obtaining available contracts and carrying out the work efficiently, but at the same time the uncertainty of new contracts made the wisdom of expensive renewal doubtful. The company never did escape this Catch-22 situation, although substantial new construction took place in the 1960s.

In 1960 Burrard built a new two-storey office building in the yard just north of No. 2 dry dock. Production staff was centralized in this office, which greatly increased the yard's efficiency. Previously offices scattered all over the yard made it difficult to co-ordinate activities. In the spring of 1965 the company called for tenders for a new plate shop and plate

storage complex at a cost of $1.1 million. The new 352-foot-by-82-foot plate shop was located along the east side of the existing unit construction shop. It included a flat steel storage area serviced by a high-speed, 110-foot-wide, semi-gantry crane with a 10-ton capacity. The crane was equipped with a magnetic floating beam that the operator could place in any position. A 90-foot section of the utility building was removed to provide access for the plate storage crane. The sheet metal shop was moved to the old No. 2 plate shop. Pipe storage, previously part of the general stores building, was relocated adjacent to the pipe shop. The main boiler plant was replaced with three automatic gas-fired heating units installed in central locations within the plant.

In 1965, after several years' negotiations, Burrard traded the property that had been its South Yard

Top: The steel storage area with a 110-foot magnetic crane feeding conveyor to shotblast, spray paint and plate and erection shop. 27-234

during the war to the National Harbours Board in return for more property on the North Shore, including land on the north side of Esplanade and east of St. Georges. Until then the company had been leasing much of this property from the National Harbours Board.

In the mid-1960s, with available business shrinking still more, Burrard turned its attention to the acquisition of Victoria Machinery Depot. Founded by Captain Joseph Spratt as Albion Iron Works in 1863, this was the oldest company of its kind in British Columbia. It had built some of the earliest paddle-wheelers that carried miners up the Fraser River during the Cariboo Gold Rush, and from 1888 under the name of Victoria Machinery Depot had continued a successful business. In the post-war years it had become a significant shipbuilder, completing 11 provincial ferries and the world's largest semi-submersible oil-drilling rig. But the company had overextended itself on this rig and wanted out. No new business was on the horizon, and the federal government's move to national tendering made future contracts less likely.

In Victoria this company was Yarrows' major competitor; its facilities for building bigger hulls helped get it the BC ferry contracts. Having VMD out of the way was a definite advantage—for Burrard as well as Yarrows—as there was simply not enough business in BC for three major shipyards. Early negotiations between VMD's owner Harold Husband and Hubert Wallace stalled as their intense competition over the years had caused distrust. Hubert was not involved with the final negotiations, and after the sale Harold Husband joined Burrard's board of directors.

On October 27, 1967, Husband sold the business, but not the land or stocks, to Burrard for $1,985,000, although the reduction in the goodwill allowance and the sale of certain assets made the actual cost $984,000. The closure of this yard and the resultant loss of jobs focussed attention on the precarious state of shipbuilding in Canada, particularly on the West Coast, where higher wages made competition with eastern yards difficult. A flurry of articles appeared in the Victoria press, and cabinet minister Jean Marchand promised an investigation, but no concrete action was taken. The sale of the yard meant Victoria moved away from heavy industry towards a greater focus on the tourist industry. Large numbers of the displaced workers moved to Edmonton, Winnipeg, Seattle, and other places where industry was more active. A few even accepted shipbuilding jobs in Mississippi, although most soon returned. This trend away from heavy industry occurred in Vancouver a generation later.

But serious problems continued. Management committee meetings frequently discussed inefficiencies and increased costs. In the late 1960s management expressed concerns that schedules were not adhered to, and the drawing office was often singled out as a cause of delays. It was difficult to find well-trained people for this department. Repairs to the *Yukon Star, Glacier Queen* and *Bainbridge* lost money, probably because of the lack of co-ordination between the estimating department and production. The repair department was often more concerned with doing a good job than staying within budget.

The boom times in BC made it difficult for Burrard to get and retain good tradesmen. While Burrard paid the standard rates, other industries generally provided better long-term stability. In a report, "Manpower Problems," dated November 25, 1964, yard manager Doug Kinvig vents his frustration at the scarcity of skilled help.

⁓

We are trying to work efficiently on *Saguenay*, Weather Ship, Barges, Block Machine, Plywood Presses. We are short of skilled platers, Machinists and engine fitters; building barges with one charge hand and helpers promoted to platers. If we lose money on a job it is taken by top Management as a sign of inattention or inefficiency of the Yard Manager and his staff. Any reasons we may put forward are naturally regarded as excuses.

It was certainly different from the family atmosphere fostered before the war. Wages for both workers and management increased more than those in Quebec and eastern Canada, which made it ever more difficult for Burrard to compete for national contracts. The multiplicity of unions following the war contributed to difficult and time-consuming negotiations, which often had to take place simultaneously on a number of different fronts. Management especially was happy when an agreement on joint certification in 1966 required all unions to negotiate as one.

The Office Employees Association was also included with this joint certification.

However, labour harmony continued to prove elusive. Many of the problems in the later years of the company arose when workers in different trades fought each other bitterly over the right to work in their area of specialty, especially as the available work diminished. This did not help the efficiency of a yard that needed to become flexible to meet the rapidly changing needs of the late twentieth century.

CHAPTER 7

Adjusting to a New World: 1972–1986

Part of the difficulty that I think, and part of the demise too, is that when the Wallaces got out and all of a sudden these people came in, these non-resident owners, for them, for the people they hire to do the job, it's just a paycheque for them. When you've got the family there and the family's involved, there's an ownership then. You try harder to make it survive.

George MacPherson,
president of the Marine Workers' Union

W hile Canadian shipbuilding experienced some good years during the 1970s, from the early 1980s the general direction was down as the federal government lost its appetite to subsidize an industry otherwise uncompetitive in a world market. Canadian shipyard employment, at 13,000 in 1977, fell to 6,956 by the end of 1986. Burrard and Yarrows reflected the national trend; their combined employment of 1,750 in July 1976 declined to 1,100 by June 1986. Halifax Industries declared bankruptcy in June 1985, Collingwood closed and Quebec's largest shipyards, Vickers and Davie, closed down in 1989 and 1998 respectively. The number of shipyards in Canada plummeted from 69 in 1980 to 20 in 1986.

Fluctuations in federal subsidies and their gradual dismantling had much to do with gyrations in employment and resulting inefficiencies. In March 1977, subsidies for new or converted vessels increased from 12 to 20 percent, causing new construction to raise the Canadian share of world tonnage to the dizzy heights of 1 percent in 1978. At 1.3 percent in 1979, Canada ranked 19th among shipbuilding nations. But then in July 1980 the subsidy was abruptly cut to 9 percent, and in June 1985 even this subsidy was removed. In 1985, Canadian yards' seven new merchant vessels were 0.3 percent of the world's total. (In 2001, the only yard doing new construction anywhere on the West Coast was Todd Shipyards in Seattle, and most of its work was in repairs.)

In the twentieth century, Canadian shipbuilding flourished in times of war or threatened war, but extended periods of peace dulled the federal government's will to finance new naval construction, while private companies could generally get their ships cheaper overseas. At the same time, reliance on the government gravy train and its generous contractual arrangements did little to make Burrard the lean and mean company it needed to be to survive in the last decades of the century, although in the early 1970s it compared favourably to other Canadian shipbuilding companies. In 1971, measured in terms of value added per employee, Burrard Yarrows stood at $18,600 compared to the rest of BC ($15,200) and all of Canada ($14,000).

Northern development fuelled much of Burrard's new construction for private accounts. Companies were eager to exploit the Arctic's immense oil and mineral wealth, and the Canadian government

displayed sporadic interest in economic development and territorial sovereignty in the face of the United States' and the Soviet Union's more consistent and aggressive exploitation of northern regions (including Canada's). But when the price of oil levelled off, exploration in the Beaufort Sea decreased and new ships were redundant, while with Canada's move to free trade, sovereignty was relegated to the back shelf.

As avenues for new construction closed off, ship repair for a time took up the slack. For most of these years Burrard Yarrows was the largest ship repair company in Canada, a position that was strengthened when Burrard bought a new dry dock in 1981. In new construction, however, it had slipped to third. Both Marine Industries in Montreal and Davie Shipbuilding in Quebec built more new tonnage than Burrard after 1970.

Further complicating Burrard's viability was the changing urban landscape. North Vancouver was no longer a resource-based community—logging had long ceased to be a major source of jobs and money, and most North Vancouverites now earned their livelihood in shops and offices. In the late 1970s a shopping and entertainment complex was developed at Lonsdale Quay, next door to the shipyard, as a place for urbanites to eat, shop and enjoy the sea air. It became more accessible when seabus service from downtown Vancouver commenced in 1978. And it raised the question: How long could a grimy shipyard co-exist with these new developments? According to Hudson, the oft-stated goal was to be out of the Lonsdale area by 2000. The short-term goal was to consolidate operations in the eastern part of the yard and sell off the western part adjacent to Lonsdale Quay. David Alsop indicates that other sites such as Roberts Bank and Britannia were being considered for new shipyard locations as early as the 1970s.

Top: The cruise ship Meteor *burned off Powell River in 1971. Although no passengers were lost, 32 members of the crew were killed. David Wallace describes the terrible sight when the ship came in to the dock. "A number of the crew had tried to escape out through the portholes, and of course their heads were there, but that was all." The ship was cleaned up and taken back to Norway, but the cost of rebuilding it was too great.* 27-3056

The End of the Wallaces

Especially since 1960, Clarence Wallace had been losing interest in the day-to-day operations of the company, preferring to enjoy the fruits of his labour in yachting trips or entertaining on his Minnekhada Estate. His son David states that by 1967 it was increasingly evident the company was adrift, with less and less executive direction from either Clarence (73) or Hubert (67). Clarence spent less than a week a month at the office, and both were out of touch with customers and persons of influence in Ottawa. In place of the cozy personal relationships with the government fostered during the war, a large impersonal bureaucracy now administered government contracts.

Neither Clarence's son Richard, who was manager of the industrial division at Burrard, nor Hubert's son John, general manager at Yarrows, had any interest in taking over the company. But David, who had been general manager at Burrard since 1956, loved the work, was ambitious and wanted nothing more than to follow in his father's footsteps. It was much to his dismay that in 1964, while going through the company's files, he came across a copy of an employment contract with Bill Hudson dated June 1962, signed under seal on behalf of Burrard and Yarrows by C. Wallace as president and H.A. Wallace as vice-president. Clauses in this contract established that Hudson was to be employed as executive vice-president of both companies until 1978. Should either Clarence or Hubert retire or be incapacitated before then, Hudson was to become president for one year and chairman of the board thereafter.

David felt betrayed, not so much because of the existence of the contract, but because he had not been told of its existence, which as a director and major shareholder he felt was his right. He and Bill Hudson had been working closely together for a number of years, but suddenly a hidden undercurrent surfaced. David made it clear that he would not support any plan that turned over the direction of the family company to someone else. When Clarence and Hubert retired, he would be in there negotiating to become president.

Hubert, and to a lesser extent Clarence, saw the future of the company in its "professionalization." This future had been initiated when they hired Bill Hudson, someone they saw as having the requisite financial expertise and management skills. Hubert was adamant that in the future no Wallace should head the company. He favoured Bill Hudson as the new head. Hubert thought "the boys"—Richard, David and John—should be satisfied with their current jobs. He and many of the board members felt strongly that making David president would not be in the best interests of the company.

At Hubert's instigation the Wallaces held a family meeting. Hubert and his three children—John, Stuart and Shirley—were on one side, while Clarence and his two sons, David and Richard, were on the other.

Above: Two generations of Wallaces in 1969. Clarence (left) and Hubert are seated. Clarence's sons Richard and David stand behind. 27-538A

Stuart and Shirley, who were not at all interested in the yard, were willing to go along with their father's wishes that Bill Hudson be the new president. John, who had been general manager of Yarrows since 1956, had a great deal more invested in his career with the yard, but that also gave his father much more control over him, especially since Hubert had loaned him substantial amounts of money for his mortgage and other expenses. (John states that he was in fact out of the country, in Nepal, at the time and was not involved in these decisions.)

As David understates, "It was not a very pleasant meeting." Hubert said that if necessary he would take the issue to a board meeting, where the majority of the directors were his supporters. Clarence, perhaps recognizing this as the best direction in the circumstances, agreed with the decision to appoint Hudson the new president.

David says that rather than work under Bill Hudson or engage in a pitched battle with their fathers for control of the company, he, John and Richard decided to force its sale. Through Wallace Enterprises they owned the majority of the shares with monetary value, so they controlled the company's destiny. Stuart and Shirley approved the plan. David remembers that when he told his father the next day, Clarence was extremely upset, and Hubert even more so. In David's opinion they had underestimated the strong sense of ownership and control David, Richard and John had developed over the years.

In March 1972, Cornat Industries offered $10 million for Burrard. About $3 million of the purchase price was in marketable securities, so the basic price was $7 million. The deal was accepted, ending nearly 80 years of the Wallace family's involvement in shipbuilding. Bill Hudson was made president the day after the sale.

Cornat's diverse interests included transportation, storage, real estate, food and mortgages. Among its other holdings were Johnston Terminals & Storage, BC Ice & Cold Storage, Coronation Credit Corporation, Pizza Products, Macor Developments and Collingwood Real Estate Corporation. CEO Peter Paul Saunders felt that Burrard's subsidiary Quadra Steel was a key to the purchase, as it could be tied to the Johnston Terminals distribution operations. The acquisition of Burrard increased Cornat's assets from $48 million to $68 million.

David Wallace was especially bitter over his shattered dream and claims he was never invited back to attend any special events or launchings. Peter Saunders feels that David may have been overreacting, pointing out that David's wife was the sister of George McKeen, the new chair of the board. Saunders says that the Wallaces did indeed attend many shipyard functions. For a while David took an office in town and also maintained his membership in the American Bureau of Shipping. Later he bought property at Palm Springs, where he played a lot of golf and tennis before moving back to Vancouver. He now lives in a modest apartment in south Vancouver.

Clarence Wallace died on November 12, 1982, while Hubert died early in July 1984.

Though no Wallaces continued working for the company, Cornat maintained a continuity of management. Bill Hudson, the new president, saw an opportunity in Canada's nationalistic post-centennial era for increased work related to the development of the North and Canada's sovereignty. Shipyard manager Ted Jones was appointed general manager of Burrard Yarrows in both North Vancouver and Esquimalt. He

> WHEN WE got the new profile-burning machine it was all tape controlled, and the guy that did that, he had a big beard and he wore a cowboy hat and he was smoking marijuana. You could smell it. He was a marvel on this bloody machine. So what do you do? He was on the wacky backy.
>
> Tom Duncan, yard manager at Burrard Dry Dock

also retained his position of shipyard manager in North Vancouver until a few months later when T.K. "Tom" Duncan was appointed to the position. Bill Maddock continued as yard manager at Yarrows.

Cornat showed much more willingness to take risks with the business than the Wallaces did. Initially it paid off. In January 1973, Pemberton Securities recommended Cornat's stock for capital gain, with Burrard's sales of $16 million in 1972 projected to rise to over $40 million the next year. By April 1974 the company had contracts for over $70 million of new construction.

To adapt to the demands of these contracts, Cornat engaged in an aggressive modernization program. The most expensive of the varied equipment and machinery acquired were a Skoda lathe, a Skoda vertical boring mill and a Washington lathe. Burrard also entered the computer world with a system purchased in 1975 for over $200,000. There was disappointingly little federal assistance for this equipment; applications for assistance under the Defence Industry Productivity Program (DIP) stalled in the bureaucracy. David Alsop, hired in 1973 to study the construction of a new dry dock, draws attention to the fact that in 1972–1973 BC received $126,354 in federal assistance compared to over $21 million for Ontario and $25 million for Quebec.

New construction in Canadian shipyards rose from $76 million in 1970 to $185 million in 1972, with Burrard sharing in the increase. Saunders was buoyed by winning a diverse array of contracts from private interests. Tom Duncan states that Saunders felt "firmly convinced that he could control world shipping and world economics." When the inevitable downturn came, he was disillusioned; by the late 1970s, euphoria had been replaced by a more subdued vision of the future. A 1980 federal report, "Interim Comparison of Shipbuilding and Ship Repair Companies," ranks the Victoria and Vancouver yards a dismal 11th and 17th out of 21 Canadian yards.

The Cornat people were primarily businessmen rather than shipbuilders. Unlike the Wallaces, whose passions and energy were indissolubly tied to the building of ships, Saunders and his colleagues were primarily interested in making money. If building ships would get them to that goal they would build ships. If not, they would move into other endeavours without regrets. This approach made the eventual demise of shipbuilding all but inevitable.

Corporate changes over the next years included the amalgamation of Cornat Industries and Versatile Manufacturing in July 1978 to become Versatile Cornat and then, less than a year later on January 1, 1979, Versatile Corporation. Burrard and Yarrows finally amalgamated to become Burrard Yarrows Corporation (and then Versatile Pacific in 1985).

The Struggle for Change

The Wallaces left behind them a group of workers who were intensely loyal to the yard but extremely traditional in their approach to shipbuilding—"a difficult cantankerous group" in Rollie Webb's words. As new construction superintendent, Webb was in a position to know. Generally they were hard-working, capable men who had been immersed in shipbuilding all their lives and did not take kindly to new ways of doing things or to the people who demanded they change. Much of this conflict stemmed from the differences between people who (like the Wallaces) had come up through the ranks and those with an academic or business grounding. The former tended to be more conservative in their approach to innovation and were skeptical of those who tried (with mixed success) to apply business and management principles to the company's operations.

A major struggle took place between powerful foremen and the new managers who wanted to whip the yard into a modern configuration. The foremen had achieved a great deal of control over how the work was done and often resisted management attempts to introduce change; some had as many as 400 people working under them and commanded intense loyalty from their men. While the foremen generally recognized that a certain amount of change was inevitable, they often resisted the latest imported management fashions. Former foreman Tom Knox considered a lot of the changes being introduced more suitable to yards (such as those in Asia) where mass production of standard ships was the norm. Burrard generally built relatively small, shaped ships. "We were rather unique because we built custom ships. We'd have a barge, and then we'd have an icebreaker, and then we'd have a dredge. All different shapes. And it's more expensive to build things custom like that."

Ted Jones brought in a lot of new technology, first as chief engineer in the 1960s and later as general manager. In the early 1980s, confronted with the financial disaster of the *Robert Lemeur* (see pp. 172–173), Jones's protege Don Challinor saw that changes in management were also essential. The workplace was extremely stratified, and one level rarely communicated effectively with another. The foremen had their own private lunchroom to which management could go only by invitation. "The whole yard was more set up in the model of the British or Scottish shipyard, where you almost expected the foremen to be wearing bowler hats," according to Dale Jenkins, who had been hired as steel superintendent in 1980. The yard needed greater flexibility to perform its increasingly complex tasks efficiently.

As the amount of foreseeable work diminished, fierce arguments over which union should be doing a particular job became frequent. Craft unions have traditionally survived by having a clear sense of what they do and their exclusive right to do it. Yard manager Tom Duncan remembers, "Every day I would have a demarcation problem. There's one reason for that—job security. They would never have worried about these demarcations if they had long-range plans." The Marine Workers, which covered all the steel trades, was the biggest and most powerful union. Duncan recalls he "fought like cat and dog" with Bill Stewart, its Communist founder.

David Alsop, who was promoted from vice-president to president in 1986, came from a Harvard MBA background. He was, in Jenkins' words, a "gentleman," friends with everyone. Many perceived this as a weakness, and conflicts at the senior management level intensified in the early 1980s as the company slid downhill. Alsop consistently casts a charitable light on difficult situations: "When you've got a craft union organization, and you're trying to introduce a production technique when you want people to do more than one thing well, you immediately have the seeds of conflict."

Barges for the North and Elsewhere

Some bright spots remained. In the 1970s the apparently boundless natural resources of the North fostered a barging boom, particularly on the Mackenzie and Hay rivers. Burrard picked up a good share of this business as its extensive experience in this relatively low-tech construction enabled it to build with speed and economy.

In December 1972, Northern Transportation

BUTCH LEROUX took over Max Pierotti's job [in personnel]. He was an American, a Vietnam pilot, shot down three times in Vietnam in his helicopter. He was on the BC Lions Grey Cup team in '64. I remember the first time I met him, I'd been advised, "Watch him, when he shakes your hand he tries to break it." So there was some kind of meeting with senior management. I'm talking about *senior* management. We were invited, so I went over there and he sticks out his hand and I stick out mine. And he's looking at you right in the eye and then he squeezes and of course all the senior managers are there. And I say, "What are you trying to do? Break my fucking hand? Let it go, you asshole." I got along with him great after then.

John Fitzpatrick, president of the Marine Workers' Union

Company contracted for five river cargo barges and one river tug, the *Johnny Hope*. This tug, the only one built by Burrard in the post-war years, was primarily for push-towing barges on the Mackenzie River system, with occasional towing of barges across Great Slave Lake. The barges, with a shallow draft of three feet, three inches, were designed to carry oil and dry cargo from Hay River on Great Slave Lake to Inuvik on the Mackenzie Delta. They left Vancouver for Tuktoyaktuk on July 10, 1973, joining with other vessels to form a convoy totalling 29 craft: 20 cargo barges, five tugs and four bow thruster barges. This operation was one of the most important to that date for serving the North, and these were the first ships for the North to be delivered by sea rather than shipped in pieces up the Mackenzie River and reassembled. It was

a disappointment when in 1977 the Mackenzie River valley was not recommended as a pipeline route, as this would have kept every BC shipbuilding facility busy for three years.

The *Rivtow Hercules*, designed by Gerry Talbot of Vancouver's Jackson, Talbot and Associates as a matching boat to *Rivtow Captain Bob*, moved logs from the Queen Charlotte forest assembly areas to Howe Sound delivery points. Designed to be towed on two towlines, it had a one-inch-thick, high-strength steel deck and two independent radio-controlled generating plants. Its crane could lift 70 tons at an 86-foot radius and could unload the 15,000-ton capacity in 40 minutes, but the cargos were getting smaller. The ship saw little use for the three years after it was launched in 1981.

Above: The Rivtow Hercules. Vancouver Maritime Museum

Burrard Builds Bigger BC Ferries Faster

The BC ferry system continued to flourish as North America's increasing affluence led to greater mobility and more tourists discovered the beauties of the northwest. Even with this growth, contracts for new ferries were scarce. During the 1970s there was excess capacity, especially on the southern routes, and renovation and expansion of existing ferries became a common, less-expensive way of increasing capacity. Burrard won the lion's share of this work.

The election of an NDP government in 1972 led to a substantial increase in the funding available for ferries. In August 1973 Burrard and Yarrows received a joint contract for $2,895,000 to stretch the *Queen of Nanaimo*; Burrard did the lengthening while Yarrows built the midsection. This increased the number of car spaces by 54 to 192, and a new sundeck restaurant,

larger cafeteria and more lounge area were added. This was the first of the stretched ferries without a formal dining room, a service that by 1976 was losing $7 million a year and serving only 10 percent of the passengers. The main function of the ferries was now to transport large numbers of people and vehicles with speed and economy—in comfort but without luxury or concern for image.

In January 1979 the *Powell River Queen* was back, along with the *Bowen Queen* and the *Mayne Queen*, for stretchings that lengthened them by 72 feet to 279 feet, increasing their capacities from 50 to 70 cars each. In this case, unlike the other stretch jobs, the superstructure remained intact and only the hull was lengthened. An added advantage to the new design was that the propulsion units could be lifted out for repair and replaced without dry docking the vessel.

A different form of jumboizing took place when

Above: The Queen of Coquitlam *takes shape.* 27-1227

in 1981 the *Queen of Vancouver* and the *Queen of Victoria* were stretched vertically. Hydraulic jacks—122 of them—raised the top section three metres. At the same time a bulbous bow, an extra bow thruster and a bigger emergency generator were added. While most of the work was done at Yarrows, the *Queen of Vancouver* was outfitted in Vancouver. *The Queen of Esquimalt* and the *Queen of Saanich* underwent similar conversions in 1982, substantially increasing their capacity to carry both cars and people.

The *Prince George* received a major $4-million refit in 1981 to make it more suitable for summer cruises between Vancouver and Alaska. An even larger $9-million conversion contract was awarded in February 1982; the *Princess of Vancouver*, built in Glasgow in 1955, had recently been acquired from Canadian Pacific by BC Ferries, which now wanted to convert the ship from stern loading to stern and bow loading. New platform decks and ramps for passenger cars were added, as well as a passenger elevator, a new sewage system and a bright new paint job of black, white and buff, the colours of the provincial department of transportation and highways. The conversion was delayed when another ship, the *Hollis Hedberg* had an accident in the Burrard dry dock. After substantial cost overruns, the *Princess* replaced the *Sechelt Queen* on the Comox–Powell River run, carrying up to 120 cars and 500 passengers. Another conversion in 1987 transformed the *Princess of Vancouver* into the British Columbia Steamship Company cruise ship *Vancouver Island Princess.*

There were some new ferries built in the 1970s, including one each by Burrard and Yarrows—bidding had been limited to BC companies. Burrard's *Queen of Coquitlam* and Yarrows' *Queen of Cowichan* were designed by Nickum and Spaulding Associates of

Above: Greasing the launchway for the Queen of Coquitlam. 27-1230

Seattle with T.A. McLaren of Vancouver. They were the largest ferries in BC's fleet, able to carry 362 cars on three levels, and 1,100 passengers. Centre lanes that were 16 feet high made it easy to move car-trailer and mobile-home traffic. Burrard's hull was launched in late November 1975 and went into service the next summer.

The ferry's design minimized the potential for environmental disaster, as it placed oil, water and sewage tanks more than one-fifth of the vessel's beam inboard from the side and left plenty of room between the bottom of the tanks and the bottom of the boat. The ship's more visible amenities included facilities for the handicapped, a first-aid room and a baby change room. Lounges had panoramic windows, while two solariums had outside seating with infrared heating units. According to a review in the May 1976 issue of *Canadian Shipping and Marine Engineering*, "Furniture is comfortably arranged to suit conversational groups and the individual."

These were the first passenger vessels in the world to use an emergency slide system for evacuating passengers, similar to those in use on jet aircraft and installed by BF Goodrich. The July 1975 issue of *Harbour and Shipping* reported that, in the event of an accident, inflatable escape chutes formed a small dock on the water from which passengers could transfer to inflatable life rafts. This all sounded great until the day came for testing. Rain had made the rubber slick, and the first people to test the slides hit the bottom at a speed that bounced them off the raft into the ocean. One of the testers broke an ankle. Although improvements were introduced, the slides were eventually abandoned.

The *Queen of Surrey*, with a capacity of 1,600, could carry even more passengers. While Burrard built this ship, Yarrows built a sister ship, the *Queen of Oak Bay*. Both entered service in the summer of 1981.

A report analyzing the costs of building these two ferries highlights the problems of the Vancouver yard. Burrard took 144,072 more man-hours to build the *Queen of Surrey* than Victoria took to build the *Queen of Oak Bay*. This resulted in a cost overrun of 24.6 percent at Burrard compared to 4.9 percent at Yarrows. Most of Vancouver's overrun was in the steel trades, sheet metal trades and joiner trades. Vancouver used 31,522 more premium and bonus overtime hours than Victoria. This was made up of 16,117 confined space and dirty money hours, 11,470 shift premium hours and 3,935 additional overtime hours. Union problems in Victoria were fewer, its management team had worked together for a number of years and a more stable workforce contributed to greater efficiency.

Trailer Ferries for Canadian Pacific

The $5-million *Carrier Princess*, Burrard's first contract with Canadian Pacific since the *Princess Louise* in 1921, was a more utilitarian hull than the *Princesses* in CPR's glory days. Designed by Jackson, Talbot and Associates, this twin-funnelled ferry's four 16-cylinder diesel engines made it the most highly powered motor ship built at Burrard to that time. Funnels at deck level to port and starboard, and separate high deckhouses forward, meant it would win no beauty contests, but they increased efficiency.

The ferry went into service in June 1973 between Swartz Bay and the new terminal at the foot of Burrard in Vancouver to support the growing commerce between the mainland and Vancouver Island; its capacity was 50 freight trailers, 30 rail cars or 150 automobiles. It also relieved the *Princess of Vancouver* on the Nanaimo run when that ship was being refitted. The passenger deck, situated amidships, had three lounges with a total seating of 284, although passenger service was discontinued in 1974.

Burrard built two similar ferries from a Jackson, Talbot design for a CP joint venture with Inchcape and Company of London to transport rail cars full of newsprint. These were designed for "intermodal service"—an efficient combination of rail and water travel. The *Incan Superior*, with a capacity of 26 50-foot railcars, travelled between Thunder Bay, Ontario, and Superior, Wisconsin, cutting from three days to 14 hours the usual time for the delivery of paper products from the Great Lakes Paper Company of Thunder Bay to American markets. The *Incan St. Laurent*, after a period spent transporting materials between New Westminster and Whittier, Alaska, for the trans-Alaska pipeline project, carried newsprint from the Baie-Comeau mill on Quebec's North Shore, near the mouth of the St. Lawrence, to tie in with the CP rail network at Quebec City.

Declining forest business led Incan Marine, a subsidiary of Canadian Pacific, to close operations at the end of 1992. *Harbour and Shipping* for July 1993 noted that the *Incan Superior* came home to Vancouver that year for a $1-million refit, which included installation of a concrete deck, overhaul of the machinery and substantial repairs to the basic structure of the hull. Renamed the *Princess Superior*, it now carried combined loads of rail cars and trailers between Vancouver and Nanaimo.

Above: The Carrier Princess *passes under the Lions Gate bridge on its way into Burrard Inlet.* 27-1298

Icebreakers: Booms and Busts

In 1969 the American ice-breaking tanker *Manhattan* made a much-publicized trip through the Northwest Passage that highlighted economic concerns and territorial issues. Subsequently, the federal government concentrated resources into developing the North and supporting oil companies' exploration. Icebreakers became increasingly powerful as oil companies and the government sought to extend the time during which operations could take place in the High Arctic. The oil shortage of the 1970s, although more chimera than reality, led to increases in the price of oil that helped finance exploration. Icebreaking was also needed in the Great Lakes and the St. Lawrence Seaway to extend the shipping season.

Burrard had already acquired experience building icebreakers with the contracts for the *Camsell* and the *Simon Fraser*, built in the 1950s. The new ventures of the 1970s were small high-tech ships suited to Burrard's limited facilities. The yard built the *Hollis Hedberg*, claimed to be the world's most advanced marine research and exploration vessel, for Cayman Islands Vessels Ltd. of Pascagoula, Mississippi, designed by William R. Brown and Associates. It used compressed air to obtain seismic readings, which eliminated environmental danger to water and aquatic life, while its on-board data-processing and interpretation ability meant researchers no longer had to wait for response from shore. The ship's primary aim was to explore new oil deposits in ice-covered waters. In early 1983 it returned for a 60-foot

Above: The Hollis Hedberg, *launched in 1974.* 27-1279

lengthening, although delays occurred when the old bow slid into the water, damaging both the new bow section and the dry dock, at considerable expense.

When bids were called for two larger R-class ice-breakers, only the Quebec yard Davie responded. Dissatisfied with this result, the federal government put the contract out for bids again, pressuring Burrard and other yards to bid. Only Burrard did so, winning the contract over Davie for the ships that became the CCGS *Pierre Radisson* and the CCGS *Franklin*. Labour problems in Quebec were cited as a reason Davie did not obtain the contract; Burrard could guarantee the work within a fixed price, while

HERBERT "BRICK" ARNOLD, foreman of the Burrard pattern shop and the last of the patternmakers at the yard, retired in 1977 after 47 years with Burrard. At this time only about 40 men in Vancouver remained in this trade, as most of the objects like pipes and valves that once required patterns for casting were now fabricated. The final castings of the patternmaker would be anywhere from less than half a pound to a stern frame weighing up to 40 tons.

Burrard-Yarrows Review, May 1977

Above: Herbert "Brick" Arnold, the patternmaker foreman, at work in October 1944. 27-380

Davie could not. This was the largest contract ever won by Burrard and it contained a "target incentive ceiling" under which Burrard would receive half of any saving the shipyard realized below the ceiling price of $94 million.

Design was by German and Milne of Montreal, and the main propulsion system by Canadian General Electric of Peterborough. The ships were of welded steel construction with cruiser sterns and ice breaking bows designed so that they rode up on the ice, forcing it under the hull, which crushed it with the ship's weight. A special rudder stock and locking pin arrangement was capable of resisting over 3-million pounds of rudder torque in the event of high-speed impact in heavy ice. Shell plating was $1\frac{1}{2}$ to 2 inches thick, and in certain areas contained special steel. An improved stabilization system counteracted the tendency of icebreaker hulls to roll. A continuous flight deck with an aluminum telescopic hangar provided a home for a Bell 212 helicopter used for ice reconnaissance.

These were Class 3 icebreakers—they could make continuous headway in ice three feet thick. This made them suitable for year-round service in the Great Lakes and the Gulf of St. Lawrence, but restricted them to summer work in the Arctic. Their primary duties included escorting ships through ice-covered waters, clearing ice from navigational channels and harbours, and flood-control duties in the St. Lawrence. Other duties included conducting ice reconnaissance; providing diving, salvage, search-and-rescue and emergency medical support to shipping; towing vessels disabled in ice; and conducting oceanographic, meteorological and other programs.

The ships were built using a new computerized management system purchased from A and P Appledore of Newcastle, England, in one of the attempts to introduce more efficient management

Top: Brick Arnold working on a stern frame pattern. 27-301

systems to Burrard. Ship Production Control System (SPCS) was coupled to a computer-based critical path networking system. Floor display boards showed what work had to be done in the following two weeks, greatly streamlining and speeding up the process of construction.

The *Pierre Radisson*, named for the eighteenth-century coureur du bois and explorer in Hudson Bay and the eastern Arctic, was launched in June 1977, replacing the *N.B. McLean*, retired after a half century

of service. The CCGS *Franklin*, named for the explorer Sir John Franklin, who died in the Arctic in 1847, was launched in March 1978 and immediately headed north to fill in for the damaged *Camsell*. Its permanent base was in St. John's, Newfoundland, from which it was used mainly in ice breaking for Northern Transportation Company vessels supplying DEW Line sites.

These were both a technical and financial success. As with other contracts, the second, or follow, ship

Above: At work on the Pierre Radisson. 27-1218

realized substantial savings, as drawing office, mould loft and welding procedures were expenses for only the first ship. This saved nearly 90,000 man-hours.

But now things took a turn for the worse. In 1979 Burrard failed to get the contracts for an ice breaking tug for Dome Petroleum (awarded to St. John Shipbuilding) and a third R-class icebreaker. In the latter contract it finished second, ahead of Quebec shipyards but $7 million behind Port Weller Dry Docks of St. Catharines, Ontario. BC's base labour rates were now three to four dollars an hour more than those of the eastern shipyards, so it was hard to compete even when overhead was cut to the bone. It was a couple of years before Burrard received another federal government contract, and before that happened the feds slashed subsidies from 20 to 9 percent in 1980.

The contract for the *Robert Lemeur*, a Class 3 icebreaker named for a village priest who had spent 35 years in Tuktoyaktuk, was tendered March 20, 1981,

and it was delivered in September 1982 to Dome Petroleum of Calgary. Arctic Offshore Limited of Vancouver designed it for work in the region of Dome's drilling operations in the Beaufort Sea. The bow had a unique spoon shape, with an ice-knife or skeg turning the hull into a tool for cutting the ice and pushing it aside. A similar shaping of the aft hull

EDDIE MCKAY retired in 1979 after 49 years of service with Burrard. He started in 1930 as a shipwright apprentice, with one of his first jobs being on the *St. Roch*, and for many years he was in charge of the shipwright's mill. Over the years the work changed, as wood gave way to steel. Demand disappeared for the wood spar ceilings or sweat battens that were once produced in large numbers.

Burrard-Yarrows Review, February 1979

Top: The Franklin *ready for ice.* 27-4193

deflected the ice up and over the propellers. A hull lubricating system and an air bubbler system reduced friction between the hull and ice or snow, as did a special Inerta 160 coating on the hull.

The ship was a financial disaster. David Alsop, again giving a bad situation the best spin possible, describes the ship as a prototype, an unusual design, and as such it cost more than was expected. Tom Duncan is more blunt. "They lost their shirt because of the complexity of the thing." Rollie Webb states it was "seriously underbid," although Vancouver Shipyards, the next lowest bidder, was only $250,000 higher. In a memo dated January 28, 1982, CEO Don Challinor discusses why the company underestimated the man-hours for the project and cites the complex nature of the hull, with closely spaced frames that required low hydrogen welding; the standard of workmanship required; the unusually high level of inspection; and the highly sophisticated painting system used inside the ship as contributing causes. Multiple changes because of a poor (in Challinor's opinion) original design increased expense. The shortage of draftsmen combined with the numerous design changes caused delays in producing working drawings for the loft. The amount of steel required increased by about 68 tons, and extended welding requirements further increased the cost, as did overtime needed to meet the September 7, 1982, delivery deadline.

Challinor, the general manager at Yarrows, had become Burrard Yarrows president and CEO in 1980, much to the chagrin of Burrard yard manager Tom Duncan, who thought he should have got the call. There was no love lost between them. Dale Jenkins, steel superintendent, recalls that they "were fighting all the time," which did little to clarify the lines of authority. While Challinor was a skilled manager and had some success in attracting new customers, Jenkins considered him more at home on the golf course, as Challinor did not have an intimate knowledge of shipbuilding. He was not, in Jenkins' words, "comfortable in the shipyard."

Whatever the reasons, the project lost a lot of money.

Man-hours ran about 30 percent over the estimate, and on October 27, 1982, the losses on the ship were listed at $7.8 million. On October 25, 1983, Burrard's claim against Dome for $2.6 million for extra costs was countered by an offer of $1.3 million. When Burrard refused, Dome withdrew all offers. Burrard's application for a stay of proceedings was dismissed and the company was left with nothing. When its expected profit had been $1,286,000, this certainly hurt. To add to its woes, the 1983 lengthening of the *Hollis Hedberg* was delayed by the accident in dry dock. This project lost $1,985,000.

THE DOCKS were a disaster. The nights I spent sleepless. And the famous night the *Coquitlam* went over [October 19, 1980]. We put her in the dock to do a docking and I got a call at five in the morning saying the dock had gone over. It was the No. 1 dry dock, the one on the east side of the wall. It went over on the wing walls and then the whole damn dock started to sink. I thought we'd lose everything because they're double enders, and the shafts are out, so the water is right all the way through the engine room, and the valves are out. So the engine's immediately flooded, the dock's going down. You can't run any of the pumps because it had gone over on the wing walls and they've got these pump drives. So finally we sank it and towed the ship out. I'll always remember George Baldwin, who was the boss of the ferries, was flying back from London. He looked down and saw the oily waters lapping the cylinder heads and he said, "What have you done to my ship?" It was a massive clean-up job and preservation of all the machinery after being in the salt water. Within a month or two she was away again. And we got the dock back in operation.

Tom Duncan, yard manager at Burrard Dry Dock

The company was far from complacent, but the solutions were as complex as the problems. An October 1981 report describes the problems in achieving production targets in the Vancouver division. Morale had declined, the hard-won credibility of the yard eroded with each cost overrun and missed deadline. Solutions proposed included adding foremen, developing better training programs, adding production planning and scheduling skills, adding more apprentices, improving communication and re-examining salary practices to ensure that first-line supervision was adequately compensated. All these ideas required cash, however, which was in short supply.

The general work ethic did not help productivity. A memo from David Alsop dated May 31, 1982, noted that "security staff do not seem to be challenging

> AT LUNCHTIME as soon as that whistle went, this was what we'd do. At half past 11 you'd be looking at your watch and then if you were working on the vessel you'd try and sneak off on the pretext you were going to the toilet, always making your way up the yard towards the gate on Lonsdale. But if you were working all the way up at the erection shop, the idea was to avoid the white hats [the foremen], because they knew what you were doing. There was a toilet there, and everybody would sneak into the toilet, and as soon as the whistle went you'd be running. We'd hit that intersection at Lonsdale and Esplanade. We didn't care for lights or anything. Just ran across there. We'd run up the hill to the St. Alice, have two or three beers and then run back down. And then they opened the Eagles at 55½ Lonsdale, so that was even better. You didn't have to go right up the hill; you'd go to the Eagles.
>
> John Fitzpatrick, president
> of the Marine Workers' Union

employees leaving the yard, outside of the lunch break, either to attend to personal business or to leave early. As a result, control is lax and employees can be seen leaving the yard, especially on second shift and on pay days, without apparent permission to do so." Theft of tools was endemic, no doubt also a sign of poor morale.

Drinking, particularly on Friday afternoons, was a common activity, although not perhaps more so than for most heavy industries of that time. Dale Jenkins recalls that when he arrived in 1980, the chief steward operated a bar in the blacksmith's shop. This problem tended to be ignored, perhaps because management often had a drink or two with its lunch as well.

Managers never tired of complaining about the non-competitive position they were placed in by the high West Coast wages. However, the cost of living, particularly housing, was substantially higher than in other shipbuilding areas, and management salaries and perks also reflected this West Coast reality. At the same time workers were being told to tighten their belts and reduce their demands, new managers were cutting some sweet deals. For example, David Cassidy was hired as general manager of operations in April 1984 at a monthly salary of $6,666.67, and several new managers received $50,000 interest-free loans for buying new houses. This did little to foster morale among the workers. Increasingly, both workers and management were trying to get what they could out of the company, sometimes without much concern about how this would affect the company's viability.

The *Terry Fox* was also a financial drain, although not to the same extent as the *Robert Lemeur*. Some in management questioned whether Roger Nairn, near retirement age and not in the best of health, still had the ability to handle his position as project manager. Perhaps more importantly, over 100 design changes requested by the owners, Gulf Canada Resources, interfered with information flow from technical offices to the production department. There were also difficulties in welding low-temperature steel. More fundamentally, the company had continuous difficulties making accurate man-hour projections, which made it impossible to estimate accurately how much a job would cost. This seriously affected its credibility.

Dale Jenkins describes the project as vastly overmanned—"there was just a mass of people and people were literally climbing over top of each other." He recalls that in management meetings, reports described the ship as on time and on budget. "I can remember walking around the yard and saying 'I don't know what *Terry Fox* they're talking about, but the one I see certainly isn't.'"

Designed by Montreal's German and Milne, and built for Beaudril, a subsidiary of Gulf Canada Resources of Calgary, the *Terry Fox* was scheduled for multi-purpose operation in the Beaufort Sea as a support vessel for Gulf's Beaufort Drilling System. *Harbour and Shipping*, November 1983, reported that the forward part of the hull was designed to prevent ice from being ingested into propellers, and the bow form developed to give maximum penetration into both level and rigid ice. On its maiden voyage it logged its first Arctic rescue. The US government research ship NOAA *Surveyor* radioed that it was trapped in ice off Point Franklin on Alaska's northwest coast. The *Terry Fox* cleared a path.

Above: The completed Terry Fox. 5069

But back in the yard, times were desperate and no icebreaker was coming to the rescue. After completion of the *Terry Fox*, layoffs "removed all hourly paid men from the yard for the first time in anyone's memory and at the same time a large number of staff employees were let go. The shock was deep, anger and resentment were the most visible emotion[s] and only a few people were willing to stand back and look at what the future really did hold." From January to August 1983, while the Victoria division made a profit of $1,156,000, the Vancouver division had racked up a whopping operating loss of $5,166,000, due in part to the overrun of man-hours on the *Terry Fox*. With no other work on the horizon, some workers may have been stretching out the only available job. The Victoria yard retained a sense of cohesion and a level of morale and commitment that the Vancouver yard had lost.

Frigate refits were assigned to Yarrows in May 1983, but splitting the work with Vancouver was not a viable option. Such was the state of crisis that a contingency plan was drawn up in which operations of

Top: The Martha L. Black *under construction.* 02-16C

the Vancouver division would be suspended for a period of six months beginning July 1, 1983. Tom Duncan, in a June 17, 1983, memo concerning work on the *Cornelius Zanen* helipad, comments, "It is evident that we are going to be in an overrun position on this contract and I would ask that everything be done to minimize our losses on this job. I know it is a very difficult situation when it is the last job in the yard, but we must be ruthless when it comes to layoffs."

A reprieve came in September 1983 with a $56-million Canadian Coast Guard contract for a Type 1100 icebreaker, part of an order of six from four Canadian yards. A memo from Don Challinor to union business agents dated September 15, 1983, does not mince words. "This could very well be our last opportunity to maintain new construction capabilities in Vancouver…Your full co-operation is expected in ensuring our return to profitability and our restored reputation as a 'good shipyard.'" It was time to

put up or shut up. In a November 29, 1983, memo, Challinor discusses improved project management, new methods of controlling design changes, ways of improving labour productivity, improved drawing office procedures and improved steel production as essential for survival.

Both this and the Yarrows sister ship *George R. Pearkes*, constructed using modular techniques, were much more successful projects than those immediately preceding. They were a more conventional hull compared to the complex design for the *Robert Lemeur* and *Terry Fox*, which led to fewer construction problems. Perhaps there was hope yet for the troubled yard.

Burrard launched the *Martha L. Black* on August 2, 1985. Named after an Independent Conservative MP for the Yukon from 1935 to 1940 who was later made an officer of the British Empire, this ship was designed for ice breaking and buoy tending,

Above: The Henry Larsen, *the last icebreaker.* 27-4188

maintaining shore aids and supplying lighthouse stations. It would be based at Prince Rupert.

That year the company also pursued possibilities for construction of Soviet icebreakers, an Antarctic vessel for India, ferries for Mexico and seabuses for Turkey. But none of these projects materialized.

Burrard's final icebreaker, the *Henry Larsen*, immortalized the long-time captain of the *St. Roch*. This ship was also built using modular techniques, with the bow and stern units fabricated at Yarrows. The heating, ventilation and other systems were built into the prefabricated units rather than being installed

> JUST BEFORE we were closing up the place, all the departments were run by ex-apprentices. To this day, there's hardly any apprentices in the trades. So you're never going to be able to build it up. Even now, when they're building the fast ferries, I went down there to see a fellow I recommended for a part of my job and I said, "Now that you got it all going here, how many apprentices have you got on the job?" And he said, "Would you believe we haven't got one?" When we were serving our time there was up to seven and eight apprentices there all the time. As soon as one got finished, another one started. Gradually as an apprentice got closer to a tradesman's wage, he got more money, and then the union steps in and says, "No, you can't do that, we've got to pay him full money after one year." Well, nobody's going to hire a fellow who's just in off the street, you can't make money off him, so you don't hire him. This was the folly of the unions. I always thought, for heaven's sake let's train them. Once he's finished his apprenticeship and gets his ticket, then get him into the union, not while he's an apprentice.
>
> George Matthews, Burrard Dry Dock foreman

in the completed hull. While much more exacting, this approach allowed more of the ship to be completed outside the berth, potentially leading to greater efficiencies.

Unfortunately, problems with construction escalated the cost. As of September 12, 1988, the loss was $663,848 on the original contract of $87,223,240. To add to its woes, the *Henry Larsen* failed dockside and sea trials in June 1987 because of a faulty propulsion system and four electric transformers that had to be removed and repaired by rewinding. Insurance damage claims amounted to $2,395,593. The fact that a similar diesel electric drive was one of the two options for the propulsion system of the proposed Polar 8 icebreaker (see Chapter 8) contributed to the trepidation that enveloped the plans for this ship.

The Class 4 *Henry Larsen* replaced the CCGS *Labrador*. Captained by Steve Gomes, the ship traversed the Northwest Passage on its maiden voyage to its base in Dartmouth.

A New Dry Dock

While improved construction, navigation and safety equipment reduced the frequency of accidents and maintenance for which ships had to be dry docked, repair and maintenance were still a large and valued part of Burrard's work. New port facilities such as Centennial Pier, Neptune Terminals, Vanterm and Lynnterm greatly increased the use of the harbour by larger ships, making Vancouver for a time the world's 12th largest port. But ships had grown, and many could not be served by Burrard's limited facilities.

The original dry dock, heralded with so much enthusiasm in the 1920s, was showing signs of serious wear by the 1950s. Teredo worms, which live off the nutrients in the wood and can grow up to six feet long, ate away at the timbers. David Wallace says that BC's "Department of Research" had been experimenting with sodium arsenate to poison the teredos and developed a highly successful system for treating dry docks that took only four hours twice a year and cost

$250 a treatment. Wallace estimates that this process, along with the use of pressure-treated plywood, extended the life of the dry dock by 10 or 15 years. But at best it was simply not large enough.

In the five years prior to 1973, Burrard's dry docking had decreased 60 percent, and man-hours on foreign repairs were down 50 percent from 1966. By the late 1960s, 70 percent of ships using the Vancouver port were too large to be repaired in what had been reduced to a 10,000-ton capacity dock. While in 1977 the dry dock's domestic sales were a healthy 285,000 man-hours, export sales, which involved mostly larger hulls, were only 95,000 man-hours.

The lifting capacity of a dry dock decreases at an accelerating but unpredictable rate in the last years of its life, and this dock was not expected to have more than another eight years left. In the original plans the pontoons were expected to have a 50-year lifespan, so they were already on borrowed time. Over the years the salt water and heavy loads had placed considerable stress and strain on the pontoons; by February 1969 some had become excessively flexible due to deterioration of fastenings. Maintenance was costly and time consuming, as the pontoons were removed each year for inspection and repairs.

At this time Burrard also had the World War II dry dock from North Van Ship Repairs, though this was in even worse shape. Its capacity had decreased from the original 12,000 tons to 9,000. A smaller dry dock, also inherited from North Van Ship Repairs, was

Above: Escorted by tugs, and towed by the Dahlia, *the new dry dock arrives.* 27-5

sold in September 1974 to General Metals of Tacoma, Washington, for the princely sum of $10.

Crandall Dry Dock Engineers of Cambridge, Massachusetts, and Swan Wooster Engineering of Vancouver had prepared a study in June 1970 that recommended a new dry dock, as the need for this facility had already been evident for many years. At that time David Wallace and Bill Hudson made a trip to Ottawa to make their pitch to government officials. But it was only after Cornat Industries purchased Burrard in 1971 that plans slowly began to solidify. Some impetus was provided by the opening of new dry dock facilities on the West Coast, including two new docks in San Francisco that were each capable of docking a ship of 150,000 dwt. The primary purpose of Burrard's planned new dock was to better serve the foreign merchant fleet, as smaller Canadian coastal vessels, including BC ferries, could be served adequately by existing docks.

A letter from Bill Hudson to Jean Marchand, federal minister of transport, was the start of an intense campaign to convince the government to fund at least part of the expensive project. In 1973, David Alsop was assigned to find ways to finance the dock. His lobbying was made more difficult by the fact that Burrard, unlike most Canadian shipbuilding companies, was not in an area that qualified for regional economic expansion grants. But Vancouver was a terminal port, where ships were often empty at some time during their stay, making it a convenient place for a ship to enter dry dock.

In 1978 federal minister Jack Horner announced the government would contribute $28.8 million to the projected $45.6 million cost. This price tag included $29.8 million for the floating dock and equipment; $10.2 million for waterfront construction, services and a 100-ton crane; $1.8 million for land creation and site preparation; and $3.8 million for land-based ancillary facilities.

Burrard hired J. Dugal Purdie as project manager commencing October 10, 1979, and by the time the agreement was finalized in June 1980, the cost had escalated to $63.3 million. The federal government's share was $40.6 million, the BC government contributed $1.5 million and Burrard Yarrows paid the remaining $21.2 million. This was the first time in Canada that a private enterprise had invested to such an extent in a facility of this size. To keep the other coast happy, Halifax Shipyards received a $40-million federal grant for a dry dock.

Swan Wooster designed the dock, and bids were called on both steel and concrete proposals. By August 31, 1979, bids for steel docks had been received from Nippon Kokan K.K., Kawasaki and Mitsubishi, all of Japan, and from G.H.H. of West Germany. Burrard Yarrows itself submitted a bid for a steel dock, and Stevenson Construction of Vancouver and Dywidag of Richmond jointly bid on a steel/concrete dock. The *Vancouver Sun* reported on January 21, 1980, that the successful bidder was Japan's Mitsubishi Heavy Industries (MHI) in Hiroshima, a world leader in shipbuilding and ship repairing that had previously constructed a dry dock for its own company. This was much to the chagrin of Stevenson Construction, the Shipyard General Workers Federation of BC and many others who had hoped for a local product. Although the lowest bid was about $10 million over the preliminary estimate of $32 million, about $5 million was saved by having the work done offshore.

In 1980, workers removed Pier No. 5 to improve water access, dismantled Pier No. 6 and began work on a replacement that would service the new dry dock. Primarily Canadian companies constructed ancillary facilities and equipment—including cranes, paint sprayers, water jets and electrical components—to prepare the area for the dry dock. The Canadian content for the whole project was about 56 percent.

On August 24, 1981, the dock arrived after a six-week 5,300-nautical-mile tow by the 12,000-horsepower *Dahlia* of Tokyo Marine Services. The load-bearing deck of the new dock was 670 feet, outside width 194 feet, the inside width 150 feet, and the height 70 feet. It was a short and wide dock, and ships sometimes hung off the ends, which a lot of

customers did not like. With a lifting capacity of 36,000 tons, the dock could take ships up to 75,000 dwt, the size of the largest ships that traverse the Panama Canal. A ship of this size could be lifted in one hour, 45 minutes.

The hefty investment soon showed signs of paying off. In its first year of operation the dock was used three-quarters of the available time, 58 percent of which involved vessels that could not have been dry docked otherwise. It was the busiest dry dock in Canada, with an estimated 30 percent of the Canadian market of $300 million. While Burrard conceded that it was not viable to compete with dry docks in ship-

yards of the Far East, business with lines serving Europe and Australia was definitely a reasonable target, as diverting their ships to the east for service would be costly. With the dearth of new construction, ship repair assumed greater importance, and Burrard considered a 50/50 balance between the two as optimal. But while the dry dock became the shipyard's most successful facility, it also became a victim of changing technology. Increased reliability of ships decreased their need for dry docking.

The most long-lasting effect of building the dry dock was that it exposed Burrard to Japanese ship-building techniques. David Alsop states that Burrard

Top: The cruise ship Britannia *just fits in the new dry dock, 1987.* 27-4196

was the first Canadian company to bring over Japanese consultants—a number were employed at Burrard in the 1980s. Rather than completing a vessel structurally and then outfitting it with all the piping and other mechanical systems, the Japanese built up units in a modular fashion. As mentioned, Burrard and Yarrows first used this method in the *Martha L. Black* and *George R. Pearkes*. Having the design virtually complete before construction started involved a radical restructuring of shipbuilding. The production department became involved in design, reducing man-hours and the total time from start of construction to completion. Alsop estimates the new techniques reduced man-hours by 25 to 35 percent. This helped for a time, but as the financial situation worsened and layoffs escalated, morale deteriorated again.

CHAPTER 8

It's a Canadian Game

It is true we got old, the colour of our feathers have faded, our combs have turned pale, the muscles of our legs and wings have softened, but that is nothing to worry about as life is everlasting, it only changes its form.

From welding foreman Mark Falconvitch's retirement speech, October 12, 1949

Polar 8: The Phantom Ship

The United States' *Manhattan*'s unchallenged passage across Canada's north in 1969 goaded the Liberal government to develop plans for an icebreaker that could protect the environment, assist northern development and assert Canadian sovereignty. Initial plans for a Class 7 icebreaker in the early 1970s were scrapped, but on the advice of an ambitious coast guard the cabinet in 1978–1979 approved designs for a nuclear-powered Class 10 icebreaker, capable of the phenomenal feat of plowing through ice 10 feet thick. In 1981 the nuclear option was rejected as too controversial in favour of a conventionally powered Polar 8 icebreaker, which could still handle a respectable eight feet of ice. In 1983 German and Milne completed a design for the coast guard. Amenities included a swimming pool, theatre and gym, and the estimated cost was $450 million.

In August 1984 the Liberal government paid three shipyards—Saint John Shipbuilding, Davie Shipbuilding and Burrard (known from 1985 as Versatile Pacific)—$450,000 each for detailed design proposals. Versatile had the luxury of vetting the bids of both Davie and Versatile Pacific since the corporation bought Davie at that time. Versatile Pacific submitted the lowest bid of $417 million. As contracts to build frigates had recently been awarded to eastern Canadian yards, politics was on Versatile Pacific's side.

When the Class 6 US icebreaker *Polar Sea* made a much-publicized and unchallenged passage through what most Canadians thought were their territorial waters of the Northwest Passage in the summer of 1985, it forced the Canadian government's hand.* On September 10, 1985, Joe Clark, the secretary of state for external affairs, announced in the House of Commons, "The government has decided to construct a Polar 8 icebreaker."

The Polar 8 was planned to be as tough as any icebreaker on the face of the planet. While the Soviets had Polar 8s, these were smaller, nuclear-powered ships. At 30,000 tons and 80,000 horsepower, the Canadian Polar 8 would indeed be a formidable vessel—so powerful that, as John Crosbie told a *Vancouver Sun* reporter in July 1989, it would be capable of "squashing nuclear submarines if it sits on one in the ice."

---

* There's a suspicion that this trip may have been intentionally unchallenged, a way of manipulating Canadian public reaction to gain support for an icebreaker project. It does indeed seem strange, if not totally out of character, that the United States would so blatantly tweak the nose of its friendly northern neighbour.

Unsolicited proposals from three companies* claiming they could build the ship more cheaply than Versatile led the ministry of transport to establish the Bruneau Commission to study the costs of building a Polar 8 icebreaker. Its conclusion was that an adequate ship could indeed be built at a substantially lower cost than Versatile Pacific's bid, which appealed to many fiscal conservatives in the Tory government. But as Versatile pointed out in an April 23, 1991, report, the statement of requirements stipulated many conditions that the Bruneau Commission did not include in its calculations. These included three propellers vs. two propellers, diesel electric vs. diesel mechanical propulsion, extensive aviation and scientific facilities and a number of other features.

Meanwhile, Versatile Pacific's parent company, Versatile Corporation, was in trouble, having lost a whopping $82 million on sales of $353 million in the first nine months of 1986. To finance a number of acquisitions and expanded investment it had floated debentures that had fixed repayment requirements. To finance these, it planned to sell Versatile Farm Equipment Company, which at the time was in difficulty because of declining world demand for four-wheel-drive tractors. It found a buyer in John Deere, but while the Canadian government approved the sale for $200 million, the American government did not, feeling it would give John Deere too dominant a share of the four-wheel-drive tractor market in North America. With no cash, the parent company went into receivership and had to sell assets to pay back its lenders. This was in spite of the fact that the shipyard itself was profitable, with a backlog in orders and cash in the bank. After undergoing another name change, the parent company, now known as BC Capital Corporation, sold its Quebec shipyards and Ottawa ship-design arm to Marine Industries for about $65 million and moved increasingly into the investment business. Versatile Pacific lent $12.6 million of its "surplus" cash to BC Capital.

* The companies were Wartsila Arctic, Canadian Marine (CAN-MAR) and Arctic Transportation (ATL).

On March 2, 1987, the government sent a draft letter of intent to Versatile Pacific, conditionally offering a contract for the construction of the Polar 8, but for a paltry $317 million (in 1985 dollars)—an even $100 million less than Versatile's original bid. The contract was to be in two stages. The first was for the design and offer to construct the icebreaker, often referred to as the contract definition contract (CDC). This was for a maximum of $8 million, to be completed within nine months of the final letter of intent. The second stage, never awarded, was the implementation contract, for the actual construction.

A major condition of the offer was that Versatile Pacific had to clear up its financial difficulties and separate itself from its troubled parent company. *Harbour and Shipping* reported in August 1987 that the government had accepted Versatile's plan, prepared with Hees International, to restructure its debt. Versatile chose Sandwell Swan Wooster and the Canadian Design Group as its partners and contractors for the Polar 8, and the yard expected to receive the pared-down contract for $317 million in late 1988. The company anticipated employing 1,000 people for four years, with projected profit as high as $50 million. A letter of intent from Monique Vezina, minister of supply and services, dated July 31, 1987, outlines the conditions for the contract but made it clear that there was no "obligation to proceed with any aspect of the Polar 8 project." Still, hopes ran high in the yard.

In November 1987 the government let a $7.85-million contract to Versatile and Sandwell Swan Wooster to produce a design and a full proposal for construction. In March 1988 *Harbour and Shipping* reported that the Norwegian firm Det Norske Veritas signed a contract with Versatile and Sandwell for the design approval and classification of a Class 8 icebreaker. (Veritas did the design classification because it had more experience in cold climate technology than Canadian Design Group did.) Work went far beyond conceptual planning. The March 10, 1988, *Vancouver Sun* reported that in early 1988, designers put three hull forms of three metres each through tank tests at the Institute for Marine Dynamics in St. John's, Newfoundland. Scale models of the hull were also given sea trials. One of the aims was to develop a hull form that would be capable of heavy ice breaking, yet would also have good sea-keeping abilities. There were suggestions the ship might be deployed in the Antarctic, which meant that long sea voyages were a definite possibility.

But the roadblocks were formidable. The department of defence lobbied hard against building the icebreaker, preferring to direct government resources to destroyers and submarines, which would have greater military use. Versatile was looking for a buyer for the shipyard, which did not instill confidence or make planning easy. In May 1988, J.D. Howe of the department of regional and economic incentives expressed serious doubts that the Canadian Icebreaker Design Group (which had been established to manage the process) would be able to come in on budget. "Failure to submit such a proposal would give the Crown the right to seek other bids and sue the parties jointly and severally for any resulting difference between the contract price and $348 million, 1988 dollars." Local politicians lobbied hard on behalf of the shipyard, with City of North Vancouver mayor Jack Loucks making two trips to Ottawa.

Sensing a disaster in the making, the bureaucrats scrambled to cover their backsides. On October 27, 1988, Versatile submitted its design proposal, but the department of supply and services was not impressed. On November 23, Aaron Rumstein, director of procurement for the Polar 8, wrote that Versatile's proposal did not comply with the requirements of the contract definition contract. "The price is subject to so many conditions, so as to make the offer meaningless." The position of the Crown was that Versatile Pacific and Sandwell Swan Wooster were "in substantial and significant default." There was definitely no question of awarding a contract for construction at this time; the noose was tightening.

As Versatile's Richard Woodhead complained in an October 26, 1989, memo, "VPSI simply does not have the resources…to stand up to DSS insatiable appetite for volumes of trivia." He characterized department of supply and services comments as "gratuitous criticism" and "all too evident attempts at bushwhacking." Versatile was caught between desperately wanting the contract and being unable to do the ship the government wanted for the stated price. The shipyard president, David Alsop, remembers how desperate the company's financial situation was at that time. Managers would sit down every Friday to decide if they had the money to open up Monday morning.

The government bureaucrats' contentious mood may have made the people at BC Capital more receptive to selling a company whose future looked dim. On December 8, 1988, after lengthy negotiations, Shieldings bought Versatile. Shieldings was a relatively small, risk-taking, venture capital investor worth $50–$60 million. Unlike Cornat Industries, which maintained some continuity when it took over 20 years earlier, Shieldings brought in a new management team to lead the company in a drastically new direction.

Terry Godsall, Shieldings' vice-president, had little respect for the way the shipyard had done business and immediately made clear his intent to move Versatile away from shipbuilding in the direction of "value added" manufacturing. One of his ideas was that it should build off-road logging trucks for use in the Pacific rain forest. He saw the dry dock as a literally moveable asset and was eager to move it to either Esquimalt or Duke Point, near Nanaimo, and shut down the North Vancouver yard. But such action required federal government approval, and that was not forthcoming. Godsall also talked about building the Polar 8 in a new facility the company would slap up at Duke Point, where it rained less and everything was cheaper. This would be "the largest dry dock outside the Orient" and would feature a 300-ton crane that would "be capable of doing phenomenal things." The model for Versatile's new direction was Coastland Wood Industries in Nanaimo, an industry leader in the production of green veneer, whose workers, Godsall proclaimed, "had elected to be union free."

The vice-president was adept at the smoke and mirrors of boardroom politics, and while much of his talk was obviously game-playing to improve his bargaining position, there's also no doubt Versatile had serious problems. In a February 16, 1989, letter to J.D. Howe, Godsall stated that Shieldings "has identified large overruns in industrial work and serious threats to shipbuilding contracts attributable to inefficient management." On June 3 he wrote, "The story of management of VPSI is one of awkward incompetence, of deliberate under-bidding, false submissions in support of bids for major government contracts…"

The CDC and all related joint venture contracts were terminated when Shieldings took over on June 29, 1989, for an acquisition price of $31 million. The contracts were replaced by an agreement with the government for Shieldings to make a proposal to construct the Polar 8. In effect, the work of the previous years was for nought.

Shieldings argued that the Polar 8 was a "transition project," a way of providing the shipyard with the "technological leverage" so it could apply its experience on this project to related but non-shipbuilding projects. The federal government, for its part, wanted to "rationalize" shipbuilding on the West Coast. This was a euphemism for getting rid of what it considered excess capacity—in other words, closing down the yard. From the feds' point of view, this made economic sense in North Vancouver, where the waterfront was of immense value for commercial and residential use. John Fitzpatrick, who had become president of the Marine Workers' Union in 1980, states that there was a move on the part of local and provincial governments to get heavy industry out of Vancouver and bring in service industries. In many ways Shieldings and the various levels of government were singing from the same songbook. They all wanted the shipyard out of North Vancouver.

Many who were around at the time agree that while some people with Shieldings wanted to build the Polar 8, others were working to kill the contract and pull money out of the federal government for a yard closure. The shipyard was a valuable piece of real estate, worth at least its $31-million purchase price, and Shieldings was an investment banker, not a shipbuilder. Others speculated that the new owners wanted to get the Polar 8 contract to improve the marketability of the company, but would then sell it and let someone else worry about building the ship. Certainly North Vancouver would see little if any action in either case, as the main construction would take place in Victoria or Nanaimo. Dale Jenkins claims he "heard stories of them purposely annoying customers just so they could go back to the federal government and get money for closing down the yard."

Godsall made his intentions for the North Vancouver yard crystal clear. "Our action in Nanaimo will allow us to release on a controlled basis the properties in North Vancouver to their highest and best use which will be a minimum of $35 million on a virtual wholesale basis, and a much higher figure ranging out beyond $65 million if we wish to do some sensitive development…There is a great deal of money to

THE ONLY one that was up front with us was [local Conservative MP] Chuck Cook. We used to lobby him, we'd march the troops up Lonsdale to his office. He'd say, "I don't care what the government's telling you, I don't know what these managers are telling you. But I'm telling you, that yard's going down. I'm telling you Fitzpatrick, you tell your men that they better all go and get other jobs. Because it's going down." Of course we thought he was fucking nuts. But he was great. He was the only honest Tory.

John Fitzpatrick, president
of the Marine Workers' Union

be made from the purchase of VPSI in a shorter time horizon given the development and sale of the North Vancouver land assets."

But the charade continued, as proposals and counterproposals flowed back and forth. The March 1989 *Harbour and Shipping* reported that two proposals aimed at cutting Polar 8 costs had been prepared: one with a diesel electric propulsion system and the other with a geared diesel drive and controllable pitch propellers. The May 8, 1989, *Vancouver Sun* expanded on the earlier story, revealing that the latter proposal was cheaper by some $30 million to build, cheaper to operate and provided more capacity in the same space, but there were worries it would not provide the power for year-round Arctic operation. The diesel electric was more technically elegant and flexible in operation, but was a far greater risk to build and operate, and took up more space.

On December 13, 1989, the North Vancouver yard was on strike, and Godsall said it was "possible that North Van will never open again." He complained that the 23 unions "believe that it is their inalienable right to work at their own pace on ships built for government." This strike played into his plan to move operations to Victoria. As early as August 1989 a memo from Godsall stated, "In the event of no Polar 8…the plan calls for an immediate withdrawal from North Vancouver and concentration of ship repair at Esquimalt/Munroe Head."

While Godsall wanted the yard in North Vancouver shut down, Versatile's new CEO, Peter Quinn, was genuinely concerned about getting the Polar 8. As late as January 8, 1990, he told the Vancouver Board of Trade the government was "looking for delivery in 1994" of the icebreaker. So it was a devastating blow to the company and to his credibility when the February 21 *Vancouver Sun* reported that the previous day the minister of finance, Michael Wilson, cancelled plans to build the ship. Kim Campbell, minister of state for Indian affairs and northern development, blamed political shifts in Eastern Europe (although the effect of these on the

thickness of ice in the north was less than clear) and Versatile's long delays in construction start-up. Perhaps Canada's political shift away from nationalism to the greater continentalism embodied in the Canada–US Free Trade Agreement diminished concern about the encroachment of foreign vessels in Canadian waters, and although not generally recognized at that time, global warming has since led to major decreases in the thickness of Arctic ice. So much for Joe Clark's September 1985 pronouncement that "The government is not about to conclude that Canada cannot afford the Arctic."

But the project seemed doomed from the start. It was so large and complex, with so many players, each with his own agenda. No one emerged as strong enough to carry it through, to surmount the large but not insuperable obstacles. Loss of the Polar 8 was a fatal blow to an already wounded company, not only for the loss of the contract, but for the loss of the opportunity to gain experience with the new technologies, which could then be applied to future projects.

I ONLY went back to Burrard once after I retired, with Ted Jones, who was my senior vice-president. The two of us went in one day to look at it. David Alsop was there, I guess. We went in that day, looked around, saw a bunch of people that we knew. Some of the people working in the shops—there wasn't much going on—they'd say, "Come on, why don't you come back and get this thing going." We both went over and had lunch and said we're never going back into that yard again, and we never did. It was just so sad.

Bill Hudson, president of Burrard Dry Dock

The Dream Dies

Less than a month after the cancellation, the federal government's agenda became clear. A March 19, 1990, letter from the industry minister, Benoit Bouchard, to Peter Quinn described a "problem of overcapacity which is affecting the Canadian shipbuilding industry across the country." Plans for shutting down North Vancouver were being formulated by the politicians at the same time as hundreds of people in both the shipyard and the government bureaucracy were spending millions thrashing out design details.

Quinn fought vigorously to see the company continue in some form. What it really needed if it was to undertake any new initiatives, though, was cash, and the next few months were a desperate search for that commodity from banks and governments that were not exactly keen to risk their money. In May 1990 the company prepared a business plan for the federal government asking for $23 million to rationalize and diversify Versatile. The plan called for the closure of the North Vancouver yard as soon as possible, and the closure of the Victoria yard once a smaller facility specializing in ship repair became operational. Optimistically, it predicted good profits from the ship repair and industrial work. The plan also went into detail about how advanced technology applications would include CASPER (an integrated CAD/CAM and Project Management System), MIRS (Medical Imaging Remote System), Smartcard and Super Smartcard Systems, Integrated Services Digital Networks and digital TV enhanced-NTSC integrated circuits.

All this sounded very trendy, with all the right buzz words. But it didn't have a lot of substance. The bureaucrats at the industry ministry dismissed the plan as "a draft overview and various pieces of ancillary information; not a business plan." They requested more information on marketing, and in spite of Quinn's plea in July for $6 million to stave off imminent financial collapse, they continued giving him the runaround. Versatile submitted a revised business plan on July 31, but more questions and requests for information followed. Since shipbuilding was being used largely as a tool to even out regional disparities, pouring money into prosperous BC made little sense—especially when the province had a dearth of Liberal members of Parliament.

Versatile lost $3.8 million in the first eight months of 1990. Efforts to secure loans from the Royal Bank and the Bank of Hong Kong using the dry dock as collateral dissolved in a morass of meetings and reports. A dry dock was not the most desirable security around. Quinn concluded that the banks did not like shipbuilding and that the Royal Bank in particular "hated Versatile." On August 8, 1990, Shieldings loaned Versatile $5 million to tide it over, but with little cash coming in, this didn't last long.

In the midst of the slow motion collapse of the company, Versatile submitted a bid for a $120-million BC super ferry in July 1990. It actually won the contract on September 5, even though a bid from the Trinity Marine group of Gulfport, Mississippi, was $10 million less. Keeping the jobs and money at home was considered worth that amount. But Quinn recognized the North Vancouver yard was in no shape to build anything, and it could not in any case get bonding for the project. The Crown created a new company, Integrated Ferry Constructors, to manage the project.

As 1990 wound down, the pursuit of cash to simply keep the doors open for another few weeks became all-consuming. Quinn turned to the provincial government, one of the company's last friends, to guarantee a $7.5-million loan. But while more receptive than the feds, the province was not quick to respond. On November 27 Quinn wrote to Godsall, "VPSI is living on the cooperation of creditors, employee health and welfare trusts and funds not advanced to the Receiver General. With no money, the place is a bloody mess. Control is not possible despite huge efforts. Karate is not done well with both legs and an arm tied."

In December 1990, at the eleventh hour, the

company received a $7.5-million loan guarantee from the provincial government to assist in restructuring. But this didn't stop the bleeding. In March 1991 the once-proud company sought court protection from its creditors for six months.

A story in the August 13, 1991, *Vancouver Sun* reports that Versatile asked the federal government to either approve sale of the dry dock or step in and buy it for $7.6 million by paying off a loan of this sum from the Hong Kong Bank of Canada. Namura Shipyards had offered $14.6 million for the dock, planning to tow it to Taiwan, but the politicians finally took action to keep it at home as without the Versatile dock the BC ferries, which needed at least 180 days of dry dock time annually, would be totally dependent on the Esquimalt dock. North Vancouver mayors Murray Dykeman and Jack Loucks, as well as BC premier Rita Johnston and others sent letters to Prime Minister Brian Mulroney, urging him to keep the dry dock where it was and to protect the shipbuilding industry.

On September 26, 1991, the federal government agreed to contribute $8 million and the BC government $6 million to save the dry dock. An additional $1.8 million came from a joint venture company formed by Vancouver Shipyards and Allied Shipbuilders. This paid off the Hong Kong Bank and re-equipped the dock.

On December 30, 1992, fewer than 10 workers left Versatile for the last time. It was a great shock to the men when the yard closed. Most believed there would be some last-minute miracle, some major new contract, as had happened so often before. But the time of miracles was over.

The February 17, 1994, *Province* reported that the final launch from the shipyards was a private undertaking, a 300-passenger aluminum dinner-cruise yacht, built by Fergus Dudley in the rented former angle shop.

In 2002, Vancouver Shipyards and Allied Shipbuilders operate the dry dock, which is the one functioning part of the former shipyard.

I DON'T THINK people believed it would close until it actually happened. I'll never forget the news coverage that was there, people coming out of the yard had been there for 30 to 35 years, they were coming out and they were crying. They just could not believe it was over. That was their whole life, their whole way of life. Some people never recovered. Their whole social structure collapsed around them. We had a couple of people who had breakdowns they haven't really fully recovered from. It was a very difficult and trying time.

George MacPherson,
president of the Marine Workers' Union

Above: The shipyard in 2002. The stern of the World War II Maintenance Ship Cape Breton, *built by Burrard Dry Dock in 1945 as the* Flamborough Head, *awaits poisitioning as part of a planned new museum in the former shipyard.* Peter A. Robson photo

Postscript

We used to say Canada has the longest sea coast and navigable waters of any country in the world, and that Canadians have no maritime conscience—and they haven't either.

Bill Hudson, president, Burrard Dry Dock

The days of major shipbuilding in Canada are over for the foreseeable future. It did not help that shipbuilding was not covered in the Canada–US Free Trade Agreement, leaving in force the Jones Act, which reserved the American market almost exclusively for US shipbuilders. This meant the US market was off-limits, and, as Rollie Webb says, "There's no way we can compete with China when they can build barges for some 40 to 50 percent less after paying duty and ocean freight." In 1998–1999, 12 Chinese-built wood barges were imported to BC for carrying wood chips.

The North Vancouver yard's success was due mainly to the energy, drive and vision of the Wallace family, particularly Andy and Clarence, and some exceptionally loyal and competent employees. Dragging at this progress was a federal government that tried to steer an all-too-Canadian course between competing regional interests, and a general skepticism on the part of some shipbuilders that mere colonials could build the most sophisticated ships at a competitive cost. While the provincial government was generally an excellent customer with its ferries, the federal government vacillated between being the profligate uncle and long periods during which it seemed to forget the West Coast existed. Municipal politicians lobbied the provincial and federal governments on behalf of the shipyard for contracts, but North Vancouver mayors do not carry a lot of clout in Ottawa, or even Victoria. And private contracts were too few to sustain the yard in a world where it could no longer compete internationally.

It's interesting to speculate on how different directions might have changed outcomes. What would have happened if the company had moved? What would have happened if David Wallace had taken over the company and it had been run by shipbuilders rather than entrepreneurs? While either of these actions may have substantially changed the last 20 years of the shipyard's life, its demise was all but inevitable. It had become ever more dependent on large federal and provincial contracts for new construction, leaving smaller yards, with their captive coastal market, to build smaller ships. While the government contracts were often lucrative, they were too few and widely spaced for any company to rely on. As the federal government moved to tighten its belt, shipbuilding was one of the first activities to be cut back. Perhaps if it had become a smaller yard, content to build fishing boats or tugs for coastal use, it might have survived in some form in another location. But for the last 80 years Burrard and then Versatile built mainly larger ships, and the company's facilities and mindset were focussed on this direction.

This is in many ways a Canadian story, another family company that like Eatons or Woodwards or Southam flourished for many years but was unwilling or unable to find the new patterns that would resonate in an international high-tech world. Our world is no longer friendly to such companies. We've created a harsher, more competitive world for ourselves—leaner, but a whole lot meaner—a world in which the buzzwords are partnerships and collaboration, but the only real story is the bottom line. The Wallaces, especially in the years up to and including World War II, remind us of a time when a few good men could successfully tackle a project, and where profit in the shipyard could co-exist with loyalty and a sense of community. North Vancouver lost not only a ship-yard, but also a part of its heart. Life moves on, but looking back can help us see where we're going.

THOSE WERE the best years of my life in the yard, bar none. It was just like a wee city. From the interaction between the guys within your department, the camaraderie. Just in the yard. Very rarely did you socialize outside the yard with them. But for eight hours it was just like a family, like a man and wife and kids. You had good guys, you had bad guys, you had ass-holes, people with hearts. It was all there. Society was there in every respect and shape. I knew the people that could support me, I knew the people that hated my guts.

John Fitzpatrick, president
of the Marine Workers' Union

Ship Repairs

By the work one knows the workman.

Jean de la Fontaine, *Fables* Volume 1, Fable 21

While shipbuilding gets most of the glory, ship repair was an essential part of Burrard's work and, on the whole, much more profitable than new construction. While fixed-price contracts for new construction became the rule in the last years of the company, the contracts for repair jobs generally covered time and materials. Ships needing repair in Vancouver were a captive market for Burrard—there was nowhere else to go, so the yard drove some hard bargains, resulting in hefty profits.

Most repair work, perhaps 75 percent, was maintenance, as a ship, like a car, needs periodic work to keep everything in good running order and to ensure the ship is "in class" and meets standards for construction, equipment, engines, etc., as defined by Lloyds, the American Bureau of Shipping, or one of the other agencies that rate ships. This ensures that the ship is at an acceptable level of safety and capability. While the major repairs were done in the shipyard, repair crews also travelled to repair ships on-site. Burrard's diesel motor expertise put it one-up on the American yards competing for non-North American business, as the American ships were steam turbine.

Converting or expanding ships was also a major activity. Burrard stretched BC ferries in both length and height, and adapted naval ships and others to new uses. Many times this meant an almost complete rebuilding of the ship, so these projects were more like new construction than repair.

For a time, Burrard was Canada's leading ship repairer as well as a builder of new vessels. It appears to have been a beneficial if sometimes strained marriage. Many of the same skills used in shipbuilding transferred to ship repair. As David Alsop says, "We were able to use the labour force in a way that provided a greater overall sense of continuity by having the two lines of business operating side by side." Rollie Webb notes that "a pure repair yard generally doesn't have the depth of management or process to do things as efficiently," although allocation of resources could be a problem if an emergency repair job arrived in the middle of a new construction project. As well, new construction tended to lower the overhead rates. A 70 percent overhead charge on labour rates was generally considered acceptable, but a high volume of new construction might decrease the overhead to 60 or 55 percent, as the fixed overhead was spread over a greater base. Ship repairs were sufficiently profitable to compensate for work that was taken at closer to cost.

While minor work could be done while a ship was at berth, major repair and maintenance required a ship to be lifted from the water so workers could get at its hull. This was when a dry dock or marine railway was necessary. George Doidge built the first marine railway for Andy Wallace in his False Creek yard, and the company built a larger 1,600-ton marine railway in the North Shore yard in 1908. Larger ships needed dry docks. These were extremely expensive to build, requiring government assistance.

The naval dockyard at Esquimalt generally had the best-equipped facility in BC. It received a dry dock in 1887 as a belated gift for BC's joining Confederation. In the 1920s a new dry dock was built that was so big it once accommodated the *Queen Elizabeth* during World War II. Large dry docks in the Seattle area, Portland, and San Francisco provided keen competition.

While its dock was often inadequate for the larger ships that visited Vancouver, Burrard did have from

THERE WAS competition from Seattle and the old chief engineer in the dry dock, Fred Menzies, wily old character, he looked up in the Lloyds register and found that these ships were due for their major inspection. So he put in a low price on the bid, knowing darn well that the age of the ship, and the time that it was, that they were in for some major repairs—overhaul. So we got the job.

Bob Logan, Burrard Dry Dock employee

Above: The barge Island Transfer No. 1 *is being repaired on the marine railway in 1958. Workers have removed a section of the bumper timber to allow a new steel plate to be fitted and welded. The new bumper is being fastened by (left to right) Ches Reynolds, Percy Reynolds and Martin Brommeland.* 27-781

1925 the only large dry dock in town. This attracted a wide variety of business that enabled the company to stay in business and keep at least a minimal crew of people employed, especially in the barren period of the 1920s and 1930s. Agreements with various lines, such as the Pacific Java Bengal and the Hoegh Silver, ensured fairly continuous work during this time. Burrard was generally the only Lower Mainland company doing deep-sea repairs before World War II. Many of the customers were Scandinavian companies whose ships plied the Pacific, often never returning to home ports. British ships, on the other hand, carried trade to and from home, so were generally repaired there. Burrard acquired a reputation for competent and efficient work. David Wallace notes that much of the work was done on a cost-plus basis, with owners' representatives generally approving the work immediately.

When Burrard purchased North Van Ship Repairs in 1951 it also inherited two smaller dry docks. The

In September 1965 the Alaska *struck a cliff after leaving Whittier, Alaska, resulting in bow damage of $219,000. The before and after photos provide a dramatic picture of the transformation of crumpled steel back to sleek and elegant lines.* 27-2782, 27-2794

larger was capable of docking ships up to 10,000 tons, while a smaller one was built out of the hulls of unfinished World War II transport ferries.

David Wallace recalls that in 1950 there were major changes to methods for cleaning and painting ships that came on dry dock. Prior to this time, manual scraping and brushing had been the rule, followed by paint applied with rollers or spray. In the 1950s, Burrard followed the lead of Todd Shipyards in Seattle, where wet sandblast machines with six-foot-long one-inch pipes that were flattened at the end were instead used to sweep the fouling away. Instead of using 30 to 40 men, it now took eight men six hours plus clean-up.

In the later years, as opportunities for new construction diminished, ship repair helped prolong the company's existence. From 1972, Burrard Yarrows consolidated its position as one of the two leading ship repair companies in Canada (the other was Canadian Vickers) with about 25 percent of the Canadian market. Yarrows was generally the steadier contributor, as it had access to the biggest dry dock. Burrard's activity declined from 515,000 man-hours in 1972 to 343,000 in 1976, although it was back up to 752,000 in 1979. The new dry dock that opened in 1981 further increased its business.

Photographs of some of the major repair jobs in the company's century of activity are included throughout the book. During one 10-year period, from 1952 to 1961, Burrard docked 4,001 ships, so only a few of the more dramatic of the thousands of clients can be represented here. They do give an indication of the mangled mess that could result when ships strayed from their proper place, and the skill of those who made things right again.

SO THIS ship came in and it was, I guess, about 15 years old, and her big main engine, a diesel, was starting to move a little bit. In other words, the holding-down bolts in some cases were broken. So I was the apprentice, the helper of the engine fitter, and we had to go into the double bottom tanks in order to get underneath those things. The double bottoms were for fuel oil and that, so we had to slosh through about six inches or so of a mixture of water and diesel, pulling an electric lamp on an extension cord. So of course I went and shoved it ahead of myself into the next compartment, dropped it into the mixture of oil and water and shorted it out. So there you are, absolute black darkness. All sorts of things come roaring through your head and all you can hear is the thumping of the generators above, so the fitter says, "Well, I'll go and get an extension, I'll go and get this fixed but you stay here." Well I sat there for about 15 minutes by myself in the mucky water, black, dark, three-quarters of an inch between me and the bottom of the ocean. Things like that come back.

Bob Logan, Burrard Dry Dock employee

Wallace/Burrard/ Versatile Hull List

Rollie Webb compiled the following hull list and notes. Rollie is the former new construction superintendent at Versatile Pacific Shipyards.

Notes Concerning the List of Ships and Vessels Built and/or Enlarged at Burrard Dry Dock

With the final demise of Burrard Dry Dock (alias Wallace and Versatile Pacific) after a century of shipbuilding, it is worthwhile reviewing the substantial accomplishments made by this company.

One aspect of this history that has never been consistently recorded was the identification of all the vessels built or enlarged in almost 100 years of "boom and bust" existence. The hull numbering system used by Wallace/Burrard/Versatile has changed at least three times. The reasons for these changes were mainly new owners' policies that were driven by business rather than historical concerns.

I believe that Wallace only started using hull numbers at the outbreak of the First War. The company made an attempt to re-create a list of all the vessels that had been built up to that time. To do so I believe they reviewed the Register of Vessels for the Port of Vancouver and assigned numbers retroactively by year of completion and registration number. Vessels registered at other ports, including Victoria, New Westminster and London, England, were ignored. Vessels such as scows that were built but not registered were also ignored. Even after the company

started using hull numbers with the construction of the *War Storm*, it did not give every vessel built a hull number. Small wooden vessels, such as the Chummie series of harbour workboats, were not included. Vessels enlarged by lengthening, reconstruction or other means were also not given hull numbers.

The list includes one vessel that remains somewhat of a mystery. The wooden sternwheeler *Fairview ON 103473*, built at Okanagan Landing in 1894 and registered at Victoria, is recorded as being built by Alfred E. Wallace of New Westminster. The city directories for New Westminster at this time do not include such a person, and Alfred (Andy) Wallace is listed as a resident of Vancouver in 1893 but is not listed in 1894. It is assumed that these two people are one and the same and hence the vessel is included in the list as the first "registered" vessel built by Andy Wallace.

This new list is as complete as possible after a review of company records, local and federal archives, shipping registers, newspapers, etc. One area where some uncertainty exists is in the identification of small vessels built in the early days that were never registered. Many wooden scows and the like built in the period before World War I were in fact registered in later years, and these have been included in the list. There is no way of knowing if all the vessels actually constructed are indeed listed.

Because of the large amount of work-sharing that went on between Burrard and Yarrows during the 45 years of common ownership, this list is best read in conjunction with a similar list prepared for Yarrows.

The serial number system used in this list is a creation of the author for the sole purpose of providing a global total of the projects undertaken. It is a simple chronological list of ships built and does not rely on hull numbers for three reasons: hull numbers were used inconsistently; the same hull number can refer to more than one ship; and some fairly major reconstruction or conversion projects were not given hull numbers and so would not be included in a list of hull numbers.

Projects other than new ships that are included in the list are those that caused the tonnage of the vessel to be re-measured and/or a reconstruction date to be included on the registration documents.

Roland H. Webb

List of abbreviations

BHP	Brake horsepower
DP	Displacement
GT	Gross tonnage
IHP	Indicated horsepower
LST	Landing ship, tank
NHP	Nominal horsepower
RHP	Reciprocating horsepower
S/D	Self-dumping
SHP	Shaft horsepower
S/L	Self-loading
STM	Steam reciprocating
STM	Steam turbine
T/S	Twin screws
Turbo El	Turbo electric

Above: Looking out from the Victory ship Fort Wallace, *1944.* 27-2323

Serial #	Hull #	Year	Reg.No.	Name	OWNERS	Tonnage	Dimensions	Propulsion	Type & Notes
1	none	1894	103473	FAIRVIEW	MARY E. COUSON	55 GT	55.0' x 15.0' x 2.9'	2 NHP JENCKS STM. REC.	WOOD STERN WHEELER (blt at Okanagan Landing, registered at Victoria)
2	1	1896	107447	LIGHTHOUSE NO. 2	FEDERATION BRAND CO.	7 GT	30.0' X 12.0' X 2.5'	NON PROPELLED	WOOD SCOW
3	2	1897	107446	LIGHTHOUSE NO. 1	FEDERATION BRAND CO.	8 GT	36.4' X 10.0' X 3.0'	NON PROPELLED	WOOD SCOW
4	3	1898	107154	JAMES DOMVILLE	KLONDIKE YUKON STEWART CO.	486 GT	121.6' X 25.8' X 4.7'	15 RHP POLSON STM. REC.	WOOD STERNWHEELER
5	4	1898	107443	DUFF	B.A. CORP. LTD	101 GT	98.6' X 23.0' X 5.8'	NON PROPELLED	WOOD BARGE
6	5	1898	107714	LIGHTHOUSE NO. 3	FEDERATION BRAND CO.	14 GT	36.0' X 14.0' X 3.7'	NON PROPELLED	WOOD SCOW
7	6	1898	111539	IDLER	S. MENHINNICK	4 GT	32.0' X 8.0' X 3.2'	2 NHP POLSON STM. REC.	WOOD TUG
8	7	1899	107716	ALBION	WURZBURG CO.LTD.	83 GT	79.2' X 18.2' X 8.3'	24 NHP INGLIS STM. REC.	WOOD TUG
9	8	1900	111538	KATIE	G.H. HARDIE	3 GT	25.5' X 7.8' X 2.4'	1 NHP THOMPSON S.R.	WOOD TUG
10	9	1901	None	Not named	unknown	not meas.	unknown	NON PROPELLED	WOOD GOLD DREDGE (blt at Lytton, B.C.)
11	none	1901	103472	CASSIAR (ex J.R.McDonald)	UNION STEAMSHIP COMPANY OF B.C.	597 GT	120.6' X 29.0' X 6.9'	43 NHP SCOTTISH STM. REC.	WOOD STEAMER (Reconstruction of wreck)
12	10	1901	111546	TERRA NOVA	D.& J. ROWAN	47 GT	68.5' X 14.7' X 6.1'	9 NHP SMITH STM. REC.	WOOD PACKER
13	11	1902	111982	GLEN ROSA	WALLACE BROS. PACKING CO. LTD.	18 GT	45.3' X 10.6' X 4.6'	2 NHP ENGLISH STM. REC.	WOOD FISH BOAT
14	12	1902	111985	HUBERT	ALFRED WALLACE	6 GT	32.9' X 8.9' X 4.0'	1 NHP POLSON STM. REC.	WOOD TUG
15	13	1902	111986	UNICAN (one)	UNITED CANNERS (B.C.) CO. LTD. & CO. STM. REC.	176 GT	89.2' X 20.0' X 8.0'	20 NHP BOW, McLACHLIN	WOOD TUG
16	14	1903	116332	KESTREL	DEPT. OF MARINE & FISHERIES	311 GT	126.0' X 24.0' X 12.2'	59 NHP POLSON STM. REC.	WOOD FISHERIES PROTECTION VESSEL
17	15	1903	112249	EDNA W	PACKERS STEAMSHIP CO. LTD.	15 GT	40.0' X 9.1' X 4.9'	3 NHP STM. REC.	WOOD TUG
18	16	1903	112256	WATER LILY	D. ROWAN	4 GT	27.6' X 7.6' X 3.4'	2 NHP ALBION STM. REC.	WOOD TUG
19	17	1903	116459	SQUID	W. ROBINSON	60 GT	72.0' X 16.4' X 5.7'	11 NHP THOMPSON S.R.	WOOD TUG
20	18	1904	116776	CLARENCE	E. WALLACE	13 GT	40.2' X 9.5' X 4.7'	2 NHP ENGLISH S.R.	WOOD TUG
21	19	1904	116782	BELFAST	T.G. MCBRIDE	105 GT	91.2' X 18.0' X 7.0'	15 NHP THOMPSON S.R.	WOOD TUG
22	20	1904	116783	HILDA	S. CHAMPION	33 GT	58.0' X 13.4' X 6.3'	8 NHP SCOTTISH S.R.	WOOD TUG
23	21	1904	116784	ST. GEORGE	NORTH VANCOUVER FERRY & POWER	544 GT	131.2' X 28.8' X 12.5'	33 NHP POLSON STM. REC.	COMPOSITE FERRY frame from Polson Iron Works, Toronto, their Hull # 65
24	22	1904	116787	IRIS (lost 1904)	JOHN FULTON	58 GT	57.0' X	6 NHP USA STM. REC.	WOOD TUG
25	23	1904	117003	RAMBLER	C. HILDEI	2 GT	23.0' X 6.2' X 2.6'	1 NHP THOMPSON S.R.	WOOD TUG
26	24	1905	117012	ELSIE	J.W. HACKETT	16 GT	53.4' X 12.3' X 5.5'	1 NHP COPP STM. REC.	WOOD TUG
27	25	1905	117017	COLUMBIA	JOHN ANTLE	40 GT	60.0' X14.0' X 4.5'	4 NHP UNION GAS ENG.	WOOD TUG
28	26	1905	117018	BURRARD	JOHN D. FOREMAN	56 GT	63.5' X 14.2' X 6.5'	10 NHP THOMPSON S.R.	WOOD TUG
29	27	1905	117113	GEORGIAN 11	MCKENZIE BROS. LTD.	649 GT	187.0' X 39.8' X 9.8'	NON PROPELLED	WOOD BARGE
30	28	1905	117117	McCULLOCH	JOHN FULTON (see # 22)	39 GT	64.0' X 14.7' X 6.7'	13 NHP STM. REC.	WOOD TUG
31	29	1905	121674	B. NO.1	J.A. RUSSELL et al	169 GT	80.0' X 30.0' X 8.0'	NON PROPELLED	WOOD SCOW
32	30	1905	121720	C.W. 3	CHAMPION & WHITE	86 GT	76.0' X 26.0' X 7.8'	NON PROPELLED	WOOD SCOW
33	31	1906	121726	IX	UNION STEAMSHIP CO. OF B.C. LTD.	164 GT	90.2' X 30.3' X 7.7'	NON PROPELLED	WOOD SCOW
34	32	1906	121741	CLAYBURN	W.H. ARMSTRONG	78 GT	73.0' X 17.9' X 8.4'	26 NHP SEMI DIESEL	WOOD TUG
35	33	1906	121750	FOUR WINDS	JAMES E. MCRAE	8 GT	26.0' X 9.7' X 5.8'	20 BHP GAS ENGINE	WOOD TUG
36	none	1906	121977	LEILA	FRANK C. STRATFORD	10 GT	36.0' X 9.0' X 3.6'	.66 HP GAS ENGINE	WOOD LAUNCH registered at Victoria
37	34	1906	122158	PROGRESSIVE	PROGRESSIVE STEAMBOAT COMPANY	79 GT	77.6' X 18.0' X 8.8'	16 NHP DOTY STM. REC.	WOOD TUG
38	35	1906	122163	VENTURE	JOHN J. HODDER	8 GT	29.1' X 9.3' X 3.4'	1 NHP GAS ENGINE	WOOD YACHT
39	36	1906	122326	KENORA	RAT PORTAGE LUMBER CO.	13 GT	31.2' X 9.0' X 4.0'	2.3 NHP GAS ENGINE	WOOD TUG
40	37	1907	122330	CARL	JAMES S. REAR	1 GT	16.4' X 5.4' X 2.6'	4 NHP GAS ENGINE	WOOD TUG
41	38	1907	122335	V.T.B. I	VANCOUVER TUG & BARGE CO. LTD.	209 GT	86.2' X 30.2' X 9.0'	NON PROPELLED	WOOD SCOW
42	39	1907	122336	V.T.B. 2	VANCOUVER TUG & BARGE CO. LTD.	212 GT	86.6' X 30.2' X 9.0'	NON PROPELLED	WOOD SCOW
43	40	1907	122375	DARING	W.W. WHITE	81 GT	72.0' X 17.8' X 8.0'	16 NHP STM. REC.	WOOD TUG
44	none	1907	122383	SPRAY	VICTORIA TUG COMPANY	118 GT	81.0' X 19.0' X 10.0'	36 NHP ROSS & DUNCAN S. R.	WOOD TUG registered at Victoria
45	41	1907	122502	LINDE	JAMES E. MCRAE	8 GT	30.8' X 8.6' X 4.2'	2 NHP GAS ENGINE	WOOD TUG
46	42	1907	122508	V.T.B. 3	VANCOUVER TUG & BARGE CO. LTD.	223 GT	86.4' X 32.1' X 9.0'	NON PROPELLED	WOOD SCOW
47	43	1907	122517	DOLA	VANCOUVER TUG & BARGE CO. LTD.	154 GT	96.3' X 21.8' X 10.9'	39 NHP McKIE & BAXTER S. R.	WOOD TUG
48	44	1907	122518	ROVER	ALFRED WALLACE	17 GT	39.0' X 11.0' X 4.8'	2 NHP GAS ENGINE	WOOD TUG
49	45	1907	122519	UNICAN (two)	JAMES E. MCRAE	15 GT	35.7' X 10.5' X 5.3'	3 NHP GAS ENGINE	WOOD TUG
50	46	1907	122537	ARMOCO	W.H. ARMSTRONG	46 GT	56.5' X 14.5' X 7.2'	10 NHP GAS ENGINE	WOOD TUG

Serial #	Hull #	Year	Reg.No.	Name	OWNERS	Tonnage	Dimensions	Propulsion	Type & Notes
51	47	1907	122538	CELTIC	COAST STEAMSHIP CO.	239 GT	89.4' X 24.5' X 8.6'	16 NHP McKIE & BAXTER STM. REC.	WOOD TUG
52	48	1907	122542	V.T.B. 4	VANCOUVER TUG & BARGE CO. LTD.	224 GT	86.5' X 32.0' X 9.1'	NON PROPELLED	WOOD SCOW
53	49	1907	122543	V.T.B. 5	VANCOUVER TUG & BARGE CO. LTD.	224 GT	86.4' X 32.0' X 9.1'	NON PROPELLED	WOOD SCOW
54	50	1907	122547	IVANHOE	GEORGE I. WILSON	186 GT	99.7' X 22.5' X 10.9'	26 NHP MCKIE & BAXTER STM. REC.	WOOD TUG
55	51	1907	126082	B.C.P.	PACKERS STEAMSHIP CO. LTD.	121 GT	80.5' X 18.0' X 7.8'	22 NHP ROSS & DUNCAN STM. REC.	WOOD TUG
56	52	1907	126086	SEMIAHMO	R.T. BURTWELL	16 GT	33.5' X 10.6' X 4.5'	1.5 NHP GAS ENGINE	WOOD TUG
57	53	1908	126071	C.W.4	CHAMPION & WHITE	176 GT	81.8' X 28.9' X 7.4'	NON PROPELLED	WOOD SCOW
58	54	1908	126076	KNIGHT	R.E. GOSSE	21 GT	44.5' X 12.0' X 5.7'	4 NHP GAS ENGINE	WOOD TUG
59	55	1908	126077	STEELHEAD	PACKERS STEAMSHIP CO. LTD.	21 GT	44.5' X 12.0' X 5.7'	5 NHP GAS ENGINE	WOOD TUG
60	56	1908	126081	NONAME	B.C.TIE & TIMBER CO. LTD.	113 GT	76.5' X 18.9' X 9.3'	26 NHP STM. REC.	WOOD TUG
61	57	1908	126507	C.PR. NO. 1	CANADIAN PACIFIC RAILWAY CO.	221 GT	106.0' X 30.0' X 8.5'	NON PROPELLED	WOOD RAILCAR BARGE
62	none	1908	158298	SKOOKUM III	ARMOUR SALVAGE & TOWING CO. LTD. (1933)	201 GT	103.5' X 30.1' X 5.6'	NON PROPELLED	WOOD SCOW, original owners unknown, registered at Vancouver in 1933
63	58	1909	126235	C.PR. NO. 2	CANADIAN PACIFIC RAILWAY CO.	252 GT	120.0' X 30.0' X 8.5'	NON PROPELLED	WOOD RAILCAR BARGE
64	59	1909	126337	V.T.B. 6	VANCOUVER TUG & BARGE CO. LTD.	183 GT	86.6' X 30.4' X 8.2'	NON PROPELLED	WOOD SCOW
65	60	1909	126339	TOTEM	PACKERS STEAMSHIP CO. LTD.	21 GT	45.2' X 12.0' X 5.9'	5 NHP GAS ENGINE	WOOD TUG
66	61	1909	126628	V.T.B. 7	VANCOUVER TUG & BARGE CO. LTD.	178 GT	82.7' X 30.1' X 7.5'	NON PROPELLED	WOOD SCOW, 1st vessel blt. In North Vancouver

SHIPYARD MOVED FROM FALSE CREEK TO NORTH VANCOUVER, HULL 62 IS LAST VESSEL BUILT ON FALSE CREEK

Serial #	Hull #	Year	Reg.No.	Name	OWNERS	Tonnage	Dimensions	Propulsion	Type & Notes
67	62	1909	126731	HELEN M. SCANLON	BROOKS SCANLON LUMBER CO. LTD.	285 GT	124.0' X 27.2' X 5'	9 NHP STM. REC.	WOOD STERNWHEELER
68	63	1909	126743	X11	UNION STEAMSHIP CO. OF B.C. LTD.	161 GT	77.2' X 28.7' X 7.7'	NON PROPELLED	WOOD SCOW
69	64	1910	126739	PYRITES	NICHOLAS CHEMICAL CO.	207 GT	89.0' X 28.2' X 9.3'	NON PROPELLED	WOOD BARGE
70	65	1910	126884	KYAC	PACKERS STEAMSHIP CO. LTD.	29 GT	55.0' X 13.3' X 6.2'	6 NHP GAS ENGINE	WOOD TUG
71	66	1910	126898	RESORT	SECHELT STEAMSHIP CO. LTD.	25 GT	45.2' X 11.8' X 5.4'	2 NHP GAS ENGINE	WOOD TUG
72	67	1910	130292	F.H. PHIPPEN	CANADIAN FISH & COLD STORAGE CO. LTD.	26 GT	54.4' X 12.3' X 6'	7 NHP GAS ENGINE	WOOD TUG
73	68	1910	130307	PANNONE	W.F. BROUGHAM	135 GT	73.4' X 28.2' X 6.7'	NON PROPELLED	WOOD SCOW
74	69	1910	130447	NORTH VANCOUVER FERRY NO.3	NORTH VANCOUVER CITY FERRIES LTD.	1176 GT	145.0' X 29.1' X 12.4'	42 NHP McKIE & BAXTER STM. REC.	STEEL FERRY
75	70	1910	133705	P.S.B. CO. NO. 2	PROGRESSIVE STEAMBOAT COMPANY	180 GT	81.5' X 29.8' X 7.7'	NON PROPELLED	WOOD SCOW
76	none	1910	151196	E.C.E. XXIV	EVANS, COLEMAN & EVANS, LTD.	27 GT	55.0' X 20.0' X 2.8'	NON PROPELLED	WOOD PILEDRIVER registered at Vancouver 1924
77	71	1911	130443	VINER	KNIGHT INLET CANNING CO. LTD.	28 GT	45.7' X 14.5' X 5.7'	6 NHP GAS ENGINE	WOOD TUG
78	72	1911	138701	C. OF V. NO.1	CORP. OF THE CITY OF VANCOUVER	136 GT	83.4' X 28.0' X 6.8'	NON PROPELLED	WOOD SCOW
79	73	1911	130749	PHRYNE	JOHN H. WRIGLEY	24 GT	47.2' X 11.8' X 6'	3 NHP GAS ENGINE	WOOD TUG
80	74	1911	130794	JERICHO	A.C. BALKWELL	44 GT	67.0' X 14.5' X 4.4'	8 NHP STM. REC.	WOOD TUG
81	75	1911	130848	McBRIDE & CO. 2	T.G. MCBRIDE	123 GT	73.4' X 28.0' X 6.6'	NON PROPELLED	WOOD SCOW
82	none	1911	150606	W.S. & D. NO. 2	WALLACE SHIPYARDS LTD.	147 GT	90.0' X 30.2' X 6.6'	NON PROPELLED	WOOD SCOW registered at Vancouver 1922
83	none	1911	none	P.W.D NO. 4	DEPT. OF PUBLIC WORKS	not meas.	70.0' X 26.0' X 8.4'	NON PROPELLED	WOOD DERRICK SCOW shown in PWD Fleet Lists
84	76	1912	137949	G. OF G. NO. 2	GULF OF GEORGIA TOWING CO. LTD.	123 GT	86.5' X 28.2' X 6.2'	NON PROPELLED	WOOD SCOW
85	77	1912	130905	NIMPKISH	PACKERS STEAMSHIP CO. LTD.	27 GT	54.2' X 13.5' X 5.4'	3 NHP GAS ENGINE	WOOD TUG
86	78	1912	130908	OLALLIE	PACKERS STEAMSHIP CO. LTD.	68 GT	72.4' X 16.5' X 7.4'	16 NHP STM. REC.	WOOD TUG
87	79	1912	130914	KAWATNA	PACKERS STEAMSHIP CO. LTD.	26 GT	54.2' X 13.9' X 5.4'	3 NHP GAS ENGINE	WOOD TUG
88	80	1912	130915	KLATAWA	PACKERS STEAMSHIP CO. LTD.	42 GT	63.9' X 14.4' X 6.5'	6 NHP GAS ENGINE	WOOD TUG
89	81	1912	130917	POINT GREY	DEPT. OF PUBLIC WORKS	238 GT	93.4' X 22.3' X 14.5'	62 NHP CAMPBELL & CALDERWOOD S. R.	STEEL TUG
90	82	1912	130919	P.S. CO. XX	PACKERS STEAMSHIP CO. LTD.	79 GT	64.0' X 23.6' X 3'	NON PROPELLED	WOOD SCOW
91	83	1912	133717	McB. NO. III	T.G. MCBRIDE	148 GT	75.1' X 30.1' X 8'	NON PROPELLED	WOOD SCOW
92	84	1912	133720	FRENO	A. WALLACE (FRENO TOW BOAT CO.LTD.)	94 GT	79.2' X 18.8' X 8.3'	24 NHP STM. REC.	WOOD TUG
93	none	1912	152526	V.D.S. NO. 5	VANCOUVER DREDGING & SALVAGE CO. LTD.	124 GT	80.2' X 24.0' X 7.8'	NON PROPELLED	WOOD SCOW registered at Vancouver 1924
94	none	1912	none	P.W.D. NO. 554	DEPT. OF PUBLIC WORKS	not meas.	61.0' X 20.9' X 5.8'	NON PROPELLED	WOOD BUNK SCOW shown on PWD Fleet lists

Serial #	Hull #	Year	Reg.No.	Name	OWNERS	Tonnage	Dimensions	Propulsion	Type & Notes
95	none	1912	none	P.W.D. NO. 555	DEPT. OF PUBLIC WORKS	not meas.	53.8' X 20.8' X 6.6'	NON PROPELLED	WOOD BUNK SCOW shown on PWD Fleet lists
96	85	1913	133942	NADEN	NAVAL SERVICE OF CANADA	88 GT	80.0' X 20.1' X 8.7'	NON PROPELLED	TWO MASTED WOOD SCHOONER
97	86	1913	134075	P.W.D. NO. 313	DEPT. OF PUBLIC WORKS	208 GT	76.0' X 35.0' X 6'	NON PROPELLED	WOOD CLAMSHELL DREDGE
98	87	1913	138295	DKS. NO. 1	JOHN P. DEEKS	141 GT	69.3' X 30.0' X 7.5'	NON PROPELLED	WOOD SCOW
99	88	1913	138296	DKS. NO. 2	JOHN P. DEEKS	142 GT	69.3' X 30.0' X 7.5'	NON PROPELLED	WOOD SCOW
100	none	1913	150277	C.W. 7	CHAMPION & WHITE	110 GT	84.0' X 26.0' X 6.0'	NON PROPELLED	WOOD SCOW registered at Vancouver in 1920
101	none	1913	135289	SIR J.J. LD. NO. 7	SIR JOHN JACKSON (CANADA) LTD.	245 GT	90.0' X 32.7' X 9.9'	NON PROPELLED	WOOD SCOW registered at London England
102	none	1913	135290	SIR J.J. LD. NO. 8	SIR JOHN JACKSON (CANADA) LTD.	283 GT	90.0' X 31.7' X 12.7'	NON PROPELLED	WOOD SCOW registered at London England
103	none	1913	135291	SIR J.J. LD. NO. 9	SIR JOHN JACKSON (CANADA) LTD.	283 GT	90.0' X 31.7' X 12.7'	NON PROPELLED	WOOD SCOW registered at London England
104	none	1913	136650	SIR J.J. LD. NO. 28	SIR JOHN JACKSON (CANADA) LTD.	231 GT	90.0' X 31.5' X 9.6'	NON PROPELLED	WOOD SCOW registered at London England
105	none	1913	170963	D.S. 310	DEPT. OF PUBLIC WORKS	224 GT	99.2' X 26.8' X 9.9'	NON PROPELLED	WOOD DUMP SCOW registered at Vancouver 1938
106	none	1913	none	P.W.D. NO. 522	DEPT. OF PUBLIC WORKS	not meas.	66.9' X 21.0' X 5.0'	NON PROPELLED	WOOD & STEEL OIL FUEL SCOW shown on PWD Fleet Lists
107	none	1913	none	P.W.D. NO. 553	DEPT. OF PUBLIC WORKS	not meas.	60.0' X 23.0' X 5.3'	NON PROPELLED	WOOD BUNK SCOW shown on PWD Fleet Lists
108	89	1914	138357	CHUMMIE II	WALLACE SHIPYARDS LTD.	14 GT	35.0' X 11.0' X 5'	2 NHP GAS ENGINE	WOOD LAUNCH
109	90	1914	134089	DRILL BOAT BURRARD	DOMINION CONTRACTING CO.	426 GT	115.0' X 30.0' X 7.8'	NON PROPELLED	STEEL DERRICK SCOW
110	none	1915	134633	RAINBOW NO. 2	THE WESTERN TRANSPORT CO. LD.	61 GT	83.0' X 26.0' X 3.7'	NON PROPELLED	WOOD BARGE registered at Victoria 1915
111	none	1915	134431	P.S.CO. XXIV	PACKERS STEAMSHIP CO. LTD.	186 GT	67.0' X 24.0' X 5.5'	NON PROPELLED	WOOD BARGE registered at Vancouver 1915
112	none	1916	138294	MANU SENA	THOMAS M. HEARD FERRY COMPANY	13 GT	43.0' X 7.5' X 4.9'	2 NHP GAS ENGINE	WOOD LAUNCH registered at Vancouver 1916
113	none	1916	156595	W.S.D. NO.4	WALLACE SHIPBUILDING & D.D. CO. LTD.	103 GT	74.7' X 26.1' X 6.3'	NON PROPELLED	WOOD SCOW registered at Vancouver 1929
114	91	1917	140388	WAR DOG	IMPERIAL MUNITIONS BOARD	3046 GT	300.0' X 45.3' X 24.9'	266 NHP WALLACE STM. REC.	STEEL FREIGHTER
115	92	1917	138351	MABEL BROWN	CANADA WEST COAST NAVIGATION CO.	1474 GT	240.0' X 43.3' X 19.0'	36 NHP T/S BOLINDER SEMI DIESEL	WOODEN AUX. SCHOONER
116	93	1917	138354	GERALDINE WOLVIN	CANADA WEST COAST NAVIGATION CO.	1472 GT	240.0' X 43.9' X 19.0'	36 NHP T/S BOLINDER SEMI DIESEL	WOODEN AUX. SCHOONER
117	94	1917	138368	JESSIE NORCROSS	CANADA WEST COAST NAVIGATION CO.	1481 GT	240.5' X 43.6' X 19.3'	36 NHP T/S BOLINDER SEMI DIESEL	WOODEN AUX. SCHOONER
118	95	1917	138369	JANET CARRUTHERS	CANADA WEST COAST NAVIGATION CO.	1466 GT	240.0' X 44.1' X 19.3'	36 NHP T/S BOLINDER SEMI DIESEL	WOODEN AUX. SCHOONER
119	96	1917	138684	MABEL STEWART	CANADA WEST COAST NAVIGATION CO.	1472 GT	243.2' X 44.0' X 19.2'	36 NHP T/S BOLINDER SEMI DIESEL	WOODEN AUX. SCHOONER
120	97	1917	138690	MARIE BARNARD	CANADA WEST COAST NAVIGATION CO.	1476 GT	243.0' X 44.0' X 19.2'	36 NHP T/S BOLINDER SEMI DIESEL	WOODEN AUX. SCHOONER
121	none	1917	130917	POINT GREY	IMPERIAL MUNITIONS BOARD/ DPW	inc 62 GT	11.6' X 21.9' X 13.3'	NON PROPELLED	STEEL MIDSECTION
122	none	1917	130897	POINT ELLICE	IMPERIAL MUNITIONS BOARD/ DPW	inc 42 GT	16.2' X 20.0' X 11.6'	NON PROPELLED	STEEL MIDSECTION
123	98	1918	142649	WAR POWER	IMPERIAL MUNITIONS BOARD	3200 GT	300.0' X 45.0' X 27.0'	226 NHP WALLACE STM. REC.	FREIGHTER
124	99	1918	143046	WAR STORM	IMPERIAL MUNITIONS BOARD	3145 GT	300.0' X 45.0' X 24.9'	226 NHP WALLACE STM. REC.	FREIGHTER
125	100	1919	141424	CANADIAN VOLUNTEER	CANADIAN GOVERNMENT MERCH. MARINE	3188 GT	320.0' X 44.2' X 22.9'	226 NHP WALLACE STM. REC.	FREIGHTER
126	101	1919	141547	CANADIAN AVIATOR	CANADIAN GOVERNMENT MERCH. MARINE	3388 GT	331.0' X 46.7' X 23.2'	235 NHP WALLACE STM. REC.	FREIGHTER
Company reorganized as Wallace Shipbuilding & Drydock Co. Ltd. May 18th, 1920									
127	102	1920	140958	CANADIAN RAIDER	CANADIAN GOVERNMENT MERCH. MARINE	3384 GT	331.0' X 46.7' X 23.2'	231 NHP WALLACE STM. REC.	FREIGHTER
128	103	1920	150265	CANADIAN HIGHLANDER	CANADIAN GOVERNMENT MERCH. MARINE	5370 GT	400.0' X 52.4' X 28.8'	266 NHP WALLACE STM. REC.	FREIGHTER
129	104	1921	150421	CANADIAN SKIRMISHER	CANADIAN GOVERNMENT MERCH. MARINE	5373 GT	400.0' X 52.4' X 28.7'	266 NHP WALLACE STM. REC.	FREIGHTER

Serial #	Hull #	Year	Reg.No.	Name	OWNERS	Tonnage	Dimensions	Propulsion	Type & Notes
130	105	1919	141710	CHILKOOT	UNION STEAMSHIP CO. OF B.C. LTD.	756 GT	172.6' X 30.2' X 12.9'	93 NHP USA STM. REC.	COASTAL FREIGHTER
131	106	1919	141431	CANADIAN TROOPER	CANADIAN GOVERNMENT MERCH. MARINE	3079 GT	320.0' X 44.2' X 22.9'	226 NHP WALLACE STM. REC.	FREIGHTER
132	107	1920	none	unnamed	CITY OF NORTH VANCOUVER	not meas.	90.0' X 34.0' X 7.8'	NON PROPELLED	WOOD COAL BARGE
133	108	1921	150555	PRINCESS LOUISE	CANADIAN PACIFIC RAILWAY CO.	4032 GT	317.2' X 48.1' X 17.4'	255 NHP T/S WALLACE STM.REC.	PASSENGER VESSEL
134	109 ?	1921	150573	CANADIAN SCOTTISH	CANADIAN GOVERNMENT MERCH. MARINE	5334 GT	Completion of outfitting of Prince Rupert Dry Dock Hull No. 1		FREIGHTER conflicting Company records show this vessel & Rio Bonito both as Hulls 109
135	109 ?	1922	150604	RIO BONITO	ALEXANDER M. DOLLAR	101 GT	94.5' X 14.6' X 7.9'	17 NHP T/S GAS ENGINES	CONVERSION OF USN WOOD S/C TO YACHT
Company reorganized as Burrard Dry Dock Co. Ltd. October 1921 but name of Wallace Sbdg. Continues to be used until 1924									
136	none	1923	150776	C.L.& R. NO. 1	COMOX LOGGING & RAILWAY COMPANY	105 GT	70.5' X 26.0' X 6.7'	NON PROPELLED	WOOD SCOW registered when built at Vancouver 1923
137	none	1923	150973	F.G. ALDER	THE MINISTER OF LANDS	7 GT	27.1' X 8.1' X 3.6'	4.66 NHP GAS ENGINE	WOOD PATROL LAUNCH Reconstruction, registered when rebuilt at Vancouver, 1923
138	none	1923	150975	E.C.E. XXII	EVANS COLEMAN & EVANS	232 GT	90.0' X 34.0' X 8.3'	NON PROPELLED	WOOD SCOW registered when built at Vancouver 1923
139	none	1923	151127	CLOYAH	MINISTER OF FISHERIES	26 GT	38.7' x 11.1' X 5.3'	2 NHP GAS ENGINE	WOOD PATROL VESSEL registered when built at Vancouver in 1923
140	none	1924	151198	CHUMMIE III	BURRARD DRY DOCK CO. LTD.	10 GT	33.2' X 9.4' X 4.7'	1 NHP GAS ENGINE	WOODEN LAUNCH registered when built at Vancouver in 1924
141	none	1924	152542	TARZAN II	SYDNEY E. JUNKINS COMPANY	474 GT	108.0' X 55.0' X 7.9'	NON PROPELLED	WOOD PILEDRIVER registered when built at Vancouver in 1924
142	none	1924	152548	COMOX	UNION STEAMSHIP CO. OF B.C. LTD.	54 GT	54.0' X 15.5' X 7.2'	3 NHP GAS ENGINE	WOOD PASSENGER VESSEL registered when built at Vancouver in 1924
143	none	1926	153011	W.S.D. NO. 5	WALLACE SHIPBUILDING & D.D. CO. LTD.	33 GT	45.6' X 20.0' X 4.7'	NON PROPELLED	WOOD SCOW registered when built at Vancouver in 1926
144	110	1926	153176	MARVOLITE	IMPERIAL OIL LTD.	131 GT	90.0' X 19.0' X 7.3'	138 NHP FAIRBANKS MORSE DIESEL	STEEL TANKER first vessel listed as built by Burrard Dry Dock Co. Ltd.
145	111	1925	153274	U.O. CO. NO.3	UNION OIL CO.	150 GT	90.0' X 30.0' X 8.9'	NON PROPELLED	STEEL OIL BARGE
146	112	1926	none	UNION OIL SCOW	UNION OIL CO.	125 GT	87.0' X 26.0' X 6.8'	NON PROPELLED	OIL SCOW
147	113A	1925	151172	BURRARD DRY DOCK	BURRARD DRY DOCK CO. LTD.	3879 GT	179.0' X 126.0' X 12.5'	NON PROPELLED	FLOATING DRYDOCK
148	113B	1925	152907	BURRARD DRY DOCK II	BURRARD DRY DOCK CO. LTD.	6798 GT	314.0' X 126.3' X 12.5'	NON PROPELLED	FLOATING DRYDOCK
149	114	1928	154809	ST. ROCH	THE MINISTER OF JUSTICE (RCMP)	197 GT	90.0' X 24.7' X 10.8'	150 NHP UNION DIESEL	WOOD ARCTIC PATROL VESSEL
150	115	1928	154944	J.H. CARLISLE	CORP. OF THE CITY OF VANCOUVER	47 GT	54.8' X 15.1' X 5.1'	150 BHP DIESEL	STEEL FIRE BOAT
151	116	1931	156480	AGASSIZ	B.C. DEPT. OF PUBLIC WORKS	140 GT	115.3' X 29.0' X 6.3'	340 BHP VIVIAN DIESEL	STEEL CAR FERRY
152	none	1934	158565	B.D.D NO. 6	BURRARD DRY DOCK CO. LTD.	36 GT	40.2' X 20.0' X 5.1'	NON PROPELLED	WOOD SCOW registered when built at Vancouver in 1934
153	117	1938	J.64	H.M.C.S. COMOX	ROYAL CANADIAN NAVY	460 DP	163.0' X 27.5' X 14.5'	850 IMP MIL STM. REC.	STEEL MINESWEEPER
154	118	1939	171815	FIFER	CAPT. W. CRAWFORD	194 GT	99.3' X 20.0' X 11.2'	240 BHP T/S MIRRLEES	STEEL DIESEL YACHT
155	none	1939	172302	CHUMMIE IV	BURRARD DRY DOCK CO. LTD.	9 GT	31.5' X 9.1' X 4.7'	60 BHP GARDNER DIESEL	WOODEN LAUNCH registered when built at Vancouver in 1939
156	119	1940	H.70	H.70 (H.C. 108)	ROYAL CANADIAN NAVY	100 DP	79.0' X 18.0' X 7.0'	70 BHP DIESEL	STEEL LIGHTER
157	120	1940	K175	H.M.C.S. WETASKIWIN (PV 55)	ROYAL CANADIAN NAVY	950 DP	190.0' X 33.0' X 13.5'd	2750 IHP BDD STM. REC.	FLOWER CLASS CORVETTE
158	121	1941	K129	H.M.C.S. AGASSIZ (PV 56)	ROYAL CANADIAN NAVY	950 DP	190.0' X 33.0' X 13.5'd	2750 IHP BDD STM. REC.	FLOWER CLASS CORVETTE
159	122	1941	K131	H.M.C.S. CHILLIWACK (PV 57)	ROYAL CANADIAN NAVY	950 DP	190.0' X 33.0' X 13.5'd	2750 IHP BDD STM. REC.	FLOWER CLASS CORVETTE
160	123	1941	K174	H.M.C.S. TRAIL (PV 58)	ROYAL CANADIAN NAVY	950 DP	190.0' X 33.0' X 13.5'd	2750 IHP BDD STM. REC.	FLOWER CLASS CORVETTE
161	124	1941	J162	H.M.C.S. WASAGA (MS 7)	ROYAL CANADIAN NAVY	672 DP	171.0' X 28.5' X 10.1'd	2400 IHP T/S CAC STM. REC.	BANGOR CLASS MINESWEEPER
162	125	1941	J165	H.M.C.S. MINAS (MS 8)	ROYAL CANADIAN NAVY	672 DP	171.0' X 28.5' X 10.1'd	2400 IHP T/S CAC STM. REC.	BANGOR CLASS MINESWEEPER
163	126	1941	J166	H.M.C.S. QUINTE (MS 9)	ROYAL CANADIAN NAVY	672 DP	171.0' X 28.5' X 10.1'd	2400 IHP T/S CAC STM. REC.	BANGOR CLASS MINESWEEPER
164	127	1941	J168	H.M.C.S. CHEDABUCTO (MS 10)	ROYAL CANADIAN NAVY	672 DP	171.0' X 28.5' X 10.1'd	2400 IHP T/S CAC STM. REC.	BANGOR CLASS MINESWEEPER
165	128	1941	J169	H.M.C.S. MIRAMICHI (MS 11)	ROYAL CANADIAN NAVY	672 DP	171.0' X 28.5' X 10.1'd	2400 IHP T/S CAC STM. REC.	BANGOR CLASS MINESWEEPER

Serial #	Hull #	Year	Reg.No.	Name	OWNERS	Tonnage	Dimensions	Propulsion	Type & Notes
166	129	1941	J170	H.M.C.S. BELLECHASE (MS 12)	ROYAL CANADIAN NAVY	672 DP	171.0' X 28.5' X 10.1'd	2400 IHP T/S CAC STM. REC.	BANGOR CLASS MINESWEEPER
167	130	1942	166053	FORT ST. JAMES	WARTIME MERCHANT SHIPPING LTD.	7128 GT	424.6' X 57.2' X 34.9'	2500 IHP DOM STM. REC.	NORTH SANDS FREIGHTER
168	131	1942	168557	FORT CHURCHILL	WARTIME MERCHANT SHIPPING LTD.	7129 GT	424.6' X 57.2' X 34.9'	2500 IHP DOM STM. REC.	NORTH SANDS FREIGHTER
169	132 VDD	1942	WAR LOSS	FORT QU'APPELLE	WARTIME MERCHANT SHIPPING LTD.	7127 GT	424.6' X 57.2' X 34.9'	2500 IHP DOM STM. REC.	NORTH SANDS FREIGHTER
170	133 VDD	1942	168827	FORT GEORGE	WARTIME MERCHANT SHIPPING LTD.	7129 GT	424.6' X 57.2' X 34.9'	2500 IHP DOM STM. REC.	NORTH SANDS FREIGHTER
171	134 VDD	1942	WAR LOSS	FORT GOOD HOPE	WARTIME MERCHANT SHIPPING LTD.	7130 GT	424.6' X 57.2' X 34.9'	2500 IHP DOM STM. REC.	NORTH SANDS FREIGHTER
172	135 VDD	1942	167860	FORT ELLICE	WARTIME MERCHANT SHIPPING LTD.	7129 GT	424.6' X 57.2' X 34.9'	2500 IHP DOM STM. REC.	NORTH SANDS FREIGHTER
173	136	1942	168725	FORT FRASER	WARTIME MERCHANT SHIPPING LTD.	7129 GT	424.6' X 57.2' X 34.9'	2500 IHP DOM STM. REC.	NORTH SANDS FREIGHTER
174	137	1942	169060	FORT McLOUGHLIN	WARTIME MERCHANT SHIPPING LTD.	7129 GT	424.6' X 57.2' X 34.9'	2500 IHP DOM STM. REC.	NORTH SANDS FREIGHTER
175	138 VDD	1942	WAR LOSS	FORT LA REINE	WARTIME MERCHANT SHIPPING LTD.	7133 GT	424.6' X 57.2' X 34.9'	2500 IHP DOM STM. REC.	NORTH SANDS FREIGHTER
176	139 VDD	1942	169065	FORT PINE	WARTIME MERCHANT SHIPPING LTD.	7133 GT	424.6' X 57.2' X 34.9'	2500 IHP DOM STM. REC.	NORTH SANDS FREIGHTER
177	140 VDD	1942	169276	FORT PEMBINA	WARTIME MERCHANT SHIPPING LTD.	7134 GT	424.6' X 57.2' X 34.9'	2500 IHP DOM STM. REC.	NORTH SANDS FREIGHTER
178	141 VDD	1942	165855	FORT KOOTENAY	WARTIME MERCHANT SHIPPING LTD.	7133 GT	424.6' X 57.2' X 34.9'	2500 IHP DOM STM. REC.	NORTH SANDS FREIGHTER
179	142	1942	169062	FORT LAC LA RONGE	WARTIME MERCHANT SHIPPING LTD.	7131 GT	424.6' X 57.2' X 34.9'	2500 IHP DOM STM. REC.	NORTH SANDS FREIGHTER
180	143	1942	168738	FORT PITT	WARTIME MERCHANT SHIPPING LTD.	7133 GT	424.6' X 57.2' X 34.9'	2500 IHP DOM STM. REC.	NORTH SANDS FREIGHTER
181	144 VDD	1942	168368	FORT RAE	WARTIME MERCHANT SHIPPING LTD.	7132 GT	424.6' X 57.2' X 34.9'	2500 IHP DOM STM. REC.	NORTH SANDS FREIGHTER
182	145 VDD	1942	168377	FORT RELIANCE	WARTIME MERCHANT SHIPPING LTD.	7134 GT	424.6' X 57.2' X 34.9'	2500 IHP DOM STM. REC.	NORTH SANDS FREIGHTER
183	146 VDD	1942	168361	FORT THOMPSON	WARTIME MERCHANT SHIPPING LTD.	7134 GT	424.6' X 57.2' X 34.9'	2500 IHP DOM STM. REC.	NORTH SANDS FREIGHTER
184	147 VDD	1942	168383	FORT WEDDERBURNE	WARTIME MERCHANT SHIPPING LTD.	7134 GT	424.6' X 57.2' X 34.9'	2500 IHP INGLIS STM. REC.	NORTH SANDS FREIGHTER
185	148	1942	168367	FORT FORK	WARTIME MERCHANT SHIPPING LTD.	7134 GT	424.6' X 57.2' X 34.9'	2500 IHP DOM STM. REC.	NORTH SANDS FREIGHTER
186	149	1942	168385	FORT POPLAR	WARTIME MERCHANT SHIPPING LTD.	7134 GT	424.6' X 57.2' X 34.9'	2500 IHP DOM STM. REC.	NORTH SANDS FREIGHTER
187	150 VDD	1942	WAR LOSS	FORT HACKETT	WARTIME MERCHANT SHIPPING LTD.	7133 GT	424.6' X 57.2' X 34.9'	2500 IHP DOM STM. REC.	NORTH SANDS FREIGHTER
188	151 VDD	1942	WAR LOSS	FORT YALE	WARTIME MERCHANT SHIPPING LTD.	7134 GT	424.6' X 57.2' X 34.9'	2500 IHP DOM STM. REC.	NORTH SANDS FREIGHTER
189	152 VDD	1942	168413	FORT ANNE	WARTIME MERCHANT SHIPPING LTD.	7134 GT	424.6' X 57.2' X 34.9'	2500 IHP DOM STM. REC.	NORTH SANDS FREIGHTER
190	153 VDD	1943	WAR LOSS	FORT JEMSEG	WARTIME MERCHANT SHIPPING LTD.	7134 GT	424.6' X 57.2' X 34.9'	2500 IHP INGLIS STM. REC.	NORTH SANDS FREIGHTER
191	154	1942	168404	FORT LIVINGSTONE	WARTIME MERCHANT SHIPPING LTD.	7135 GT	424.6' X 57.2' X 34.9'	2500 IHP DOM STM. REC.	NORTH SANDS FREIGHTER
192	155	1943	169883	FORT LAWERENCE	WARTIME MERCHANT SHIPPING LTD.	7134 GT	424.6' X 57.2' X 34.9'	2500 IHP DOM STM. REC.	NORTH SANDS FREIGHTER
193	156 VDD	1943	169734	FORT GASPEREAU	WARTIME MERCHANT SHIPPING LTD.	7134 GT	424.6' X 57.2' X 34.9'	2500 IHP DOM STM. REC.	NORTH SANDS FREIGHTER
194	157 VDD	1943	168431	FORT CHARNISAY	WARTIME MERCHANT SHIPPING LTD.	7133 GT	424.6' X 57.2' X 34.9'	2500 IHP DOM STM. REC.	NORTH SANDS FREIGHTER
195	158 VDD	1943	168441	FORT AKLAVIK	WARTIME MERCHANT SHIPPING LTD.	7132 GT	424.6' X 57.2' X 34.9'	2500 IHP DOM STM. REC.	NORTH SANDS FREIGHTER
196	159 VDD	1943	168448	FORT CADOTTE	WARTIME MERCHANT SHIPPING LTD.	7128 GT	424.6' X 57.2' X 34.9'	2500 IHP DOM STM. REC.	NORTH SANDS FREIGHTER
197	160	1943	168428	FORT NASHWAAK	WARTIME MERCHANT SHIPPING LTD.	7134 GT	424.6' X 57.2' X 34.9'	2500 IHP DOM STM. REC.	NORTH SANDS FREIGHTER
198	161	1943	168447	FORT BEDFORD	WARTIME MERCHANT SHIPPING LTD.	7127 GT	424.6' X 57.2' X 34.9'	2500 IHP DOM STM. REC.	NORTH SANDS FREIGHTER
199	162 VDD	1943	168456	FORT CHESTERFIELD	WARTIME MERCHANT SHIPPING LTD.	7127 GT	424.6' X 57.2' X 34.9'	2500 IHP CAC STM. REC.	NORTH SANDS FREIGHTER
200	163 VDD	1943	168472	FORT DEASE LAKE	WARTIME MERCHANT SHIPPING LTD.	7126 GT	424.6' X 57.2' X 34.9'	2500 IHP DOM STM. REC.	NORTH SANDS FREIGHTER
201	164	1943	168350	FORT McMURRAY	WARTIME MERCHANT SHIPPING LTD.	7133 GT	424.6' X 57.2' X 34.9'	2500 IHP DOM STM. REC.	NORTH SANDS FREIGHTER
202	165	1943	168376	FORT VERMILLION	WARTIME MERCHANT SHIPPING LTD.	7133 GT	424.6' X 57.2' X 34.9'	2500 IHP DOM STM. REC.	NORTH SANDS FREIGHTER
203	166	1943	WAR LOSS	FORT HOWE	WARTIME MERCHANT SHIPPING LTD.	7133 GT	424.6' X 57.2' X 34.9'	2500 IHP CAC STM. REC.	NORTH SANDS FREIGHTER
204	167	1943	168438	FORT LAJOIE	WARTIME MERCHANT SHIPPING LTD.	7134 GT	424.6' X 57.2' X 34.9'	2500 IHP CAC STM. REC.	NORTH SANDS FREIGHTER
205	168	1943	168429	FORT MEDUCTIC	WARTIME MERCHANT SHIPPING LTD.	7134 GT	424.6' X 57.2' X 34.9'	2500 IHP DOM STM. REC.	NORTH SANDS FREIGHTER
206	169	1943	WAR LOSS	FORT BUCKINGHAM	WARTIME MERCHANT SHIPPING LTD.	7122 GT	424.6' X 57.2' X 34.9'	2500 IHP DOM STM. REC.	NORTH SANDS FREIGHTER
207	170	1943	168466	FORT CONNOLLY	WARTIME MERCHANT SHIPPING LTD.	7133 GT	424.6' X 57.2' X 34.9'	2500 IHP CAC STM. REC.	NORTH SANDS FREIGHTER
208	171 VDD	1943	168485	FORT CARIBOU	WARTIME MERCHANT SHIPPING LTD.	7132 GT	424.6' X 57.2' X 34.9'	2500 IHP CAC STM. REC.	NORTH SANDS FREIGHTER
209	172 VDD	1943	169575	FORT CUMBERLAND	WARTIME MERCHANT SHIPPING LTD.	7134 GT	424.6' X 57.2' X 34.9'	2500 IHP DOM STM. REC.	NORTH SANDS FREIGHTER
210	173	1943	168480	FORT ASSINIBOINE	WARTIME MERCHANT SHIPPING LTD.	7128 GT	424.6' X 57.2' X 34.9'	2500 IHP DOM STM. REC.	NORTH SANDS FREIGHTER
211	174	1943	168470	FORT ASH	WARTIME MERCHANT SHIPPING LTD.	7131 GT	424.6' X 57.2' X 34.9'	2500 IHP DOM STM. REC.	NORTH SANDS FREIGHTER
212	175	1943	WAR LOSS	FORT ATHABASKA	WARTIME MERCHANT SHIPPING LTD.	7132 GT	424.6' X 57.2' X 34.9'	2500 IHP INGLIS STM. REC.	NORTH SANDS FREIGHTER
213	176 VDD	1943	169565	FORT DAUPHIN	WARTIME MERCHANT SHIPPING LTD.	7133 GT	424.6' X 57.2' X 34.9'	2500 IHP INGLIS STM. REC.	NORTH SANDS FREIGHTER
214	177 VDD	1943	174163	MOHAWK PARK	PARK STEAMSHIP COMPANY	7128 GT	424.6' X 57.2' X 34.9'	2500 IHP CAC STM. REC.	NORTH SANDS FREIGHTER
215	178	1943	169580	FORT BELL	WARTIME MERCHANT SHIPPING LTD.	7128 GT	424.6' X 57.2' X 34.9'	2500 IHP INGLIS STM. REC.	NORTH SANDS FREIGHTER
216	179	1943	169585	FORT BRANDON	WARTIME MERCHANT SHIPPING LTD.	7129 GT	424.6' X 57.2' X 34.9'	2500 IHP INGLIS STM. REC.	NORTH SANDS FREIGHTER
217	180	1943	169609	FORT COLUMBIA	WARTIME MERCHANT SHIPPING LTD.	7155 GT	424.6' X 57.2' X 34.9'	2500 IHP INGLIS STM. REC.	VICTORY FREIGHTER
218	181 VDD	1943	169616	FORT YUKON	WARTIME MERCHANT SHIPPING LTD.	7153 GT	424.6' X 57.2' X 34.9'	2500 IHP INGLIS STM. REC.	VICTORY FREIGHTER

Serial #	Hull #	Year	Reg.No.	Name	OWNERS	Tonnage	Dimensions	Propulsion	Type & Notes
219	182	1943	WAR LOSS	FORT BELLINGHAM	WARTIME MERCHANT SHIPPING LTD.	7150 GT	424.6' X 57.2' X 34.9'	2500 IHP DOM STM. REC.	VICTORY FREIGHTER
220	183 VDD	1943	174798	WASCANA PARK	PARK STEAMSHIP COMPANY	7152 GT	424.6' X 57.2' X 34.9'	2500 IHP INGLIS STM. REC.	VICTORY FREIGHTER
221	184	1943	174802	STRATHCONA PARK	PARK STEAMSHIP COMPANY	7150 GT	424.6' X 57.2' X 34.9'	2500 IHP INGLIS STM. REC.	VICTORY FREIGHTER
222	185 VDD	1943	169992	FORT MASSAC	WARTIME MERCHANT SHIPPING LTD.	7157 GT	424.6' X 57.2' X 34.9'	2500 IHP CAC STM. REC.	VICTORY FREIGHTER
223	186	1943	WAR LOSS	FORT ST. NICHOLAS	WARTIME MERCHANT SHIPPING LTD.	7154 GT	424.6' X 57.2' X 34.9'	2500 IHP DOM STM. REC.	VICTORY FREIGHTER
224	187 VDD	1943	169706	FORT PRUDHOMME	WARTIME MERCHANT SHIPPING LTD.	7167 GT	424.6' X 57.2' X 34.9'	2500 IHP DOM STM. REC.	VICTORY FREIGHTER
225	188	1943	169945	FORT SAKISDAC	WARTIME MERCHANT SHIPPING LTD.	7160 GT	424.6' X 57.2' X 34.9'	2500 IHP DOM STM. REC.	VICTORY FREIGHTER
226	189 VDD	1943	169733	FORT VENANGO	WARTIME MERCHANT SHIPPING LTD.	7166 GT	424.6' X 57.2' X 34.9'	2500 IHP CAC STM. REC.	VICTORY FREIGHTER
227	190	1943	180009	FORT MACHAULT	WARTIME MERCHANT SHIPPING LTD.	7160 GT	424.6' X 57.2' X 34.9'	2500 IHP INGLIS STM. REC.	VICTORY FREIGHTER
228	191 VDD	1943	180045	FORT ORLEANS	WARTIME MERCHANT SHIPPING LTD.	7180 GT	424.6' X 57.2' X 34.9'	2500 IHP CAC STM. REC.	VICTORY FREIGHTER
229	192	1943	174820	BEATON PARK	PARK STEAMSHIP COMPANY	7164 GT	424.6' X 57.2' X 34.9'	2500 IHP INGLIS STM. REC.	VICTORY FREIGHTER
230	193 VDD	1943	169769	FORT ST. CROIX	WARTIME MERCHANT SHIPPING LTD.	7160 GT	424.6' X 57.2' X 34.9'	2500 IHP INGLIS STM. REC.	VICTORY FREIGHTER
231	194	1943	169839	FORT BILOXI	WARTIME MERCHANT SHIPPING LTD.	7161 GT	424.6' X 57.2' X 34.9'	2500 IHP INGLIS STM. REC.	VICTORY FREIGHTER
232	195 VDD	1944	175355	SAPPERTON PARK	PARK STEAMSHIP COMPANY	7166 GT	424.6' X 57.2' X 34.9'	2500 IHP DOM STM. REC.	VICTORY FREIGHTER
233	196	1944	169828	FORT DEARBORN	WARTIME MERCHANT SHIPPING LTD.	7160 GT	424.6' X 57.2' X 34.9'	2500 IHP INGLIS STM. REC.	VICTORY FREIGHTER
234	197 VDD	1944	175360	GREEN HILL PARK	PARK STEAMSHIP COMPANY	7168 GT	424.6' X 57.2' X 34.9'	2500 IHP INGLIS STM. REC.	VICTORY FREIGHTER
235	198	1944	175361	MEWATA PARK	PARK STEAMSHIP COMPANY	7161 GT	424.6' X 57.2' X 34.9'	2500 IHP CAC STM. REC.	VICTORY FREIGHTER
236	199 VDD	1944	175363	LOUISBOURG PARK	PARK STEAMSHIP COMPANY	7160 GT	424.6' X 57.2' X 34.9'	2500 IHP CAC STM. REC.	VICTORY FREIGHTER
237	200	1944	169854	FORT WALLACE	WARTIME MERCHANT SHIPPING LTD.	7161 GT	424.6' X 57.2' X 34.9'	2500 IHP CAC STM. REC.	VICTORY FREIGHTER
238	201 VDD	1944	175367	TIPPERARY PARK	PARK STEAMSHIP COMPANY	7161 GT	424.6' X 57.2' X 34.9'	2500 IHP DOM STM. REC.	VICTORY FREIGHTER
239	202	1944	169912	FORT LA HAVE	WARTIME MERCHANT SHIPPING LTD.	7166 GT	424.6' X 57.2' X 34.9'	2500 IHP DOM STM. REC.	VICTORY FREIGHTER
240	203 VDD	1944	169867	FORT ISLAND	WARTIME MERCHANT SHIPPING LTD.	7167 GT	424.6' X 57.2' X 34.9'	2500 IHP INGLIS STM. REC.	VICTORY FREIGHTER
241	204	1944	169893	FORT BRISEBOIS	WARTIME MERCHANT SHIPPING LTD.	7157 GT	424.6' X 57.2' X 34.9'	2500 IHP DOM STM. REC.	VICTORY FREIGHTER
242	205 VDD	1944	175373	ASPEN PARK	PARK STEAMSHIP COMPANY	7158 GT	424.6' X 57.2' X 34.9'	2500 IHP DOM STM. REC.	VICTORY FREIGHTER
243	206	1944	180002	FORT DUNVEGAN	WARTIME MERCHANT SHIPPING LTD.	7225 GT	424.6' X 57.2' X 34.9'	2500 IHP CAC STM. REC.	VICTORY FREIGHTER
244	207 VDD	1944	169996	FORT CONSTANTINE	WARTIME MERCHANT SHIPPING LTD.	7221 GT	424.6' X 57.2' X 34.9'	2500 IHP CAC STM. REC.	VICTORY FREIGHTER
245	208	1944	169995	FORT KILMAR	WARTIME MERCHANT SHIPPING LTD.	7200 GT	424.6' X 57.2' X 34.9'	2500 IHP DOM STM. REC.	VICTORY FREIGHTER
246	209 VDD	1944	180003	FORT PROVIDENCE	WARTIME MERCHANT SHIPPING LTD.	7201 GT	424.6' X 57.2' X 34.9'	2500 IHP CAC STM. REC.	VICTORY FREIGHTER
247	210	1944	169999	FORT McDONNELL	WARTIME MERCHANT SHIPPING LTD.	7203 GT	424.6' X 57.2' X 34.9'	2500 IHP INGLIS STM. REC.	VICTORY FREIGHTER
248	211 VDD	1944	170000	FORT ALABAMA	WARTIME MERCHANT SHIPPING LTD.	7202 GT	424.6' X 57.2' X 34.9'	2500 IHP CAC STM. REC.	VICTORY FREIGHTER
249	212	1944	180001	FORT EDMONTON	WARTIME MERCHANT SHIPPING LTD.	7202 GT	424.6' X 57.2' X 34.9'	2500 IHP CAC STM. REC.	VICTORY FREIGHTER
250	213 VDD	1944	175397	BOWNESS PARK	PARK STEAMSHIP COMPANY	7165 GT	424.6' X 57.2' X 34.9'	2500 IHP CAC STM. REC.	VICTORY FREIGHTER
251	214	1944	175573	WESTEND PARK	PARK STEAMSHIP COMPANY	7166 GT	424.6' X 57.2' X 34.9'	2500 IHP DOM STM. REC.	VICTORY FREIGHTER
252	215 VDD	1944	175578	DUNLOP PARK	PARK STEAMSHIP COMPANY	7165 GT	424.6' X 57.2' X 34.9'	2500 IHP DOM STM. REC.	VICTORY FREIGHTER
253	216	1944	175587	TOBIATIC PARK	PARK STEAMSHIP COMPANY	7163 GT	424.6' X 57.2' X 34.9'	2500 IHP DOM STM. REC.	VICTORY FREIGHTER
254	217 VDD	1944	175595	MOHAWK PARK	PARK STEAMSHIP COMPANY	7128 GT	424.6' X 57.2' X 34.9'	2500 IHP CAC STM. REC.	VICTORY FREIGHTER
255	218	1944	175597	KOOTENAY PARK	PARK STEAMSHIP COMPANY	7162 GT	424.6' X 57.2' X 34.9'	2500 IHP CAC STM. REC.	VICTORY FREIGHTER
256	219 VDD	1944	175602	SEACLIFF PARK	PARK STEAMSHIP COMPANY	7163 GT	424.6' X 57.2' X 34.9'	2500 IHP GEN. MACH. STM. REC.	VICTORY FREIGHTER
257	220	1944	175607	CORONATION PARK	PARK STEAMSHIP COMPANY	7162 GT	424.6' X 57.2' X 34.9'	2500 IHP GEN. MACH. STM. REC.	VICTORY FREIGHTER
258	221 VDD	1944	179218	FORT WRANGELL	WARTIME MERCHANT SHIPPING LTD.	7213 GT	424.6' X 57.2' X 34.9'	2500 IHP GEN. MACH. STM. REC.	STORES ISSUING SHIP
259	none	1944	175640	CHUMMIE V	BURRARD DRY DOCK CO. LTD.	13 GT	38.6' X 10.1' X 5.3'	100 BHP CUMMINS DIESEL	WOODEN LAUNCH registered when built at Vancouver in 1944
260	222	1945	CN 998	H.M.S. BEACHY HEAD	ROYAL NAVY	8580 DP	424.6' X 57.2' X 34.9'	2500 IHP GEN. MACH. STM. REC.	MAINTENANCE SHIP
261	223 VDD	1945	CN 1004	H.M.S. FLAMBOROUGH HEAD	ROYAL NAVY	8580 DP	424.6' X 57.2' X 34.9'	2500 IHP STM. REC.	MAINTENANCE SHIP
262	224	1945	CN 999	H.M.S. BERRY HEAD	ROYAL NAVY	8580 DP	424.6' X 57.2' X 34.9'	2500 IHP CAC STM. REC.	MAINTENANCE SHIP
263	225 VDD	1945	CN 1005	H.M.S. HARTLAND POINT	ROYAL NAVY	8580 DP	424.6' X 57.2' X 34.9'	2500 IHP CAC STM. REC.	MAINTENANCE SHIP
264	226	1945	CN 1000	H.M.S. DUNCANSBY HEAD	ROYAL NAVY	8580 DP	424.6' X 57.2' X 34.9'	2500 IHP CAC STM. REC.	MAINTENANCE SHIP
265	227 VDD	1945	176004	FAIRMOUNT PARK	PARK STEAMSHIP COMPANY	7145 GT	424.6' X 57.2' X 34.9'	2500 IHP DOM STM. REC.	CANADIAN TYPE FREIGHTER
266	228	1945	176006	CROMWELL PARK	PARK STEAMSHIP COMPANY	7147 GT	424.6' X 57.2' X 34.9'	2500 IHP DOM STM. REC.	CANADIAN TYPE FREIGHTER
267	229 VDD	1945	176007	PRINCETON PARK	PARK STEAMSHIP COMPANY	7149 GT	424.6' X 57.2' X 34.9'	2500 IHP DOM STM. REC.	CANADIAN TYPE FREIGHTER
268	230	1945	176011	GARDEN PARK	PARK STEAMSHIP COMPANY	7148 GT	424.6' X 57.2' X 34.9'	2500 IHP DOM STM. REC.	CANADIAN TYPE FREIGHTER
269	231 VDD	1945	176014	ALBERT PARK	PARK STEAMSHIP COMPANY	7145 GT	424.6' X 57.2' X 34.9'	2500 IHP DOM STM. REC.	CANADIAN TYPE FREIGHTER

Serial #	Hull #	Year	Reg.No.	Name	OWNERS	Tonnage	Dimensions	Propulsion	Type & Notes
270	232	1945	176017	RUPERT PARK	PARK STEAMSHIP COMPANY	7148 GT	424.6' X 57.2' X 34.9'	2500 IHP DOM STM. REC.	CANADIAN TYPE FREIGHTER
271	233 VDD	1945	CN 1006	H.M.S. GIRDLE NESS	ROYAL NAVY	8580 DP	424.6' X 57.2' X 34.9'	2500 IHP DOM STM. REC.	MAINTENANCE SHIP
272	234	1945	CN 1001	H.M.S. DODMAN POINT	ROYAL NAVY	8580 DP	424.6' X 57.2' X 34.9'	2500 IHP CAC STM. REC.	MAINTENANCE SHIP
273	235 VDD	1945	CN 1007	H.M.S. FIFE NESS	ROYAL NAVY	8580 DP	424.6' X 57.2' X 34.9'	2500 IHP DOM STM. REC.	MAINTENANCE SHIP
274	236	1945	CN 1002	H.M.S. PORTLAND BILL	ROYAL NAVY	8580 DP	424.6' X 57.2' X 34.9'	2500 IHP DOM STM. REC.	MAINTENANCE SHIP
275	237 VDD	1945	CN 1008	H.M.S. SPURN POINT	ROYAL NAVY	8580 DP	424.6' X 57.2' X 34.9'	2500 IHP CAC STM. REC.	MAINTENANCE SHIP
276	238	1946	CN 1003	H.M.S. SELSEY BILL	ROYAL NAVY	8580 DP	424.6' X 57.2' X 34.9'	2500 IHP DOM STM. REC.	MAINTENANCE SHIP
277	239 VDD	1945	CN 1027	L.S.T. 3538	ROYAL NAVY			LD. APR.2/45 LAUNCHED JUL. 11/45 FOR COMP. AS LOG BARGE BY WCSB	LST MARK 3 (ISLAND LOGGER, ON 176661 or ISLAND YARDER, ON 177982)
278	240	SCRAP	CN 1028	L.S.T. 3539	ROYAL NAVY			LD. APR.15/45 SCRAPPED ON BERTH	LST MARK 3
279	240 VDD	SCRAP	CN 1030	L.S.T. 3541	ROYAL NAVY			LD. MAY 23/45 SCRAPPED ON BERTH	LST MARK 3
280	242	SCRAP	CN 1031	L.S.T. 3542	ROYAL NAVY			LD. MAY 5/45 SCRAPPED ON BERTH	LST MARK 3
281	243 VDD	1946	176563	OTTAWA PAGE	BRITISH MINISTRY OF WAR TRANSPORT	1340 GT	214.1' X 36.7' X 19.8'	900 IHP CAC STM.REC.	B TYPE COASTER
282	244	SCRAP	CN 1051	L.S.T. 3555	ROYAL NAVY			LD. JUL.24/45 SCRAPPED ON BERTH	LST MARK 3
283	245 VDD	1946	CHINA	OTTAWA PALMER	BRITISH MINISTRY OF WAR TRANSPORT	1340 GT	214.1' X 36.7' X 19.8'	900 IHP CAC STM.REC.	B TYPE COASTER
284	246	CANC	CN 1052	L.S.T. 3556	ROYAL NAVY				LST MARK 3
285	247 VDD	1946	CHINA	OTTAWA PARADE	BRITISH MINISTRY OF WAR TRANSPORT	1340 GT	214.1' X 36.7' X 19.8'	900 IHP CAC STM.REC.	B TYPE COASTER
286	248	CANC	CN 1053	L.S.T. 3557	ROYAL NAVY				LST MARK 3
287	249 VDD	1946	PHILIP.	OTTAWA PATIENCE	BRITISH MINISTRY OF WAR TRANSPORT	1340 GT	214.1' X 36.7' X 19.8'	900 IHP CAC STM.REC.	B TYPE COASTER
288	250	CANC	CN 1054	L.S.T. 3558	ROYAL NAVY				LST MARK 3
289	251	1946	PHILIP.	OTTAWA PANGIS	BRITISH MINISTRY OF WAR TRANSPORT	1340 GT	214.1' X 36.7' X 19.8'	900 IHP CAC STM.REC.	B TYPE COASTER
290	252	CANC	CN 1055	L.S.T. 3559	ROYAL NAVY				LST MARK 3
291	253	1946	PHILIP.	OTTAWA PAGEANT	BRITISH MINISTRY OF WAR TRANSPORT	1340 GT	214.1' X 36.7' X 19.8'	900 IHP CAC STM.REC.	B TYPE COASTER
292	254	1947	177872	CANADIAN CONSTRUCTOR	CANADIAN NATIONAL STEAMSHIPS	6745 GT	418.0' X 59.2' X 32.3'	6000 BHP CV/DOXFORD DIESEL	CARGO/PASSENGER FREIGHTER
293	none	1946	176903	CAMOSUN	UNION STEAMSHIP COMPANY	1835 GT	235.7' 36.0' X 22.2'	2800IHP S/S STEAM REC. PASSENGER VESSEL	CONVERSION OF CORVETTE TO
294	255	1948	FRANCE	VAIRES	GOV' T OF FRANCE	3630 GT	372.0' X 48.0' X 20.0'	1560 IHP CV UNIFLOW STM	COLLIER
295	256	1948	FRANCE	LONGEAU	GOV' T OF FRANCE	3630 GT	372.0' X 48.0' X 20.0'	1560 IHP CV UNIFLOW STM	COLLIER
296	257	1948	FRANCE	TERGNIER	GOV' T OF FRANCE	3630 GT	372.0' X 48.0' X 20.0'	1560 IHP CV UNIFLOW STM	COLLIER
297	258	1948	FRANCE	S.N.A.3 (ACHERES)	GOV' T OF FRANCE	3630 GT	372.0' X 48.0' X 20.0'	1560 IHP CV UNIFLOW STM	COLLIER
298	259	1948	FRANCE	SOTTEVILLE	GOV' T OF FRANCE	5630 GT	413.0' X 51.0' X 24.0'	2900 SHP INGLIS STM TURB.	COLLIER
299	260	1948	FRANCE	VENISSIEUX	GOV' T OF FRANCE	5547 GT	413.0' X 51.0' X 24.0'	2900 SHP INGLIS STM TURB.	COLLIER
300	261	1948	FRANCE	CARONTE	GOV' T OF FRANCE	5370 GT	413.0' X 51.0' X 24.0'	2900 SHP INGLIS STM TURB.	COLLIER
301	262	1948	FRANCE	PENZE	GOV' T OF FRANCE	5435 GT	413.0' X 51.0' X 24.0'	2900 SHP INGLIS STM TURB.	COLLIER
302	263	1948	FRANCE	ASTREE'	GOV' T OF FRANCE	5438 GT	413.0' X 51.0' X 24.0'	2900 SHP INGLIS STM TURB.	COLLIER
303	264	1948	FRANCE	BAREE'	GOV' T OF FRANCE	5438 GT	413.0' X 51.0' X 24.0'	2900 SHP INGLIS STM TURB.	COLLIER
304	265	1949	FRANCE	HEBE	GOV' T OF FRANCE	5437 GT	413.0' X 51.0' X 24.0'	2900 SHP INGLIS STM TURB.	COLLIER
305	266	1950	192757	ALEXANDER MACKENZIE	DEPT. OF TRANSPORT	576 GT	142.6' X 30.2' X 12.6'	1000 BHP T/S VIVIAN DIES.	BUOY TENDER
306	267	1957	DDE 207	H.M.C.S. SKEENA	ROYAL CANADIAN NAVY	2263 DP	366.0' X 42.0' X 13.1'd	30,000 SHP T/S ST.TURB.	DESTROYER ESCORT
307	268	1957	DDE 233	H.M.C.S. FRASER	ROYAL CANADIAN NAVY	2263 DP	366.0' X 42.0' X 13.1'd	30,000 SHP T/S ST.TURB.	DDE (COMPLETED BY YARROWS)
308	269	1952	YMG 185	H.M.C.S. PORTE QUEBEC	ROYAL CANADIAN NAVY	429 DP	125.5' X 26.3' X 13.0'd	600 SHP DIESEL ELECT.	GATE VESSEL
309	270	1959	DDE 258	H.M.C.S. KOOTENAY	ROYAL CANADIAN NAVY	2366 DP	366.0' X 42.0' X 13.5'd	30,000 SHP T/S ST.TURB.	DESTROYER ESCORT
310	271	1959	DDE 260	H.M.C.S. COLUMBIA	ROYAL CANADIAN NAVY	2366 DP	366.0' X 42.0' X 13.5'd	30,000 SHP T/S ST.TURB.	DESTROYER ESCORT
311	272	1951	194664	HARMAC 50	MACMILLAN & BLOEDEL LTD.	419 GT	120.0' X 40.0' X 10.1'	NON PROPELLED	CHIP SCOW
BURRARD DRY DOCK BOUGHT PACIFIC DRYDOCK CO. LTD. MAY 02/51 AND OVER THE NEXT THREE YEARS OPERATED BOTH FACILITIES AND BUILT SEVEN HULLS AT THAT SITE									
312	273	1952	194865	K. 42	MCKEEN & WILSON LTD.	506 GT	124.0' X 42.1' X 10.7'	NON PROPELLED	CHIP SCOW
313	274	1956	YMF 250	YMF 250	ROYAL CANADIAN NAVY	650 DP	120.0' X 60.0' X 9.3'	NON PROPELLED	DERRICK BARGE (blt. at PACIFIC DD. Site)
314	275	1952	195441	B.A. 10	THE BRITISH AMERICAN OIL CO.	104 GT	75.0' X 26.0' X 4.6'	NON PROPELLED	OIL SCOW
315	276	1956	YMF 252	YMF 252	ROYAL CANADIAN NAVY	650 DP	120.0' X 60.0' X 9.3'	NON PROPELLED	DERRICK BARGE (blt. at PACIFIC DD. Site)

Serial #	Hull #	Year	Reg.No.	Name	OWNERS	Tonnage	Dimensions	Propulsion	Type & Notes
316	none	1952	194688	C.C.C.-WOODS NO. 1	COLUMBIA CELLULOSE CO. LTD.	66 GT	60.0' X 25.1' X 5.3'	NON PROPELLED	WOODEN SCOW (blt. at PACIFIC DD. Site, registered when built)
317	277	1951	195890	STRAITS NO. 9	STRAITS TOWING LTD.	395 GT	110.1' X 40.0' X 10.7'	NON PROPELLED	WOODEN CHIP SCOW (blt. at PACIFIC DD. Site)
318	none	1957	FEE 303	H.M.C.S. BEACON HILL	ROYAL CANADIAN NAVY	1570 DP			Conversion Of WWII frigate into PRESTONIAN class escort vessel
319	278	1954	198075	POWELL NO.1	POWELL RIVER CO.	3730 GT	342.7' X 63.1' X 19.3'	NON PROPELLED	S/D LOG BARGE
320	279	1954	198105	POWELL NO. 2	POWELL RIVER CO.	3731 GT	342.7' X 63.1' X 19.3'	NON PROPELLED	S/D LOG BARGE
321	280	1954	197671	K. 40	MCKEEN & WILSON LTD.	546 GT	126.0' X 44.0' X 11.2'	NON PROPELLED	WOODEN CHIP SCOW (blt. at PACIFIC DD. Site)
322	281	1954	197709	K. 41	MCKEEN & WILSON LTD.	545 GT	126.0' X 44.0' X 11.2'	NON PROPELLED	WOODEN CHIP SCOW (blt. at PACIFIC DD. Site)
323	282	1954	198073	K. 43	MCKEEN & WILSON LTD.	540 GT	126.0' X 44.0' X 11.1'	NON PROPELLED	WOODEN CHIP SCOW (blt. at PACIFIC DD. Site)
324	283	1956	188698	SIR JAMES DOUGLAS	DEPT. OF TRANSPORT	564 GT	142.6' X 30.1' X 11.6'	1140 BHP T/S CROSSLEY DIESEL	BUOY TENDER
325	284	1954	198106	STRAITS NO. 24	STRAITS TOWING LTD.	508 GT	130.0' X 43.0' X 10.1'	NON PROPELLED	CHIP SCOW
326	285	1955	198646	SKEENA NO. 1	COLUMBIA CELLULOSE CO. LTD.	97 GT	90.0' X 28.0' X 4.4'	NON PROPELLED	FLAT SCOW
327	286	1955	198984	STRAITS NO. 26	STRAITS TOWING LTD.	564 GT	140.0' X 44.1' X 10.1'	NON PROPELLED	CHIP SCOW
328	287	1955	198991	V.P.D. DERRICK NO. 1	VANCOUVER PILE DRIVING & CON. CO. LTD.	210 GT	190.0' X 34.0' X 7.5'	NON PROPELLED	DERRICK SCOW
329	288	1956	188319	V.T. NO. 57	VANCOUVER TUG BOAT CO. LTD.	1055 GT	235.0' X 43.1' X 12.0'	NON PROPELLED	COVERED PAPER BARGE
330	289	1956	188354	V.T. NO. 58	VANCOUVER TUG & BARGE CO. LTD	1055 GT	235.0' X 43.1' X 12.0'	NON PROPELLED	COVERED PAPER BARGE
331	290	1956	none	not named	DEPT. OF TRANSPORT	not meas.	28.0' X 14.0' X 4.5'	NON PROPELLED	SCOW
332	291	1956	198840	ISLAND TUG 55	ISLAND TUG & BARGE LTD.	545 GT	140.0' X 43.1' X 10.0'	NON PROPELLED	CHIP SCOW
333	292	1956	198841	ISLAND TUG 56	ISLAND TUG & BARGE LTD.	545 GT	140.0' X 43.1' X 10.0'	NON PROPELLED,	CHIP SCOW
334	293	1956	188244	H.B.C. BARGE NO. 260	HUDSON'S BAY CO.	216 GT	115.0' X 30.1' X 7.0'	NON PROPELLED	RIVER BARGE
335	294	1956	188245	H.B.C. BARGE NO. 261	HUDSON'S BAY CO.	216 GT	115.0' X 30.1' X 7.0'	NON PROPELLED	RIVER BARGE
336	295	1956	188663	H.S.P. NO. 1	CANADIAN FOREST PRODUCTS LTD.	595 GT	150.0' X 43.1' X 10.1'	NON PROPELLED	CHIP SCOW
337	296	1956	188664	H.S.P. NO. 2	CANADIAN FOREST PRODUCTS LTD.	595 GT	150.0' X 43.1' X 10.1'	NON PROPELLED	CHIP SCOW
338	297	1956	189239	V.T. NO. 56	VANCOUVER TUG BOAT CO. LTD.	922 GT	175.0' X 48.1' X 12.9'	NON PROPELLED	FLAT DECK SCOW
339	298	1957	189296	STRAITS COLD DECKER	STRAITS TOWING LTD.	2389 GT	285.3' X 60.1' X 15.8'	NON PROPELLED	S/D LOG BARGE
340	299	1957	189969	STRAITS WATER SKIDDER	STRAITS TOWING LTD.	2390 GT	285.3' X 60.1' X 15.8'	NON PROPELLED	S/D LOG BARGE
341	300	1957	189998	CROWN ZELLERBACH NO. 5	CROWN ZELLERBACH CANADA LTD.	2385 GT	285.3' X 60.1' X 15.8'	NON PROPELLED	S/D LOG BARGE
342	301	1957	189999	CROWN ZELLERBACH NO. 6	CROWN ZELLERBACH CANADA LTD.	2384 GT	285.3' X 60.1' X 15.8'	NON PROPELLED	S/D LOG BARGE
343	302	1957	189978	CROWN ZELLERBACH NO. 7	CROWN ZELLERBACH CANADA LTD.	264 GT	90.0' X 48.0' X 6.5'	NON PROPELLED	CRANE LIGHTER
344	303	1957	310352	CROWN ZELLERBACH NO. 8	CROWN ZELLERBACH CANADA LTD.	811 GT	175.0' X 48.1' X 11.0'	NON PROPELLED	CHIP SCOW
345	304	1957	310354	STRAITS NO. 102	STRAITS TOWING LTD.	592 GT	150.0' X 43.1' X 10.1'	NON PROPELLED	CHIP SCOW
346	305	1959	310150	CAMSELL	DEPT. OF TRANSPORT	2022 GT	210.4' X 48.2' X 18.1'	5332 BHP T/S DIESEL EL.	ICEBREAKER (outfitted at Yarrows)
347	306	1959	313105	SIMON FRASER	DEPT. OF TRANSPORT	1353 GT	193.3' X 42.1' X 16.1'	3332 BHP T/S DIESEL EL.	ICEBREAKER/BUOY TENDER
348	307	1958	310428	G. of G. NO. 100	GULF OF GEORGIA TOWING CO. LTD.	352 GT	110.0' X 36.0' X 10.1'	NON PROPELLED	FLAT DECK SCOW
349	308	1958	310429	G. of G. NO. 101	GULF OF GEORGIA TOWING CO. LTD.	152 GT	110.0' X 36.0' X 10.1'	NON PROPELLED	FLAT DECK SCOW
350	309	1960	312277	TSAWWASSEN	B.C. TOLL HIGHWAYS & BRIDGES AUTH.	3127 GT	310.2' X 74.2' X 16.8'	6000 BHP T/S DIESEL	PASS/CAR FERRY
351	310	1963	DDE 263	H.M.C.S. YUKON	ROYAL CANADIAN NAVY	2380 DP	366.0' X 42.0' X 13.0'd	30,000 SHP T/S TURBINE	DESTROYER ESCORT
352	311	1962	318636	CITY OF VANCOUVER	B.C. TOLL HIGHWAYS & BRIDGES AUTH.	3541 GT	310.5' X 76.1' X 16.8'	6664 BHP T/S DIESEL	PASS/CAR FERRY
353	312	1961	313905	FORT LANGLEY	DEPT. OF PUBLIC WORKS	1788 GT	226.6' X 45.1' X 19.1'	4026 BHP T/S DIESEL EL.	SUCTION/HOPPER DREDGER
354	none	1963	DDH 205	H.M.C.S. ST. LAURENT	ROYAL CANADIAN NAVY	2400 DP			Conversion of DDE into DDH class escort vessel
355	none	1964	DDH 206	H.M.C.S. SAGUENAY	ROYAL CANADIAN NAVY	2400 DP			Conversion of DDE into DDH class escort vessel
356	313	1963	318541	READY	DEPT. OF TRANSPORT	139 GT	95' X 20.0' X 10.8'	2400 BHP T/S DIESEL	SAR CUTTER
357	314	1963	320164	NORTHLAND PRINCE	NORTHLAND SHIPPING (1962)CO. LTD.	3150 GT	312.0' X 46.1' X 22.4'	4200 BHP T/S DIESEL	PASSENGER/CARGO VESSEL
358	315	1962	314901	G. of G. 230	GULF OF GEORGIA TOWING CO. LTD.	567 GT	120.0' X 44.1' X 12.1'	NON PROPELLED	FLAT DECK SCOW

Serial #	Hull #	Year	Reg.No.	Name	OWNERS	Tonnage	Dimensions	Propulsion	Type & Notes
359	316	1962	314902	G. of G. 231	GULF OF GEORGIA TOWING CO. LTD.	567 GT	120.0' X 44.1' X 12.1'	NON PROPELLED	FLAT DECK SCOW
360	317	1962	314908	G. of G. 232	GULF OF GEORGIA TOWING CO. LTD.	567 GT	120.0' X 44.1' X 12.1'	NON PROPELLED	FLAT DECK SCOW
361	318	1962	314919	G. of G. 233	GULF OF GEORGIA TOWING CO. LTD.	567 GT	120.0' X 44.1' X 12.1'	NON PROPELLED	FLAT DECK SCOW
362	319	1962	319343	LAKELSE	NORTHLAND SHIPPING (1962)CO. LTD.	803 GT	160.0' X 48.1' X 11.6'	NON PROPELLED	COVERED BARGE
363	320	1963	320045	QUEEN OF THE ISLANDS	B.C. TOLL HIGHWAYS & BRIDGES AUTH.	1717 GT	222.7' X 52.0' X 17.5'	4000 BHP T/S DIESEL	PASS/CAR FERRY
364	321	1963	320193	B.A. STEVESTON	THE BRITISH AMERICAN OIL CO.	285 GT	102.5' X 34.0' X 6.5'	NON PROPELLED	FLOATING SERVICE STATION
365	322	1963	320170	G. of G. 240	HARBOUR INDUSTRIES LTD.	563 GT	120.0' X 44.1' X 12.1'	NON PROPELLED	FLAT DECK SCOW
366	323	1963	320192	G. of G. 241	HARBOUR INDUSTRIES LTD.	563 GT	120.0' X 44.1' X 12.1'	NON PROPELLED	FLAT DECK SCOW
367	324	1963	320240	G. of G. 242	JAMES S. BYRN	563 GT	120.0' X 44.1' X 12.1'	NON PROPELLED	FLAT DECK SCOW
368	325	1963	320241	G. of G. 243	JAMES S. BYRN	563 GT	120.0' X 44.1' X 12.1'	NON PROPELLED	FLAT DECK SCOW
369	326	1966	320965	VANCOUVER	DEPT. OF TRANSPORT	5537 GT	372.8' X 50.0' X 19.1'	7500 SHP T/S TURBO EL.	WEATHER SHIP
370	327	1967	328071	QUADRA	DEPT. OF TRANSPORT	5536 GT	372.8' X 50.0' X 19.1'	7500 SHP T/S TURBO EL.	WEATHER SHIP
371	328	1964	323240	V.T.NO. 140	VANCOUVER TUG BOAT CO. LTD.	760 GT	168.0' X 48.1' X 10.3'	NON PROPELLED	CHIP SCOW
372	329	1965	323249	V.T.NO. 141	VANCOUVER TUG BOAT CO. LTD.	760 GT	168.0' X 48.1' X 10.3'	NON PROPELLED	CHIP SCOW
373	330	1965	323291	V.T.NO. 142	VANCOUVER TUG BOAT CO. LTD.	760 GT	168.0' X 48.1' X 10.3'	NON PROPELLED	CHIP SCOW
374	331	1965	323318	V.T.NO. 143	VANCOUVER TUG BOAT CO. LTD.	760 GT	168.0' X 48.1' X 10.3'	NON PROPELLED	CHIP SCOW
375	332	1967	328076	PARIZEAU	DEPT. OF MINES & TECHNICAL SURVEYS	1314 GT	198.8' X 40.0' X 18.9'	3400 BHP T/S DIESEL	SURVEY VESSEL
376	333	1966	327237	V.T.NO. 173	VANCOUVER TUG BOAT CO. LTD.	774 GT	168.0' X 48.1' X 10.5'	NON PROPELLED	CHIP SCOW
377	334	1966	321238	V.T.NO. 174	VANCOUVER TUG BOAT CO. LTD.	774 GT	168.0' X 48.1' X 10.5'	NON PROPELLED	CHIP SCOW
378	335	1969	AGOR 192	C.N.A.V. QUEST	ROYAL CANADIAN NAVY	2320 DP	235.0' X 42.0' X 21.0'	2900 BHP T/S DIESEL EL.	RESEARCH VESSEL
379	336	1967	327897	V.T.NO. 202	BARCLAY INDUSTRIES LTD.	4101 GT	298.6' X 68.1' X 22.3'	NON PROPELLED	BULK CARGO BARGE
380	337	1967	327950	GOLD RIVER II	VANCOUVER TUG BOAT CO. LTD.	3279 GT	244.4' X 54.0' X 15.0'	NON PROPELLED	PULP/CHEMICAL BARGE
381	338	1968	329198	ISLAND TUG 128	ISLAND TUG & BARGE LTD.	819 GT	175.0' X 48.0' X 11.3'	NON PROPELLED	CHIP SCOW
382	339	1968	329199	ISLAND TUG 129	ISLAND TUG & BARGE LTD.	819 GT	175.0' X 48.0' X 11.3'	NON PROPELLED	CHIP SCOW
383	340	1968	329200	ISLAND TUG 130	ISLAND TUG & BARGE LTD.	819 GT	175.0' X 48.0' X 11.3'	NON PROPELLED	CHIP SCOW
384	341	1968	329201	ISLAND TUG 131	ISLAND TUG & BARGE LTD.	819 GT	175.0' X 48.0' X 11.3'	NON PROPELLED	CHIP SCOW
385	342	1968	329526	RIVTOW 103	JAMES DOUGLAS	760 GT	168.0' X 48.0' X 10.7'	NON PROPELLED	GRAVEL BARGE
386	343	1969	330840	WILLIAM DENNY	RAYMOND CONCRETE PILE LTD.	8100 GT	350.0' X 100.0' X 25.0'	NON PROPELLED	DERRICK BARGE
387	344	1970	331938	IMPERIAL SKEENA	IMPERIAL OIL LTD.	3047 GT	290.0' X 53.0' X 21.0'	3000 BHP T/S DIESEL	COASTAL TANKER
388	none	1969	331164	N.T. 1016	NORTHERN TRANSPORTATION CO. LTD.	642 GT	200.0' X 50.0' X 7.5'	NON PROPELLED	RIVER CARGO BARGE, subcontract from Dominion Bridge Co. shipped in pieces to Arctic
389	none	1969	318673	QUEEN OF ESQUIMALT	B.C. FERRY AUTHORITY	inc1344 GT	84.0' X 76.1' X 16.8'	NON PROPELLED	MID BODY SECTION
390	345	1969	330419	V.T. NO. 191	VANCOUVER TUG BOAT CO. LTD.	858 GT	180.0' X 48.5' X 11.3'	NON PROPELLED	CHIP SCOW
391	342Y	1969	330620	ISLAND FORESTER	YARROWS LTD.	not meas.	150.0' X 96.0' X 27.0'	NON PROPELLED	BOW SECTION
392	346	1970	344573	N.T. 1503	NORTHERN TRANSPORTATION CO. LTD.	1250 GT	250.0' X 56.0' X 10.0'	NON PROPELLED	RIVER CARGO BARGE
393	347	1970	344574	N.T. 1504	NORTHERN TRANSPORTATION CO. LTD.	1250 GT	250.0' X 56.0' X 10.0'	NON PROPELLED	RIVER CARGO BARGE
394	348	1970	344585	G. of G. 480	HARBOUR BARGES LTD.	912 GT	180.0' X 48.0' X 12.0'	NON PROPELLED	FLAT DECK BARGE
395	349	1970	344586	G. of G. 481	HARBOUR BARGES LTD.	912 GT	180.0' X 48.0' X 12.0'	NON PROPELLED	FLAT DECK BARGE
396	none	1970	314040	QUEEN OF VICTORIA	B.C. FERRY AUTHORITY	inc 1359 GT	84.0' X 76.1' X 16.8'	NON PROPELLED	MID BODY SECTION
397	352Y	1971	331572	ROTHESAY CARRIER	YARROWS LTD.	not meas.	150.0' X 82.0' X 22.0'	NON PROPELLED	BOW SECTION
398	350	1971	345178	CATES ARK	C.H. CATES & SONS LTD.	44 GT	55.0' X 22.0' X 4.5'	NON PROPELLED	FLAT DECK SCOW
399	none	1971	310431	ISLAND PRINCESS	B.C. FERRY AUTHORITY	inc 339 GT			lengthening and widening of existing ferry
400	351	1971	none	not named	CHUTTER HYDR.& MACH. LTD	not meas.	32.0' X 24.0' X 5.0'	NON PROPELLED	PUMP FLOAT
401	none	1971	318669	QUEEN OF SAANICH	B.C. FERRY AUTHORITY	inc 1360 GT	84.0' X 76.1' X 16.8'	NON PROPELLED	MID BODY SECTION
402	352	1973	347756	CARRIER PRINCESS	CANADIAN PACIFIC LTD,	4353 GT	368.0' X 66.0' X 24.0'	11500 BHP T/S DIESEL	RAIL CAR/TRUCK FERRY
403	none	1973	322978	QUEEN OF BURNABY	B.C. FERRY AUTHORITY	inc 1361 GT	84.0' X 76.1' X 16.8'	NON PROPELLED	MID BODY SECTION
404	none	1973	322953	QUEEN OF NEW WESTMINSTER	B.C. FERRY AUTHORITY	inc 1360 GT	84.0' X 76.1' X 16.8'	NON PROPELLED	MID BODY SECTION
405	353	1973	346516	N.T. 1523	NORTHERN TRANSPORTATION CO. LTD.	1252 GT	250.0' X 56.0' X 10.0'	NON PROPELLED	RIVER CARGO BARGE
406	354	1973	346517	N.T. 1524	NORTHERN TRANSPORTATION CO. LTD.	1252 GT	250.0' X 56.0' X 10.0'	NON PROPELLED	RIVER CARGO BARGE
407	355	1973	346518	N.T. 1525	NORTHERN TRANSPORTATION CO. LTD.	1252 GT	250.0' X 56.0' X 10.0'	NON PROPELLED	RIVER CARGO BARGE
408	356	1973	346519	N.T. 1526	NORTHERN TRANSPORTATION CO. LTD.	1252 GT	250.0' X 56.0' X 10.0'	NON PROPELLED	RIVER CARGO BARGE
409	357	1973	346520	N.T. 1527	NORTHERN TRANSPORTATION CO. LTD.	1252 GT	250.0' X 56.0' X 10.0'	NON PROPELLED	RIVER CARGO BARGE

Serial #	Hull #	Year	Reg.No.	Name	OWNERS	Tonnage	Dimensions	Propulsion	Type & Notes
410	358								not used due to predicted confusion with Yarrows hull 358
411	359	1973	347537	JOHNNY HOPE	NORTHERN TRANSPORTATION CO. LTD.	783 GT	154.5' X 52.0' X 9.5'	4500 BHP Q/S DIESEL	RIVER TUG
SYSTEM CHANGED BY NEW OWNERS TO REDUCE CONFUSION WITH YARROWS NUMBERS									
412	210	1974	Foreign	HOLLIS HEDBERG	CAYMAN ISLAND VESSELS LTD.	1410 GT	176.0' X 42.0' X 19.0'	3900 BHP T/S DIESEL	RESEARCH VESSEL
413	211	1974	348515	INCAN SUPERIOR	INCAN MARINE LTD.	3838 GT	372.0' X 66.0' X 24.0'	4360 BHP T/S DIESEL	RAIL CAR FERRY
414	212	1975	369371	INCAN ST. LAURENT	INCAN MARINE LTD.	7892 GT	372.0' X 66.0' X 24.0'	5700 BHP T/S DIESEL	RAIL CAR FERRY
415	213	1974	348862	N.W.D. 308	NORTH WESTERN DREDGING CO. LTD.	1349 GT	194.0' X 42.3' X 19.1'	NON PROPELLED	HOPPER DUMP BARGE
416	214	1974	348863	N.W.D. 309	NORTH WESTERN DREDGING CO. LTD.	1349 GT	194.0' X 42.3' X 19.1'	NON PROPELLED	HOPPER DUMP BARGE
417	215	1974	348864	N.W.D. 310	NORTH WESTERN DREDGING CO. LTD.	1349 GT	194.0' X 42.3' X 19.1'	NON PROPELLED	HOPPER DUMP BARGE
418	216	1974	348865	N.W.D. 311	NORTH WESTERN DREDGING CO. LTD.	1349 GT	194.0' X 42.3' X 19.1'	NON PROPELLED	HOPPER DUMP BARGE
419	217	1974	348866	N.W.D. 312	NORTH WESTERN DREDGING CO. LTD.	1349 GT	194.0' X 42.3' X 19.1'	NON PROPELLED	HOPPER DUMP BARGE
420	218	1974	348025	N.T. 1802	NORTHERN TRANSPORTATION CO. LTD.	1949 GT	210.0' X 56.0' X 13.0'	NON PROPELLED	CARGO/OIL BARGE
421	219	1976	370060	QUEEN OF COQUITLAM	B.C. FERRY AUTHORITY	6551 GT	404.0' X 88.9' X 26.0'	13060 BHP T/S DIESEL	PASS/CAR FERRY
422	220	1975	370260	CANMAR SUPPLIER III	DOME PETROLEUM LTD.	1190 GT	185.0' X 45.0' X 18.3'	7000 BHP T/S DIESEL	OFFSHORE SUPPLY SHIP
423	221	1978	383326	PIERRE RADISSON	DEPT. OF TRANSPORT	5910 GT	288.5' X 64.0' X 26.5'	13600 BHP T/S DIESEL	ICEBREAKER
424	222	1979	383347	FRANKLIN	DEPT. OF TRANSPORT	5910 GT	288.5' X 64.0' X 26.5'	13600 BHP T/S DIESEL	ICEBREAKER
425	223	1975	370335	SALISH NO.1	GREENLEES PILEDRIVING CO.LTD.	715 GT	160.0' X 48.0' X 10.8'	NON PROPELLED	FLAT DECK BARGE
426	224	1978	383476	CROWN ZELLERBACH	CROWN ZELLERBACH CANADA LTD.	525 GT	100.0' X 64.0' X 9.0'	NON PROPELLED	CRANE BARGE LOADER # 3
427	225	1978	none	none	CHUTTER HYDR.& MACH. LTD	not meas.	36.0' X 26.0' X 6.0'	NON PROPELLED	PUMP FLOAT
428	226	1978	384021	ECLIPSE 104	McDONALD CEDAR PRODUCTS LTD.	229 GT	101.0' X 40.0' X 6.5'	NON PROPELLED	LOG BUNDLING BARGE
429	227	1978	391339	CAPTAIN VERNON	MENZIES BAY MARINE SERVICES LTD.	1579 GT	300.0' X 50.0' X 12.0'	NON PROPELLED	S/D LOG BARGE
430	228	1979	393558	CROWN ZELLERBACH # 14	built at Yarrows as Hull no. 386	1102 GT	208.6' X 50.0' X 12.0'	NON PROPELLED	CHIP SCOW
431	229	1979	392783	CROWN ZELLERBACH # 15	NORSK PACIFIC STEAMSHIP CO.	1102 GT	208.6' X 50.0' X 12.0'	NON PROPELLED	CHIP SCOW
432	230	1979	392974	CROWN ZELLERBACH # 16	NORSK PACIFIC STEAMSHIP CO.	1102 GT	208.6' X 50.0' X 12.0'	NON PROPELLED	CHIP SCOW
HULL NUMBERING SYSTEM CHANGED AGAIN TO BE COMPATIBLE WITH NEW COMPUTER COSTING SYSTEM									
433	100	1980	369048	QUEEN OF SURREY	B.C. FERRY AUTHORITY	6969 GT	404.0' X 88.9' X 26.0'	13060 BHP T/S DIESEL	PASS/CAR FERRY
434	none	1979	323841	POWELL RIVER QUEEN	B.C. FERRY AUTHORITY	inc 361 GT	72.0' X 61.1' X 12.5'	NON PROPELLED	MID BODY SECTION
435	none	1979	323848	MAYNE QUEEN	B.C. FERRY AUTHORITY	inc 351 GT	72.0' X 61.1' X 12.5'	NON PROPELLED	MID BODY SECTION
436	none	1979	323854	BOWEN QUEEN	B.C. FERRY AUTHORITY	inc 352 GT	72.0' X 61.1' X 12.5'	NON PROPELLED	MID BODY SECTION
437	101	1979	none	not named	CHUTTER HYDR.& MACH. LTD	not meas.	36.0' X 26.0' X 6.0'	NON PROPELLED	PUMP FLOAT
438	none	1979	347185	IMPERIAL TOFINO	IMPERIAL OIL LTD.	inc 114 GT	28.0' X 33.9' X 15.0'	NON PROPELLED	MID BODY SECTION
439	102	1981	800204	RIVTOW HERCULES	RIVTOW STRAITS LTD,	9043 GT	400.0' X 100.0' X 25.0'	NON PROPELLED	S/L & S/D LOG BARGE
440	103	1981	800201	CROWN ZELLERBACH # 17	NORSK PACIFIC STEAMSHIP CO.	1077 GT	208.6' X 50.0' X 12.0'	NON PROPELLED	CHIP SCOW
441	104	1981	800202	CROWN ZELLERBACH # 18	NORSK PACIFIC STEAMSHIP CO.	1077 GT	208.6' X 50.0' X 12.0'	NON PROPELLED	CHIP SCOW
442	105	1981	800203	CROWN ZELLERBACH # 19	NORSK PACIFIC STEAMSHIP CO.	1077 GT	208.6' X 50.0' X 12.0'	NON PROPELLED	CHIP SCOW
443	none	1982	Foreign	HOLLIS HEDBERG	CAYMAN ISLAND VESSELS LTD.	unknown	40.0' X 42.0' X 19.0'	NON PROPELLED	LENGTHENED, Mid body from Victoria Division (YARROWS)
444	106	1982	801810	ROBERT LEMEUR	CANMAR DRILLING LTD.	3186 GT	270.6' X 59.0' X 24.6'	9800 BHP T/S DIESEL	ICEBREAKER/SUPPLY SHIP
445	107	1983	803579	TERRY FOX	GULF CANADA RESOURCES LTD.	4234 GT	266.3' X 57.4' X 32.8'	22000 BHP T/S DIESEL	ICEBREAKER/SUPPLY SHIP
446	108	1986	806313	MARTHA L.BLACK	CANADIAN COAST GUARD	3818 GT	257.0' X 53.1' X 25.4'	7500 SHP T/S DIESEL EL.	ICEBREAKER/NAVAIDS TENDER
447	109	1984	none	not named	CHAMCO ENGINEERING SALES LTD.	not meas.	40.0' X 28.0' X 6.0'	NON PROPELLED	PUMP FLOAT
448	110	1988	808731	HENRY LARSEN	CANADIAN COAST GUARD	6167 GT	288.5' X 64.6' X 26.5'	16000 SHP T/S DIESEL EL.	ICEBREAKER
449	111	1990	813730	MATTHEW	Built at Yarrows as Hull 511	857 GT			HYDROGRAPHIC VESSEL
450	none	1988	none	not named	CHAMCO ENGINEERING SALES LTD.	not meas.	40.0' X 28.0' X 6.0'	NON PROPELLED	PUMP FLOAT

Notes

To avoid burdening the reader with an overabundance of notes, I identified sources in the text whenever possible. Where this could not easily be done, I have cited the source(s) that provided information contained in a particular paragraph in the following list. The relevant passage in the text is indicated by the first few words of the paragraph. This does not mean, of course, that everything in that paragraph came from the source(s).

All archival sources are North Vancouver Museum and Archives unless otherwise noted.

Chapter 1
Laying the Foundations: 1894–1913

Alfred Wallace: His Early Years

When he was 11 ... James Marshall, *Burrard Dry Dock Company*, 2–3.

In 1889 the young couple ... Marshall, 6

Alfred Wallace, an energetic ... Marshall, 13; Gerald Rushton, *Whistle up the Inlet*, 20.

Alfred and Eliza's first ... Marshall, 14; NVMA J.D.V. Kinvig fonds 97, File 1, Family, Friends, and Ships, 187.

In 1894, with the profits ... Marshall, 16.

Sidebar: Two generations of McColls ... Interview with David Wallace.

The Beginning: The False Creek Yards

The burgeoning fishing ... Marshall, 16.

When Wallace started ... *Burrard-Pacific News*, August 1953.

In 1898 Wallace expanded ... *Vancouver Sun,* November 15, 1946; Marshall, 20.

Doidge lived a rich ... *Wallace Shipbuilder*, July 1942 and March 1944.

The ship transported ... *Wallace Shipbuilder*, July 1943; *Kings County Record* [Sussex, New Brunswick], July 15, 1997.

Other projects soon ... Rushton (1974), 41.

Relaunched on September 28 ... Rushton (1974), 17–18.

One of the *Kestrel's* ... Marshall, 28.

Wallace's business prospered ... S.W. Jackman, *The Men at Cary Castle*, 165.

North Vancouver Ferry No. 2

The ship's life ... *Vancouver News Herald*, March 1, 1937; James Barr, *Ferry Across the Harbour*, 61.

Moving to the North Shore

Wallace's business required ... Information at end of paragraph from Rollie Webb.

In 1904 Wallace ... Kathleen Woodward-Reynolds, "A History of the City and District of North Vancouver," 125–126.

North Vancouver Ferry No. 3

I would remind you ... NVMA City of North Vancouver fonds 20, clerk's correspondence, February 28, 1918.

The *No. 3 Ferry* stayed ... Gordon Newell *The H.W. McCurdy Marine History of the Pacific Northwest*, xxiii.

Adapting to Local Needs

Elsewhere tugs were . . . Information from Rollie Webb.

The Terminal Steamship Company . . . *Harbour and Shipping*, October 1987.

The *Progressive*, captained by . . . Ken Drushka, *Against Wind and Weather*, 220.

Arthur H. Moscrop . . . *Harbour and Shipping*, April 1974.

The *Cheslakee* joined . . . Tom Henry, *The Good Company*, 48, 50.

Surviving Fire and Leaner Times

Wallace hinted that . . . Marshall, 1945.

In spite of the general . . . *Harbour and Shipping*, May 1988.

The history of Burrard . . . G.W. Taylor, *Shipyards of British Columbia*, 66, 68; Eileen Marcil, *Tall Ships and Tankers*, 141.

Chapter 2
Ocean Ventures: 1914–1920

Early War Years: The Wallace Yards Expand

Before World War I . . . Taylor, 86.

War was the engine . . . Marshall, 55.

One of the junior . . . Jackman, 166.

Sidebar: Big Jim Andrews . . . Marine Workers and Boilermakers, *A History of Shipbuilding in B.C.*, 91.

Meanwhile, Clarence's younger . . . Marshall, 54.

No. 2 Yard: The *Mabel Brown* and its Sisters

Sailing ships were definitely . . . Taylor, 86.

In June 1916 . . . Taylor, 87.

We would therefore . . . Fonds 20, clerk's correspondence.

Wallace soon contracted . . . Marshall, 56.

The keel for the first . . . Dick Hammond, *Tales from Hidden Basin*, 243.

When it came time . . . Hammond, 246; *Wallace Shipbuilder*, July 1942.

On its maiden voyage . . . Hammond, 249–250.

The *Janet Carruthers* . . . Jim Gibbs, *West Coast Windjammers*, 134–135.

The *Jessie Norcross* . . . *Harbour and Shipping*, June 1986.

The schooners were not . . . "History of Burrard Dry Dock," 6.

The "Mabel Brown" vessels . . . *Harbour and Shipping*, June 1986.

The War Ships

In April 1917 . . . Michael Moss, *Shipbuilders to the World*, 193; William Kaplan, *Everything that Floats*, 4.

The Imperial Munitions Board . . . Taylor, 92–93.

While these ships . . . *Vancouver Province*, September 28, 1939.

In early 1918 . . . Marshall, 67.

He also continued . . . Fonds 20, clerk's correspondence, August 15, 1918.

Merchant Marine Contracts

These were good years . . . Margaret Ormsby, *British Columbia: A History*, 406.

In March 1918 . . . Marshall, 66.

In late March 1918 . . . and [We] have come . . . National Archives RG42, Vol. 282, file 45304, Item 41.

In January 1921 . . . Marshall, 68–69.

Between 1918 and 1920 . . . Eric Sager, *Ships and Memories*, 4.

The ships were sold . . . *Burrard-Yarrows Review*, May 1977.

In 1939 the *Canadian Skirmisher* . . . Robert Halford, *The Unknown Navy*, 18.

The *Chilkoot*

As the lucrative . . . Rushton (1974), 81.

Built for service . . . Rushton (1974), 81.

The *Chilkoot* served . . . Rushton, *Echoes of the Whistle*, 123; Newell (1966), 624.

Changing Times

In May 1918 . . . Taylor, 103.

A series of agreements . . . NVMA Versatile Pacific Shipyards Inc., fonds 27, Box 48, A12-12.

Chapter 3
A Few Good Ships: 1921–1939

Princess Louise: It *Is* Possible

While neither the size . . . Taylor, 101.

It has been the ambition . . . *Vancouver Sun*, June 14, 1963.

Its great flaring bow . . . *Harbour and Shipping*, July 1963; Robert Turner, *The Pacific Princesses*, 125.

Premier Duff Pattullo . . . Turner, 199.

But even *Princesses* . . . *Harbour and Shipping*, December 1989; Robert Schwemer, "Death of a Princess," 18.

The Long Walk to a Dry Dock

On September 17, 1921 . . . Marshall, 99.

W.T. Donnelly of New York . . . Marshall, 100.

The recently opened . . . *Harbour and Shipping*, January 1923.

Leaner and Meaner

Equipping a Canadian . . . Nicholas Tracy, *Canada's Naval Strategy*, 15.

Throughout the world . . . Marcil, 199.

St. Roch: Creation of a Legend

Burrard had not built . . . James Delgado, *Across the Top of the World*, 185.

Small and stubby . . . Bill White, "Sailing on the St. Roch," 94; *Wallace Shipbuilder*, November 1944.

Bill White, one of . . . White (1983), 89.

The *Roch* with her bathtub . . . White (1983), 93.

A steel shoe . . . *Harbour and Shipping*, November 1944.

J.H. Carlisle

The September 1928 . . . *Harbour and Shipping*, January 1928.

Burrard launched . . . Marshall, 116.

HMCS Comox

As the 1930s . . . Marcil, 221.

The building of the Basset . . . Taylor, 74.

In spite of the rapidly . . . Marcil, 222.

The Fifer: Elegant Beauty

Before the war . . . Peter Vassilopoulos, *Antiques Afloat*, 103.

In 1948 San Francisco . . . *Harbour and Shipping*, October 1991.

At various times . . . Vassilopoulos, 107.

An Era Ends

In 1926 Alfred Wallace . . . Alfred's more sedentary . . . Eliza Wallace died . . . Interview with David Wallace.

What made Alfred Wallace . . . Fonds 97, 187.

He was a tough . . . *Wallace Shipbuilder*, July 1942.

"Nerve" characterized . . . *Burrard-Pacific News*, August 1953.

Chapter 4
Paths of Glory: 1939–1946

Great Britain declared . . . Newell (1966), 475.

Corvettes: "Cheap but Nasties"

After the 1938 Munich . . . K.R. Macpherson, *Canada's Fighting Ships*, 48; Gilbert Tucker, *Activities on Shore During the Second World War*, 31; *Harbour and Shipping*, February 1941.

The standard corvette . . . Thomas Lynch, *Canada's Flowers*, 7–8.

Corvettes have been described . . . David Bercuson, *Maple Leaf Against the Axis*, 25.

The Canadian War Supply . . . Tucker, 38–39.

Workers laid the keel . . . Lynch, 95.

On March 11, 1944 . . . Lynch, 52.

Bangor Minesweepers

More naval construction . . . Tucker, 32, 43.

Like the corvettes . . . Macpherson, 76.

North Sands: 10,000 Tons and What Do You Get?

But more, much more . . . Newell (1966), 478.

In late 1940 . . . Fonds 27, Box 210, Amendments, Agreements.

evolved from the stark . . . Newell (1966), 479.

In March 1941 . . . Marshall, 164.

Burrard, like other shipyards . . . Marine Workers and Boilermakers, 78.

The 10,000-ton supply ships . . . George Edwards, *From Waterfront to Warfront*, 4.

As the war progressed . . . Edwards, 34–35.

Plant Development

A new copper . . . Marshall, 151.

Hugh Lewis was appointed . . . Edwards, 15–16.

Victory Ships

As the war progressed . . . Marshall, 170; *Wallace Shipbuilder*, May 1943.

The keel for Burrard's . . . Marshall, 175.

Beginning in June . . . Marshall, 180.

Women in the Yards

The North Yard hired . . . *Vancouver Sun*, March 20, 1943.

A Job Well Done

Although they had to be . . . *Wallace Shipbuilder*, October 1944.

These ships were built . . . Halford, 143.

In a 1942 estimate . . . Halford, 144; Robert Gardiner, *The Golden Age of Shipping*, 149.

The success of the west . . . *Harbour and Shipping*, January 1943.

But that takes away . . . *Harbour and Shipping*, August 1945.

Sidebar on *Green Hill Park*: By June 1946 . . . Taylor, 120; Stephanie Heal, *Conceived in War*, 99.

At the same time . . . NVMA fonds 104 William Wardle.

The company's drive . . . David Wallace interview.

Conversion of Aircraft Carriers at LaPointe Pier

Allied experience . . . Tucker, 89.

In the first seven . . . David Wallace interview.

The changes went beyond . . . Kinvig, 92.

At its peak . . . Tucker, 98–99.

The *Puncher* left Norfolk . . . Macpherson, 19.

Conversion of the *Princes*

During the late 1930s . . . Tucker, 10, 34, 35.

Work began . . . Tucker, 36.

Each ship received . . . Tucker, 36, 37; Taylor, 106.

As the war entered . . . Tucker, 88; *Harbour and Shipping*, March 1974.

Other Conversions

Other ships needed . . . Kinvig, 88.

Kaiser may have had . . . Stephanie Heal, *A Great Fleet of Ships*, 40.

The Party's Over

In September 1944 . . . Halford, 141.

Immense transportation . . . Halford, 145.

Chapter 5
Peacetime Retrenchment: 1946–1960

The Pace Slows

Except for the recession . . . Rollie Webb, "The Rise and Demise of Vancouver's Biggest Shipyard," 12.

Federal contracts buried . . . Webb, 15.

A Few Old Ships Made New Again

Union Steamship had purchased . . . Henry (1995), 131–133.

Buying out the Competition: Purchase of Yarrows and Pacific Drydock

Burrard's main North Shore . . . David Wallace interview.

When Clarence Wallace . . . David Wallace interview.

Naval Engagements

When the last . . . Marshall, 337.

The Canadian Shipbuilding . . . Taylor, 75.

In naval heritage . . . Taylor, 76.

Burrard laid the keel . . . Marshall, 383.

Construction of HMCS *Fraser* . . . Fonds 27, Box 12, MC meeting July 9, 1957.

The other two . . . Fonds 27, Box 12, MC meeting May 27, 1958.

Page 3 of the agreement . . . Fonds 27, Box 7, Hull 310 Yukon 1962.

A decade later . . . Marcil, 336.

Log Barges Replace Log Rafts

In 1936 . . . Tom Henry, *Westcoasters*, 118.

After World War II . . . McAllister in Westwood, *A History of Canadian Marine Technology*, 133–134.

The Industrial Division

One of its first major . . . Marshall, 333.

As the shipbuilders . . . Fonds 27, Box 12, MC meeting January 8, 1957.

Burrard pioneered . . . Marshall, 556.

For the petrochemical . . . Marshall, 334.

Chapter 6
Last Years of the Wallaces: 1961–1972

BC Ferries Go Provincial

The *Tsawwassen* cost . . . Turner, 187.

This set the pattern . . . Kinvig, 202.

On September 1, 1961 . . . Gary Bannerman, *The Ships of British Columbia*, 69.

At $2.1 million . . . Bannerman, 96.

Haste in the ferry's . . . Bannerman, 171.

BC government ferries . . . Bannerman, 69.

Burrard won the contract . . . Marshall, 634.

The *Fort Langley* Dredge

Burrard's original bid . . . David Wallace interview.

But the ship was built . . . Marshall, 427.

Taking Care of Number One

In 1947 Burrard . . . Bill Hudson interview.

The Many Lives of the *Northland Prince*

In December 1986 . . . Includes information from Len McCann.

Coast Guard Contracts

Although it had operated . . . Snider in Westwood, p. 219.

Partway through construction . . . Fonds 97, file 8.

The *Quadra* and *Vancouver* . . . *Victoria Times*, August 18, 1978.

The $8.6 million auxiliary . . . Marshall, 516.

Bigger Better Barges

Burrard's skill and innovation . . . Marshall, 436.

Imperial Skeena: First Tanker in 40 Years

The *Imperial Skeena* . . . Marshall, 525.

A decade later . . . *Harbour and Shipping*, May 1980.

Struggling to Remain Competitive

In 1960 Burrard built . . . David Wallace interview; Marshall, 466.

In 1965, after several . . . Bill Hudson interview.

In the mid-1960s . . . Rollie Webb interview.

We are trying . . . Fonds 97, File 10.

Chapter 7
Adjusting to a New World: 1972–1986

The End of the Wallaces

To adapt to the demands . . . Fonds 27, Box 12, Modernization.

Barges for the North and Elsewhere

In December 1972 . . . Marshall, Chapter 11, 31.

The *Rivtow Hercules* . . . McAllister in Westwood, 141.

Burrard Builds Bigger BC Ferries Faster

In January 1979 . . . Marshall, Chapter 12, 146.

These were the first . . . Bannerman, 134.

Trailer Ferries for Canadian Pacific

Burrard built two . . . Turner, 226.

Icebreakers: Booms and Busts

Burrard had already . . . Kinvig, 197.

The ship was a financial . . . Fonds 27, Box 20, M.3.2. memos DWC.

The general work ethic . . . Fonds 27, Box 20, M.3.3 Memos—D.J. Alsop.

Managers never tired . . . Fonds 27, Box 20, M.3.2 Memos DWC.

The *Terry Fox* . . . Fonds 27, Box 20, January 26, 1983 Challinor Dailies.

But back in the yard . . . Fonds 27, Box 12, MC meeting September 29, 1983.

Frigate refits . . . Fonds 27, Box 20, 1983 T.K. Duncan Dailies.

A reprieve came . . . Fonds 27, Box 20, M.3.2 Memos DVC.

Unfortunately, problems . . . *Vancouver Sun*, May 11, 1988.

A New Dry Dock

At this time . . . Fonds 27, Box 48, A45, Documents.

A letter from Bill Hudson . . . Fonds 27, Box 7, Government Correspondence, 1972.

In 1978 federal . . . Marshall, Chapter 12, 199.

On August 24, 1981 . . . Tom Duncan interview.

The hefty investment . . . Webb, 10.

Chapter 8
It's a Canadian Game

Polar 8: The Phantom Ship

Unsolicited proposals . . . Fonds 27, chronological files.

Meanwhile, Versatile Pacific's . . . Alsop interview.

A major condition . . . Fonds 27, chronological files.

Sensing a disaster . . . Fonds 27, chronological files.

Terry Godsall, Shieldings' . . . Fonds 27, chronological files.

The vice-president was adept . . . Fonds 27, chronological files.

The CDC and all . . . Fonds 27, chronological files.

Many who were . . . MacPherson interview; Jenkins interview.

Godsall made his . . . Fonds 27, chronological files.

On December 13, 1989 . . . Fonds 27, chronological files.

The Dream Dies

Less than a month . . . Fonds 27, chronological files.

All this sounded . . . Fonds 27, chronological files.

In the midst . . . Vicki Jensen, *Ships of Steel*, 138.

Appendix 1
Ship Repairs

Most repair work . . . Hudson interview.

For a time . . . David Wallace interview.

While its dock . . . Bob Logan interview.

Works Cited

Bannerman, Gary, and Patricia Bannerman. *The Ships of British Columbia: An Illustrated History of the British Columbia Ferry Corporation.* Surrey, BC: Hancock House, 1985.

Barr, James. *Ferry Across the Harbour.* Vancouver: Mitchell Press, 1969.

Bercuson, David J. *Maple Leaf Against the Axis.* Toronto: Stoddart, 1995.

Burnes, Rodger J. *Echoes of the Ferries: A History of the North Vancouver Ferry Service.* n.d.

Dalcor Group. *A Study of the Ocean Industry in British Columbia.* Victoria: BC Ministry of Economic Development, January 1978.

Delgado, James. *Across the Top of the World: The Quest for the North West Passage.* Vancouver: Douglas & McIntyre, 1999.

——. *Dauntless St. Roch, The Mountie's Arctic Schooner.* Victoria: Horsdal & Schubart Ltd., 1992.

Drushka, Ken. *Against Wind and Weather: The History of Towboating in British Columbia.* Vancouver: Douglas & McIntyre, 1981.

Edwards, George N. *Waterfront to Warfront: Burrard Dry Dock Company During World War II.* North Vancouver, BC: G.N. Edwards, 1995.

Elphick, Peter. *Liberty: The Ships That Won the War.* Annapolis, MD: Naval Institute Press, 2001.

Evenden, L.J., ed. *Vancouver: Western Metropolis.* Victoria: University of Victoria, Department of Geography, 1978.

Gardiner, Robert, ed. *The Golden Age of Shipping. The Classic Merchant Ship 1900–1960.* London, England: Conway Maritime Press, 1994.

Gibb, George S. "Canadian Ferry Services." In *A Half Century of Maritime Technology,* edited by Harry Berford. Jersey City, NJ: The Society of Naval Architects and Marine Engineers, 1993.

Gibbs, Jim. *West Coast Windjammers in Story and Pictures.* New York: Bonanza Books, 1968.

Gosnell, R.E. *A History of British Columbia.* Lewis Publishing Co., 1906.

Granatstein, J.L., and Desmond Morton. *A Nation Forged in Fire.* Toronto: Lester & Orpen Denys, 1989.

Greene, Ruth. *Personality Ships of British Columbia.* West Vancouver: Marine Tapestry Publications, 1969.

Halford, Robert G. *The Unknown Navy: Canada's World War II Merchant Navy.* St. Catharines, ON: Vanwell Publishing, 1995.

Hammond, Dick. *Tales from Hidden Basin.* Madeira Park, BC: Harbour Publishing, 1996.

Heal, Stephanie. *Conceived in War: Born in Peace: Canada's Deep Sea Merchant Marine.* Vancouver: Cordillera Publishing, 1992.

——. *A Great Fleet of Ships: The Canadian Forts and Parks.* St. Catharines, ON: Vanwell Publishing, 1999.

Henry, Tom. *The Good Company: An Affectionate History of the Union Steamships.* Madeira Park, BC: Harbour Publishing, 1995.

——. *Westcoasters: Boats That Built BC.* Madeira Park, BC: Harbour Publishing, 1998.

"History of Burrard Dry Dock Company Limited." Taken from installments printed in the *Yarrows Review*, 1953.

International Longshore Workers Union Local 500 Pensioners. *"Man Along the Shore!" The Story of the Vancouver Waterfront as told by the Longshoremen Themselves 1860s–1975.* Vancouver: ILWU Local 500 Pensioners, 1865 Franklin Street, circa 1975.

Jackman, S.W. *The Men at Cary Castle.* Victoria: Morriss Printing Company, 1972.

Jensen, Vicki. *Ships of Steel: A British Columbia Shipbuilder's Story.* Madeira Park, BC: Harbour Publishing, 2000.

Kaplan, William. *Everything That Floats.* Toronto: University of Toronto Press, 1987.

Kettle, Capt. (James H. Hamilton). *Western Shores: Narratives of the Pacific Coast.* Vancouver: Progress Publishing Company, 1932.

Lynch, Thomas G. *Canada's Flowers: History of the Corvettes of Canada.* Halifax: Nimbus, 1981.

MacIntosh, Robert. *Boilermakers in British Columbia.* Vancouver: Boilermakers Lodge No. 359, February 1976.

Macpherson, K.R. *Canada's Fighting Ships.* Toronto: Samuel Stevens, Hakkert & Company, 1975.

Marcil, Eileen Reid. *Tall Ships and Tankers. The History of the Davie Shipbuilders.* Toronto: McClelland and Stewart, 1997.

Marine Workers and Boilermakers Industrial Union Local No. 1. *A History of Shipbuilding in British Columbia: As told by Shipyard Workers 1927–1977.* (Published for the 50th anniversary of the Marine Workers and Boilermakers Industrial Union Local No. 1.) Vancouver: College Printers, 1977.

Marshall, James. *Burrard Dry Dock Company.* Unpublished history.

Mitchell, W.H., and L.A. Sawyer. *The Oceans, the Forts and the Parks.* London, England: Journal of Commerce and Shipping Telegraph, 1966.

Moss, Michael, and John R. Hulme. *Shipbuilders to the World: 125 Years of Harland and Wolff, Belfast, 1861–1986.* Belfast: The Blackstaff Press, 1986.

National Archives. Correspondence. RG42, Vol. 282, files 453204, items 40, 41.

Newell, Gordon, ed. *The H.W. McCurdy Marine History of the Pacific Northwest.* Seattle: The Superior Publishing Co., 1966.

——. *The H.W. McCurdy Marine History of the Pacific Northwest 1966–1976.* Seattle: The Superior Publishing Company, 1977.

North Vancouver Museum and Archives. Clipping files, records of J.D. Kinvig, David Wallace, Versatile Pacific Shipyards, and the City of North Vancouver.

Ormsby, Margaret. *British Columbia: A History.* Toronto: Macmillan, 1958.

Progress 1894–1946. North Vancouver: Burrard Dry Dock, 1947.

Rushton, Gerald. *Echoes of the Whistle: An Illustrated History of the Union Steamship Company.* Madeira Park, BC: Harbour Publishing, 1995.

——. *Whistle Up the Inlet.* North Vancouver: J.J. Douglas Ltd., 1974.

Sager, Eric W. *Ships and Memories. Merchant Seafarers in Canada's Age of Steam.* Vancouver: University of British Columbia Press, 1993.

Schwemer, Robert V. "Death of a Princess." *Mains'l Haul* (Maritime Museum of San Diego) (Winter 1991), 13–18.

Taylor, G.W. *Shipyards of British Columbia: The Principal Companies.* Victoria: Morriss Printing, 1986.

Tracy, Nicholas. *Canada's Naval Strategy: Rooted in Experience.* Maritime Security Occasional Paper No. 1. Halifax: Dalhousie University, Centre for Foreign Policy Studies, 1995.

Tucker, Gilbert Norman. *Activities on Shore During the Second World War.* Volume II of *The Naval Service of Canada: Its Official History.* Ottawa: King's Printer, 1952.

Turner, Robert D. *The Pacific Princesses: An Illustrated History of Canadian Pacific Railway's Princess Fleet on the Northwest Coast.* Victoria: Sono Nis Press, 1977.

Tweedale, Aitken, ed. *Shipbuilding and Shipbuilders of British Columbia with Allied Industries.* Vancouver: Tower Publishing, 1918.

Twigg, A.M. *Union Steamships Remembered 1920–1958.* Campbell River: Author, 1997.

Vassilopoulos, Peter. *Antiques Afloat. From the Golden Age of Boating in British Columbia.* Vancouver: Panorama Publications, 1980.

Webb, Roland H. "The Rise and Demise of Vancouver's Biggest Shipyard." Paper presented at the annual meeting of the Canadian Nautical Research Society, Toronto, May 27–29, 1993.

Westwood, Roger, Keith Farrell, and Abigail Fyfe, eds. *A History of Canadian Marine Technology.* Ottawa: Society of Naval Architects and Marine Engineers, Eastern Canadian Section, 1995.

White, Bill, and Howard White. "Sailing on the St. Roch." In *Raincoast Chronicles Six/Ten,* edited by Howard White. Madeira Park, BC: Harbour Publishing, 1983. Originally published in *Raincoast Chronicles* 7 (n.d.), 89–98.

White, Howard. *A Hard Man to Beat. The Story of Bill White: Labour Leader, Historian, Shipyard Worker, Raconteur.* Vancouver: Pulp Press, 1983.

Williams, Robin. *A Vancouver Boyhood.* Vancouver: Peanut Butter Publishing, 1997.

Woodward-Reynolds, Kathleen. "A History of the City and District of North Vancouver." Master's thesis, University of British Columbia, 1943.

Newspapers

Canadian Shipping and Marine Engineering, May 1976.

Harbour and Shipping (Vancouver), 1918–1998.

Kings County Record (Sussex New Brunswick), July 15, 1997.

Monde Ouvrier (Montreal), 1924.

North Shore News (North Vancouver), 1976–

North Shore Press (North Vancouver), 1913–1958.

North Vancouver Citizen, 1959.

North Vancouver Express, 1906–1912.

Ship and Shop, December 1961.

Vancouver Daily World, 1898–1903.

Vancouver Morning Star, 1926.

Vancouver News Herald, 1939–1957.

Vancouver Province, 1910–1994.

Vancouver Sun, 1944–1991.

Victoria Times, 1978.

Company newsletters

Wallace Shipbuilder. North Vancouver: Burrard Dry Dock, 1942–1945.

Burrard-Pacific News. North Vancouver: Burrard Dry Dock, 1953–1954.

Burrard Dry Dock News. North Vancouver: Burrard Dry Dock, 1955.

Burrard News. North Vancouver: Burrard Dry Dock, 1956–1965.

Burrard-Yarrows Review. North Vancouver: Burrard Yarrows Corporation, 1969–1983.

By Word. North Vancouver: Burrard Yarrows Corporation, 1984.

VPSI Monthly Bulletin. North Vancouver: Versatile Pacific Shipyards, 1985.

Interviews

Alsop, David. Interviewed at his place of business, RSL Com Canada Ltd., North Vancouver, May 28, 1999.

Cash, Jack. Interviewed in the cafeteria at Nanaimo General Hospital, Nanaimo, BC, April 29, 2001.

Downing, Robert. Interviewed in the North Vancouver Museum and Archives, July 16, 1999.

Duncan, Tom. Interviewed in the North Vancouver Museum and Archives, June 23, 1999.

Fitzpatrick, John. Interviewed at the Maritime Labour Centre, Vancouver, August 20, 1999.

Hudson, Bill. Interviewed at his home in Vancouver, January 22, 2000.

Jenkins, Dale. Interviewed at his place of business, Canadian Weld-Vent Systems Ltd., North Vancouver, November 1, 2000.

Knox, Tom. Interviewed with George Matthews in the North Vancouver Museum and Archives, January 29, 2001.

Logan, Bob. Interviewed at his home in North Vancouver, March 7, 2000.

MacPherson, George. Interviewed at the Maritime Labour Centre, Vancouver, September 3, 1999.

Matthews, George. Interviewed with Tom Knox in the North Vancouver Museum and Archives, January 29, 2001.

Saunders, Peter. Interviewed at his place of business in Vancouver, 2000.

Wallace, David. Interviewed at his home in Vancouver, March 17 and March 21, 2000.

Wallace, John. Interviewed at his home in Vancouver, September 10, 2001.

Webb, Rollie. Interviewed at his home in White Rock, BC, May 7, 1999.

Index

Other Marine History Titles
from Harbour Publishing

Dangerous Waters: Wrecks and Rescues off the BC Coast

by Keith Keller

6 x 9 · 304 pages, 50 photos, 24 maps, 12 illustrations, index · paper · 1-55017-288-3 · $24.95

These twenty-one hair-raising accounts of amazing marine disasters and near-disasters come from those who lived through them and those who were there. They are harrowing and very moving.

Burrard Inlet: A History

by Doreen Armitage

6 x 9 · 324 pages, photos, index · cloth · 1-55017-272-7 $32.95

Vancouver has one of the world's finest natural, deep-water harbours in the world. Its port handles more cargo than any in Canada. Much of the area's history centers on the waterfront and this book is both a carefully researched history and an entertaining read.

Ships of Steel: A British Columbia Shipbuilder's Story

by T.A. McLaren with Vickie Jensen

8½ x 11 · 288 pages, 300+ photos, index · cloth 1-55017-242-5 · $39.95

The wisdom, experience and memories of three generations of McLarens, a major West Coast shipbuilding family, bring the story of BC steel shipbuilding to life in this illustrated history of Allied Shipbuilders Ltd.

Westcoasters: Boats That Built BC

by Tom Henry

8½ x 11 · 192 pages, 120 photos, index · paper 1-55017-233-6 · $28.95

Here is the story of the unique vessels that make up BC history's fleet, from the *Beaver* and the *Lady Alexandra* to Bill Reid's *Lootaas.* Informative and amusing, *Westcoasters* brings the province's strange and romantic nautical history to life.

The Good Company: An Affectionate History of the Union Steamships

by Tom Henry

9 x 12 · 152 pages, 100+ photos, index · cloth 1-55017-111-9 · $35.95

The un-put-downable story of the legendary Union Steamship Company, which operated up and down the BC coast between 1890 and 1955.

Working the Tides: A Portrait of Canada's West Coast Fishery

Edited by Peter A. Robson and Michael Skog

8½x 11 · 216 pages, 200+ photos, index · cloth 1-55017-153-4 · $34.95 Can, $24.95 US

Gripping insider views not just of the familiar salmon trollers, gillnetters and seiners, but of the people and boats that harvest herring, halibut, rockfish and many other species.

High Seas, High Risk: The Story of the Sudburys

by Pat Wastell Norris

6 x 9 · 240 pages, 80 photos, index · cloth
1-55017-208-5 · $28.95

This is the story of Island Tug & Barge, BC's most famous deepsea salvage company and once the largest employer in Victoria. This riveting story is told through the anecdotes of family, friends and former crew members.

Fishing for a Living

by Alan Haig-Brown

8½ x 11 · 200 pages, 150 photos, index · cloth
1-55017-093-7 · $36.95

On the West Coast, catching fish is a way of life, celebrated in these writings, oral histories and photographs about the people who build the boats and bring in the fish.

God's Little Ships: A History of the Columbia Coast Mission

by Michael Hadley

6 x 9 · 308 pages · cloth · 1-55017-133-X · $28.95

To deliver medical care and spiritual support to logging camps, Native villages and white settlements in 20,000 square miles of rugged coastline, the men and women of the Columbia Coast Mission ships had to be as tough and unconventional as those they served.

Available from your local bookstore or

Harbour Publishing
P.O. Box 219
Madeira Park, BC, Canada V0N 2H0

Phone (604) 883-2730
Fax (604) 883-9451
Toll-free order line 1 800 667-2988
Toll-free fax order line 1 877 604-9449
E-mail orders@harbourpublishing.com
Website www.harbourpublishing.com